# TEACHABLE MOMENTS

# Studies in the Postmodern Theory of Education

Joe L. Kincheloe and Shirley R. Steinberg
*General Editors*

Vol. 297

PETER LANG
New York • Washington, D.C./Baltimore • Bern
Frankfurt am Main • Berlin • Brussels • Vienna • Oxford

Eunsook Hyun

# TEACHABLE MOMENTS

## Re-conceptualizing Curricula Understandings

PETER LANG
New York • Washington, D.C./Baltimore • Bern
Frankfurt am Main • Berlin • Brussels • Vienna • Oxford

**Library of Congress Cataloging-in-Publication Data**

Hyun, Eunsook.
Teachable moments: re-conceptualizing curricula understandings / Eunsook Hyun.
p. cm. — (Counterpoints: studies in the postmodern theory of education; vol. 297)
Includes bibliographical references and index.
1. Early childhood education—Curricula. I. Title.
LB1139.4.H975 372.19—dc22 2006018959
ISBN 0-8204-8141-6
ISSN 1058-1634

Bibliographic information published by **Die Deutsche Bibliothek**.
**Die Deutsche Bibliothek** lists this publication in the "Deutsche Nationalbibliografie"; detailed bibliographic data is available on the Internet at http://dnb.ddb.de/.

Cover art by Eunsook Hyun

The paper in this book meets the guidelines for permanence and durability of the Committee on Production Guidelines for Book Longevity of the Council of Library Resources.

29 Broadway, New York, NY 10006
www.peterlang.com



Printed in the United States of America

**This book is dedicated to my son, Yevin A. Roh**

# Table of Contents


List of Figures ix

List of Tables xi

Acknowledgments xiii

Preface xv

Section I: Toward Curriculum Re-conceptualization

Chapter 1 Cultural Complexity and Early Childhood 3

Chapter 2 Curriculum Understanding: Its Relationship to Teaching 17

Chapter 3 Influences in Modern Early Childhood: Curriculum and Teaching 33

Chapter 4 Curricula Understandings 53

Section II: Re-conceptualizing Curricular Practices

Chapter 5 Teachable Moment-Oriented Curriculum 69

Chapter 6 Emergent-Oriented Curriculum 89

Chapter 7 Negotiation-Oriented Curriculum 115

Section III: Curricula Re-conceptualization and Interconnectedness

Chapter 8 Recursive Movement Among Positions 135

Chapter 9 Reflectivity and Multiple Perspective-Taking 151

Chapter 10 Summary and Conclusion 167

References 177

Author Index 189

Subject Index 193

# Figures

Figure 2.1. Dewey's View on Instruction and Pedagogy 19

Figure 2.2. Instruction Versus Pedagogy 23

Figure 2.3. Various Views Used in Understanding Curriculum Definitions 26

Figure 2.4. Various Views Used in Understanding Curriculum Purposes 27

Figure 3.1. Example of Isa 40

Figure 3.2. Three Major Theoretical Traditions Influencing U.S. Early Childhood Curriculum 42

Figure 3.3. A Brief Comparison for Curricula Understanding 43

Figure 4.1. What Curriculum *Is*, What It *Does*, Thus, the Lived Curriculum 60

Figure 4.2. Elements of Developmentally Meaningful and Culturally Congruent Curriculum Understanding 66

Figure 5.1. Conventional Dynamics of Teachable Moment-Oriented Curriculum 83

Figure 5.2. Dynamics of a Developmentally Meaningful and Culturally Congruent Teachable Moment-Oriented Curriculum Practice 86

Figure 6.1. Dynamics of Emergent-Oriented Curriculum Practice 105

Figure 6.2. Brief Comparison of Teachable Moment-Oriented Curriculum Practice and Emergent-Oriented Curriculum Practices 106

Figure 7.1. Relationship and Interconnectedness Among a Teacher's Study-Based Pedagogical Practice, Inner and Outer Dialogue, Negotiation, and Teacher Reflectivity 120

Figure 8.1. Recursive Cycle 145

Figure 9.1. Recursive and Interconnected Relationship Between Reflectivity and Perspective-Taking 160

Figure 10.1. An Illustration of Power Issues and Teachable Moments in the Three Different Understandings of Curriculum 173

# Tables

Table 3.1. Main Characteristics of Existing ECE Curriculum Models/Approaches 44

Table 8.1. Teacher's Constructivist Teaching Accompanied by Various Curricular Practices 142

Table 9.1. Parallel Dynamics of Perspective-Taking 154

Table 9.2. Teacher's Perspective-Taking Implemented in Pedagogical Reflective Thinking and Action 155

Table 9.3. Examples of the Teacher's Inner Dialogue at the Elementary Cognitive Level with First-Person Perspective-Taking 162

Table 9.4. Examples of the Inner Dialogue Occurring in Reflection-in-Action with Second-Person Perspective-Taking 162

Table 9.5. Examples of Narrative Elements in the Inner Dialogue Occurring in Reflection-on-Action with First-Person Perspective-Taking 163

Table 9.6. Examples of Critical Elements in the Inner Dialogue Occurring in Reflection-for-Practice 164

Table 10.1. Negotiation-Oriented Practice in Comparison with Teachable Moment-Oriented and Emergent-Oriented Practice 169

Table 10.2. Teachable Moments in the Three Different Curricular Practices 171

Table 10.3. Power Issues in the Three Different Curricula Practices 172

## Acknowledgments

As I sit at my desk looking at my finished but perhaps never truly complete manuscript, so many moments flood my mind like a tsunami—a powerful learning experience. My heart pounding and my eyes filling with tears, I feel the overwhelming desire to revisit the moments and retell the stories with a different perspective.

So many children, teachers, parents, and colleagues from many different places have invited me to share their moments of unexpected teaching and learning as they pondered and strived for developmentally meaningful (not "appropriate") and culturally congruent human schooling experiences from diverse learners' points of view. I deeply appreciate all they have given me. I wish I could name the hundreds of people who have inspired and helped me on this book project, but because I cannot do so, I will name only a few. First of all, I will hear the voices of Angelo, Jeffrey, Jenny, Newly, Syler, and their family members and friends in my heart always. These children helped me understand the organic nature of developmentally meaningful and culturally congruent lived curriculum. I also appreciate all of my former students and cooperating teachers in the early childhood teacher education programs at the Pennsylvania State University (1992–1995), Clarion University of Pennsylvania (1995–1997), Florida Gulf Coast University (1997–2001), in particular Karen McGreevy and L.D., and Kent State University (2001–2006). Each one helped me to articulate the powerful notion of teachable moments through their field experiences. I am truly grateful to all the participants in the National Association of Early Childhood Teacher Educators (NAECTE) Research Net group entitled "Early Childhood Teacher Preparation for Developmentally and Culturally Appropriate Practice (DCAP)" (1995–2003) for their nationwide collaborative project to articulate DCAP-based teacher preparation. These include, to name a few, Dr. Ardley from North Carolina Department of Health and Human Services; Dr. Saundra DiPento, Southeastern Oklahoma State University-Station A; Dr. Georgianna Duart, University of Texas-Brownsville; Dr. Celeste Matthews, Winona State University, MN; Dr. Rosario Morales, California State University-LA; and Dr. Jocelynn Smrekar, Clarion University of Pennsylvania. In addition, my deepest appreciation goes to Dr. J. Dan Marshall at the Pennsylvania State University, who has helped me to develop a deep and profound understanding of the notion of organic and lived curriculum. His scholarly and collegial collaboration set the groundwork for this book. I am indebted to these people for their help in this ever-evolving work.

During the editing process, Dr. Linda Meixner, a wonderful colleague, provided excellent editing. I appreciate her invaluable professional help. I also appreciate my graduate assistant Ji-Young Choi, who is a C&I doctoral candidate; and postdoctoral research fellow Dr. Yoo-Jin Shon, who helped me with the tedious task of indexing.

My special appreciation goes to Dr. Shirley Steinberg and Dr. Joe Kincheloe, the two editors who have decided to include this book in Peter Lang's series *Counterpoints: Studies in the Postmodern Theory of Education*. I am truly honored to have my work included in this series. My thanks also go to Mr. Chris Myers, Managing Director of Peter Lang Publishing Company, whose responses are always thoughtful, prompt, and professional.

Last but hardly least, my son Yevin A. Roh continuously inspires me to ponder and appreciate diverse worldviews of human endeavor, and that is the foundation of this book. I will be forever indebted to him.

# Preface

This book opens with several questions: How do we understand what curriculum *is* and *does* for both learners and teachers? How do we prepare future teachers to be fully aware of what curriculum *is* and *does* in relation to teaching in a diverse school context? How can teachers understand developmentally meaningful and culturally congruent curriculum practice from the perspectives of both the child and the culturally cognizant adult? Furthermore, how might teachers infuse this developmentally meaningful and culturally congruent curriculum practice into their everyday teaching?

Since 1979 the U.S. national accrediting body has expected teacher education programs to prepare teachers for Education that is Multicultural (ETM) in order to respond to the complexities of "diversity" in schools, and doing so has been a significant task in initial teacher preparation (National Council for Accreditation of Teacher Education, 2002). In addition, NCATE standards discuss the necessity of addressing what the National Association for the Education of Young Children (NAEYC) christened Developmentally Appropriate Practice (DAP) (Bredekamp, 1987; Bredekamp & Copple, 1997) in conjunction with ETM in programs designed for the initial preparation of early childhood teachers (Hyson, 2003; NAEYC, 1997). For almost two decades since its inception, DAP has been the primary philosophical basis and related pedagogical framework for early childhood education, emphasizing age appropriate, individually appropriate, and socially and culturally appropriate curricula for young children. Since its inception, however, many early childhood educators have suggested the need for greater attention to cultural differences and related attention to more culturally appropriate practices that are fair and *meaningful* to all children (e.g., Bowman, 1994, 1992; Bredekamp & Rosegrant, 1992, 1995; Cannella, 1997; Delpit, 1988, 1995; Derman-Sparks, 1989; 1992; Hyun, 1998; Jipson, 1991; Mallory & New, 1994; Spodek & Brown, 1993; Swadener & Miller-Marsh, 1993; York, 1991).

Furthermore, we must articulate how to transform teachers' knowledge of DAP into a pedagogy-based teaching and curriculum practice that would pluralistically promote developmentally meaningful and culturally congruent learning experiences from diverse learners' points of view (Hyun, 2004, 2006, in press). Some postmodern educators have viewed the tendency of DAP to support adult privilege, (e.g., Cannella, 1997) justifying what is appropriate and what is not, without a full awareness of diverse human cultural influences that shape each child's developmental meaningfulness, growth, and learning. The NAEYC guidelines underlying the notion of what is "developmentally appropriate" must further articulate teachers' processes of *becoming* developmentally appropriate practitioners who value and embrace the developmental meaningfulness of each child as it has been shaped by family and ethnic cultural influences and who can work toward culturally congruent pedagogical interactions with all young learners (Hyun, 1998).

How can teachers understand multiple forms of curricula and pedagogical practices that are developmentally meaningful and culturally congruent from the child's perspective as well as from the culturally cognizant adult's perspective? How might we (teacher educators, teachers, school administrators, educational policy makers, and so on) articulate and infuse the notion of developmentally meaningful and culturally congruent curriculum practice into teachers' everyday action? One way to accomplish this goal involves reorienting programs for the initial preparation of early childhood educators. Toward this end several teacher educators (Hyun, 1996, 1998; Hyun & Marshall, 1996, 1997; Hyun, Marshall, & Dana, 1995) have developed and implemented an initial teacher preparation model (e.g., Hyun et al., 2000), which moves students beyond DAP toward developmentally meaningful and culturally congruent teaching and learning approaches, known as "developmentally and culturally appropriate practice (DCAP)."

The proposal for teacher preparation for DCAP represents a much-needed contemporary teacher education effort designed to help prospective teachers know themselves directly and their own cultural and ethnic backgrounds more immediately (e.g., Baker, 1994; Banks, 1994; Britzman & Pitt, 1996; Brown, 1998; Kincheloe, 1993; Nieto, 1992; Sleeter & Grant, 1999) in order to better understand and value the diverse cultural backgrounds and characteristics of the children they will teach. The intent of the DCAP teacher education model is to help prospective teachers develop multiple/multiethnic perspective-taking abilities as a move toward more culturally congruent curriculum and pedagogy that incorporate the contemporary cultural diversity of the children into their teaching and learning.

This new book is an extension of the early childhood teacher education model I presented in my 1998 book *Making sense of developmentally and culturally appropriate practice (DCAP) in early childhood education.* The current volume focuses on the articulation of developmentally meaningful and culturally congruent curricula practices based on field-based images of U.S. pre-K-3$^{rd}$ grade teachers' curriculum work, which I have collected over the course of 13 years in multicultural/multiethnic/multilingual school contexts. Most of the teachers described in this book are former students in teacher education programs with which I was previously affiliated, and they not only knew about and valued NAEYC's notion of DAP, but they were also aware of the critical limitations of DAP for culturally congruent practice as a result of their teacher education curriculum. Their work in the field inspired me to articulate developmentally meaningful and culturally congruent curriculum practice in three different aspects: teachable moment-oriented, emergent-oriented and negotiation-oriented, which differ distinctly from one another in the classroom curriculum practice. These three forms of curriculum practice are, however, interconnected by the different intentions of teachers capitalizing on teachable moments. In a nutshell, this book is about articulating these particular phenomena.

Ordinarily when we deal with developmentally appropriate practice (DAP), we must consider *whose appropriateness, whose guidelines of appropriateness we are referring to* and in many cases without realizing the limitation, we usually refer to "dominant" cultural values of appropriateness. Thus, children from diverse background and underprivileged contexts become unfairly and inappropriately cared for, interacted with, and educated (Bowman, 1994; Cannella, 1997; Hyun, 1998). As a result, their schooling experience suffers, leading to further complex social, cultural, and economic consequences in their lives. In order to overcome the critical limitations, we need to articulate developmental appropriateness as developmental meaningfulness from a child's point of view, reflecting the cultural congruency that has shaped growth, learning, and change in the child. For this reason I have changed the phrase from developmentally and culturally appropriate practice (DCAP) to *developmentally meaningful and culturally congruent practices.* The book introduces multiple new ways of understanding early childhood curricula and practices that are developmentally meaningful and culturally congruent from the perspectives of diverse children and families and also describes ways teachers can infuse developmentally meaningful and culturally congruent curricula practices into their everyday actions that include teachable moment-, emergent-, and negotiation-oriented curricula practices.

Postmodernism has provided us with an intellectual space where we conclude that we cannot continue as we have been (Constas, 1998; Lather, 1991; Slattery, 1995). Many leading early childhood educators have clearly expressed the need to strengthen and elaborate all that is good about "developmentally appropriate practice" for young children in light of this country's increasingly diverse and ever-changing population of children and families (Bowman, 1994; Cannella, 1997; Hyun, 1998; Lubeck, 1996; Mallory & New, 1994). Postmodern early childhood educators ask this key question: What are the contemporary sociocultural conditions within which a human act takes place, and how might those conditions support a person's capability to construct, deconstruct, reconstruct, and interpret new meanings of that act? Some postmodern critical discourse occurred in the late 1990s. Even so, the critical deconstruction of the conventional early childhood curriculum and practice has been very slowly manifested in the process of reconceptualizing early childhood education for teachers.

Most widely used early childhood curriculum textbooks are either traditional subject-based texts promoting curriculum integration or developmental sequence-based texts designed to introduce early childhood curriculum typically by incorporating early intervention and inclusion, multiple intelligences, DAP, and play. By and large, these popular textbooks primarily reflect a monocultural or single-perspective orientation (i.e., White European American) with some consideration of multiculturalism as an additional component relative to the early childhood curriculum and teaching. We, however, need to articulate teachers' understanding of curriculum (what curriculum *is* and what curriculum *does*) in conjunction with their pedagogical decision-making processes for the multidirectional dynamics of curriculum change affected by diverse young children's contemporary culture, family, identities, or emergent meaning-making (e.g., Delpit, 1995). ECE curriculum studies related literatures need to discuss the fundamental aspects of what curriculum *is* and *does* in light of learners' and teachers' points of view in diverse school and social contexts.

The current book illustrates the phenomenon of teachers' multiple/multiethnic perspective-taking ability as it pertains to curricular decision-making and ever-changing sociocultural phenomena affecting culturally congruent curricula understandings and practices in multiple forms, such as teachable moment-, emergent-, and negotiation-oriented. In the field of early childhood teacher education, as well as the field of curriculum studies in general, we need a curriculum textbook that moves beyond the traditional textbook based in the single subject, in several elements, or in program name. Instead, senior level prospective teachers and future ECE leaders need to explore and learn the fundamentals of ECE critical pedagogy through contemporary curricula understandings derived from real life-based emerging phenomena brought by contemporary children living together in multidimensional, multicultural, and multiethnic cultural environments with developmental characteristics shaped by multifaceted cultural influences (e.g., Greenfield & Cocking, 1994). This book aims to meet that need.

In this book I question what curriculum *is* and *does* and describe three positions from which to understand, orchestrate, and enact early childhood curriculum that promotes developmentally meaningful and culturally congruent practice based on my previous curriculum theorizing works: Teachable Moments-Oriented Curriculum (e.g., Hyun & Marshall, 2003), Emergent-Oriented Curriculum (e.g., Hyun & Marshall, 2003), and Negotiation-Oriented Curriculum (e.g., Hyun, 2004, 2006, in press). I situate the discussion of these forms of curriculum thought and practice within the broader discussion of re-conceptualizing early childhood curriculum and practice in light of developmentally meaningful and culturally congruent practice with young children. In doing so, I intend to both celebrate and critique the field's "developmentally appropriate practice (DAP)" mantra while simultaneously imagining and toying with multiple ways of promoting

DAP as developmentally meaningful and culturally congruent curriculum experiences from the points of view of diverse learners.

Field-based case studies and vignettes are infused into the chapters to connect ECE curriculum matters with contemporary children's lives and their learning experiences. Each chapter is also accompanied by initial thought-provoking questions and chapter-ending reflective questions for group discussion. Each chapter has tables, figures, and footnotes to elucidate the complexity of the discussion effectively.

This book is designed for

1. junior and senior ECE undergraduates in early childhood curriculum courses who require a reality-based understanding of teaching and curriculum practice;
2. graduate students in curriculum studies who are interested in learning the fundamentals of curriculum (what curriculum *is* and *does*) and social, cultural, political, and historical influences on ECE as well as the influence of developmental theories;
3. early childhood teacher educators who teach current issues in ECE curriculum and re-conceptualizing ECE; and
4. graduate faculty who teach curriculum studies courses and are interested in including ECE contemporary curricula discourses.

This book is divided into three sections. Section I: Toward Curriculum Re-conceptualization is composed of four chapters (Chapters 1–4). "Chapter 1: Cultural Complexity and Early Childhood" redefines education that is multicultural for young children. Theoretical understandings of DAP versus developmentally and culturally appropriate practice (DCAP) are reviewed, and curricular images of developmentally meaningful and culturally congruent practices in early childhood education are foreshadowed.

"Chapter 2: Curriculum Understanding: Its Relationship to Teaching" reviews understanding of curriculum (what it *is* and *does*) in relationship with instruction-oriented versus pedagogy-based teaching.

"Chapter 3: Influences in Modern Early Childhood Curriculum and Teaching" reviews preexisting understandings of curriculum in light of what curriculum *is* and *does* to articulate critical limits that have pervasively influenced early childhood curricula.

In "Chapter 4: Curricula Understandings Toward Developmentally Meaningful and Culturally Congruent Practices," the reader comes to see how developmentally meaningful and culturally congruent practices intersect with notions of contemporary postmodern curriculum. Three different curricula perspectives—teachable moment-oriented curriculum, emergent-oriented curriculum, and negotiation-oriented curriculum—are explained in terms of their relationship to the theorizing of developmentally meaningful and culturally congruent practices and early childhood pedagogy.

Section II: Re-conceptualizing Curricula Practices presents three different images of curricula practices in Chapters 5—7. Chapter 5 introduces teachable moment-oriented curriculum practice, which is based on teachers' observations and interpretations of diverse learners' individual voices and identities, their developmental growth and change, and their intellectual cultures, needs, interests, and curiosities. The chapter challenges readers (teachers) to reexamine their own understanding of teachable moments in order to question their congruence with learners' learnable moments.

Chapter 6 deals with emergent-oriented curriculum practice, which entails an expansion of teachable moment-oriented curriculum work led by children's continuation of learnable moments. Not all teachable moments lead to emergent-oriented curriculum. Here, the teacher captures children's moments of emerging interests and works to preserve, nurture, and transform these moments while maintaining the core idea of "child initiation" (e.g., Coles & Nixon, 1998; Hyun & Marshall, 2003b; Peterson, 2002). In comparison with teachable moment-oriented curriculum practice, emergent-oriented curriculum practice represents an effort to engage diverse children's emerging interests within a social learning context through large- and small-group sharing, exploration, and discussion of learner-generated topics and issues.

Chapter 7 covers negotiation-oriented curriculum practice in conjunction with reference to Chapter 2. It contains a discussion of pedagogy-based teaching (as opposed to instruction-oriented teaching), which entails study-based, ethical, socially just, and morally sound practice resulting from inner and outer negotiation among the teacher, students, and others. Chapter 7 articulates negotiation-oriented curriculum for pedagogy-based teaching that illuminates developmentally meaningful and culturally congruent practice. In negotiation-oriented curriculum, teachers deliberately look for a particular kind of moment as a teachable moment that is equally a learnable moment.

Section III: Curricula Re-conceptualization and Interconnectedness comprises three chapters (Chapters 8–10) that introduce the interrelationship among the three different curricula understandings in light of various types of constructivist approaches and teacher reflectivity. "Chapter 8: Recursive Movement Among Positions" contains a discussion of teachers' manifestations of constructivism related to their sense-making of teachable moments and how their approaches shape their curriculum practice. The chapter also explores what drives teachers to engage in the recursive mode of de-construction, re-construction, and new construction of their teaching, and how it leads to changes in their curriculum practice.

"Chapter 9: Reflectivity and Multiple Perspective-Taking" articulates teachers' metacognitive infrastructure (multiple forms of reflectivity and perspective-taking) that supports free and fluid ransacking of the three curricula notions. Key to bringing developmentally meaningful and culturally congruent practice into teachers' everyday curriculum work is their willingness and ability to transform instruction-oriented teaching into pedagogy-based teaching through the pedagogical habit of multiple/multiethnic perspective-taking (Hyun & Marshall, 1997). Chapter 9 describes the way multiple/multiethnic perspective-taking combines with the reflective functions (Hyun & Marshall, 1996) basic to these varied curriculum perspectives to promote reconstructing an early childhood curriculum that is developmentally meaningful and culturally cognizant.

Based on discussions of different types of curricula approaches in the first nine chapters in light of teacher reflectivity and multiple perspective-taking, "Chapter 10: Summary and Conclusion" compares and contrasts the three different curricula understandings in conjunction with power-sharing and negotiation. Further articulation on the key characteristics of negotiation-oriented curriculum practice in comparison with teachable moment-oriented curriculum and emergent-oriented curriculum is discussed in the chapter.

The chapter concludes with a question to ponder: How would an informed educator move toward pedagogically sound curriculum leadership for young learners? Beginning in the late 1980s, we have faced a conflicting reality and paradoxical behaviors in curriculum practice influenced by the law and politics (e.g., The U.S. No Child Left Behind Act, 2002; The U.K. National Curriculum, 1988) that heavily emphasize standardized curriculum practices and assessments (Bassey, 2003; Hyun, 2003). As well-informed educators we need to learn how to negotiate and go beyond the political scrutiny of narrowly defined curriculum implementation in order to cultivate and enhance democratically and pedagogically sound curriculum leadership for all learners with multiethnic, multilingual, multidimensional, and multidirectional learner characteristics.

# Section I: Toward Curriculum Re-conceptualization

# Chapter One

# Cultural Complexity and Early Childhood

## Initial Inquiries

- How do we see cultural complexity in young children's lives?
- Why should teachers embrace cultural complexity in their practice?
- What needs to be considered to promote developmentally meaningful and culturally congruent curriculum practices for all young children?

## Orientation Toward Cultural Complexity

As long as human society depends upon and values the practice we have come to know as "schooling," we will continue to practice it as a crucial social activity, using "teachers" as critical agents in overseeing its functioning. As such, the initial preparation of teachers will remain crucial, and teacher education programs responsible for this preparation should acknowledge and welcome their fundamental responsibility for readying new teachers to experience and learn reflectively about themselves and the human diversity they will encounter in schools and classrooms. When this consciousness becomes a part of pedagogical knowledge, skills, and dispositions presented to new teachers, they will be better equipped to construct a curriculum that is more likely to lead to equal, fair, developmentally meaningful, and culturally congruent schooling experiences for all learners.

One of the most profound aspects of U.S. education today is its cultural complexity. Since the late 1970s, a massive body of literature and numerous programs dealing with teacher preparation for education that is "multicultural" (ETM) have emerged (Banks, 1994, Gollnick & Chinn, 1998; Grant, 1992; Ladson-Billings, 1992, 1994; National Council for Accreditation of Teacher Education, 1979, 2002; Ramsey, 1987; Sleeter, 1991; Sleeter & Grant, 1994, 1999; Zeichner, 1993; 1981–1982; Zeichner & Grant, 1998; Zeichner, & Liston, 1987). Most related materials and practices designed toward this end, however, are based on conventional multicultural education typically derived from an orientation toward human "grouping" (Giroux, 1997).

Group orientation usually results from a view of pluralistic human society based on unequal positions of power in the United States. People's thinking and visual images of "multiculturalism" are typically shaped by classification in terms of "at-risk status," ethnicity, race, language, gender, social class, disability, and exceptionality, religion, sexual orientation, and the like. In addition, when materials and programs represent education that is multicultural from a social meliorist or a social reconstructionist perspective (Kliebard, 1995), the traditional orientation pertains to notions of power struggle, and equal opportunity (Sleeter & Grant, 1994, 1999). Influenced by this tradition, school reform is represented through actions such as desegregation, affirmative action, racially balanced cooperating groups, mainstreaming and inclusion, ESE (Exceptional Students Education) classes, ESOL (English Speakers of Other Languages) programs, and bilingual education, to name a few.

As a result of these necessary reforms, we have acknowledged human diversity by identifying individual disabilities, differences, ethnic identities and unique characteristics of specific groups of people and by revisiting our democratic ideal of equity and cultural pluralism through schooling. A typical quotation representing this group-oriented position regarding pluralistic multiculturalism follows:

> For cultural pluralism to be a reality, the nation would recognize many ethnic, religious, [and other groups] that could coexist. It would require that power and resources be shared somewhat equitably across those groups. (Gollnick & Chinn, 1998, p. 17)

The tone of acknowledging pluralism in schooling from this perspective, however, always reflects a dominant power-holder's perspective—as in the need for compensatory help from the dominant society such as "We need to respect other groups' right to coexist with us and do this (whatever 'this' happens to be at the moment) for them so that we can live together more equitably." In this regard, Giroux (1997) advocated schooling to avoid such superficial pluralism resulting from a notion of multiculturalism structured around dominance:

> Multiculturalism doesn't simply mean numerical plurality of different cultures, but rather a community which is creating, guaranteeing, encouraging spaces within which different communities are able to grow at their own

> pace. At the same time it means creating a public space in which these communities are able to interact, enrich the existing culture and create a new consensual culture in which they recognize reflections of their own identity. (Bhabha & Parekh, 1989, cited in Giroux, 1997, p. 247)

Giroux believed that teacher education programs should nurture future teachers' pedagogical practices, allowing

> schools to become places where students and teachers can become border crossers engaged in critical and ethical reflection about what it means to bring a wider variety of cultures into dialogue with each other, to theorize about cultures in the plural, within rather than outside antagonistic relations of domination and subordination. (Giroux, 1997, p. 247)

This pluralistic orientation works to unsettle many overly simplistic practices of schooling such as "one-size-fits-all" curriculum packages, the one-shot-deal-based "traveler approach" to professional development for teachers, and the celebratory subject approach to diversity (e.g., Black History Month, Women's History Month, Study of China, Study of Native Americans, and so on). In their place pluralism requires teachers to search for multiple forms of "good" practice (Gardner, 1983, 1999) and culturally appropriate, thus culturally responsive, curricula (see, for example, Bowman, 1992, 1994; Delpit, 1995; Ladson-Billings, 1992). Within the pluralistic orientation, NAEYC's Developmentally Appropriate Practice (DAP) (Bredekamp & Copple, 1997) is no longer viewed as the single best approach to educating young children (Cannella, 1997; Delpit, 1988, 1995; Derman-Sparks, 1989, 1992; Hyun, 1998; Jipson, 1991; Mallory & New, 1994; Swadener & Miller-Marsh, 1993).

No matter how well these group-oriented practices have succeeded in moving us toward schooling that serves a multicultural, pluralistic human society, we still face almost the same struggles in maintaining equal, fair, developmentally meaningful, and culturally congruent schooling environment for all students. We still count the number of Blacks, Hispanics, Native Americans, and Asians in each classroom, the number of children identified as English Speakers of Other Languages (ESOL), children with special needs, children who receive free lunch, and so on. Although a good deal of this counting helps institutions provide various forms of support for students and teachers, it also creates and maintains the grouping orientation in the minds and practice of education professionals. Much worse, however, it helps to reinforce group stereotyping because it promotes a kind of institutionalized patronization that maintains the very power differential struggles (i.e., dominance over students in general, and certain groups of students in particular). This grouping framework seldom allows teachers or schools to see and acknowledge diverse children's unique capabilities and differences, nor can it accept the individual ways children share and learn from one another, building self-identity while learning to appreciate and experiment with the identities of others. The important and increasingly popular group orientation to education that is multicultural is limited in terms of helping children develop an intellectual framework for realizing positive self-identity and developing an eventual repertoire of other identities which underlie the dynamic nature of a human organism.

## Cultural Complexity in Early Childhood

In contemporary U.S. culture, young children are not only oriented by their own multiple cultures (racial, ethnic, age, gender, and family to name several) but also by living and learning within a socioculturally conditioned world filled with many different conditions of cultural difference. The following vignettes serve to illustrate these points.[1]

> Story of Yoko
>
> Eight-month-old Yoko wears cotton diapers at home. When she goes to day care, she wears disposable diapers. Yoko appears to sense the different diapers and has learned that she can use both kinds. At home Yoko's Japanese American mother holds Yoko on her back and speaks to her in both Japanese and English languages. Her Spanish speaking Native American grandmother holds Yoko on her sides as well as on her back. At day care, Yoko's English speaking Mexican-American teacher holds Yoko on her stomach. (Los Angeles, CA, 1998)

The world of young Yoko is an already complex one that permits her to feel differently in different places, see things from different vantage points, interact with others in various modes, and listen to at least three different linguistic patterns as she grows.

Story of Tony and Jane

Five-year-old Jane visited Tony's home, where she watched Tony use chopsticks to eat chicken nuggets and carrots. Tony's mom gave Jane a fork as well as a set of chopsticks, but Jane used her fingers when she ate her chicken nuggets. Tony said to Jane, "At my home I use chopsticks for food. I don't use my fingers. But at school I use a fork or my fingers." Tony showed Jane how to use chopsticks, and later she asked Tony's mom if she could take the chopsticks home. "They are hard to use, but they are fun to use, too. And, I know how to use them now. I like to use them." At their full day kindergarten, Tony and Jane asked the teacher if they could use chopsticks when they ate lunch. Tony's mother brought a box of plastic chopsticks as well as a box of bamboo chopsticks for the children. Tony and Jane demonstrated how to use chopsticks for the other children. Afterward, the children could then use chopsticks, silverware, and their fingers when having their meals at school. (State College, PA, 1994)

When young children discover and acquire new knowledge, they tend to gather information without making value judgments (e.g., chopsticks are not funny or a strange things, but simply different tools for the same purpose of eating food). Their expression of new knowledge at school enriches the "schooling" environment.

Story of Syler

When Syler, who is African American, was 5 years old, he and his two fathers attended story time every Saturday at their local library. One day a storyteller read a book entitled *Between Earth and Sky: Legends of Native American Sacred Places* (Bruchac & Locker, 1996). Syler loved the story so much that after hearing it, he preferred to be called Little Bear like the main character in the story. From this story Syler and his fathers learned about the seven directions: north, south, east, west, earth, sky, and the seventh direction within us all, the place where we distinguish right from wrong and maintain balance in life by choosing to live in a good way. Two years later when Syler was in the second grade, his class learned about directions. When the teacher and the textbook referred only to four directions (north, south, east, and west, based on the Sunshine State [Florida] Social Studies Content Standards), Syler disagreed, explaining to his teacher and classmates that he knew about three other directions: earth, sky, and the judging of right and wrong. The teacher answered, "Syler, we are learning about north, south, east, and west. These are the main directions we need to learn." Puzzled, Syler went home at the end of the day and explained what had happened at school. He and his father Jeffray returned to the local library and checked out the book they remembered so well. The next day Syler took the book to school and asked the teacher whether he and his father Jeffray could read the book together to the class. Because there were some big words in the book that Syler couldn't yet read by himself, he needed his father's help. The teacher agreed, not to change the content but to support parental involvement in the classroom; however, she wanted to read the book before making a decision about letting Syler and his father read the book. The following day Syler and his father Jeffray read the book together to the class. Syler's classmates and teacher listened to the story and learned of seven directions. When Syler and his father finished reading the book, the teacher captured a teachable moment and genuinely asked the children to tell what they knew about the new directions, how they were different from the first four directions, and what they thought about the other three directions. Wanting to add the three directions, the children asked their teacher to change the bulletin board to reflect the three new directions along with the previous four. Later the children talked not only about which directions Christopher Columbus took to get to North America but also which direction they should take to make good decisions for building (not "keeping") peace on earth and in their classroom (Fort Myers, FL, 1997). (See Chapter 7 for further analysis of this case.)

A child's personally compelling inquiry led him and his father to be socially proactive about bringing new knowledge into the learning process in his *schooling*. The children and the teacher had an unexpected but powerful learning experience in which the learning community of *schooling* went beyond the single perspective of knowledge.

Story of Newly

Newly's Haitian family lives in a migrant farm workers' community. Because of their extremely limited income, two other families (12 people in all) live in Newly's very old mobile home, which has one toilet, a sink, a stove, two small rooms, and a TV. Five-year-old Newly attends a nonprofit community day care each day from 7:30 a.m. to 5:30 p.m. There, some of her friends who have lighter-colored skin than she speak English, with which she is familiar because of her favorite TV program *Barney*, while other friends with skin colored closer to hers speak Spanish or Creole, the Haitian language; or Black English, Ebonics (African American Vernacular English), Newly's teachers at the day care all speak English and Spanish or Creole. Newly and her friends have learned that, for example, *thank you*, *gracias*, and *mèsi* have the same meaning. She and most of her friends have also learned what kinds of languages and words to use and when, and they count numbers in the three different languages. Watching a TV program on the Learning Channel, they observe many different-looking children on the TV screen count numbers in other unfamiliar languages. After viewing, they are able to count numbers in Swahili as well as Japanese. One day, Newly listened to

> her parents and teacher talking about her next year at kindergarten in the public school. Suddenly, Newly asked her teacher, "Why do I have to use only English at the big school?" Why does the big school teach only English? I know more than English. I also see many people speak differently on TV, and I know what they are saying. We can say and write words in many ways. Look at this book! The iguana brothers speak in English and Spanish in this book (*The Iguana Brothers*, written by Tony Johnston, illustrated by Mark Trague, 1995). It's my favorite! In the computer center I also play games with English and Spanish words when I read stories. I know them. (Immokalee, FL, 1999)

The child lives in an environment filled with multiple linguistic resources, which have led her to question the limits that schooling holds for her and other children in the very near future. The child may have perceived the limits in schooling more deeply than adults have. The young child exhibits a powerful and critical capability of problematizing the previously organized body of knowledge through a particular cultural lens and possibly alters the knowledge in a way that makes sense to her.

> Story of Jake
>
> Eight-year-old Jake likes to play with computers. Recently, his family purchased a new computer, and under his parents' supervision Jake has learned how to find certain Internet Web sites. One Saturday morning he watched a TV cartoon called *Pokémon,* which he liked very much. He remembered that many of his school friends play Pokémon with their Gameboys and play with Pokémon cards. Later that day he turned on the computer, searching for information about Pokémon. He learned that a Pokémon League gathered every Saturday in a local book store to play with Pokémon cards. When Jake went there with his parents, he played with many other kids—some younger, some older, and some the same age as he, some using wheelchairs or wearing aids, some African American, Asian American, and Hispanic American kids, and a girl with two moms! "I am going to attend every Saturday for the league," he announced later. "It's a cool game. I thought those kids were different from me. I see them at my school, but I don't play with them much. I thought I could never be friends with any of them. But they are all same as me. I played with most of them! I also thought girls didn't like to play Pokémon, but the girl I played with and her mom knew almost every Pokémon name. They are cool, too. Later, Jake said to his parents, "I think she has two moms. I noticed that she was calling them 'Mom Jenny' and 'Mom Susan.' I also saw Pokémon cards written in other languages [Chinese, Japanese, and Korean] which I did not know about before, but we still played with those.

> Somehow we learned about each card's information when we played together. It was like magic. I am going back next week." (Fort Myers, FL, 1998)

The commercialization of the contemporary culture of children's play and their personal interests have motivated greater and inclusive friendship-making experiences. In the foregoing example neither Jake's schooling nor family culture had influenced him to build inclusive friendship-making experiences voluntarily.

*Multicultural* and *multiethnic* are the words we now use to describe young children's identities in contemporary U.S. society, yet young children can no longer be seen as having a single ethnic identity (e.g., Mexican American). Our predominant, group-oriented view of multiculturalism, wherein an everlasting power struggle exists, no longer provides us with a congruent intellectual framework for appreciating young children's current and future living and learning situations. As illustrated in the above vignettes, if we carefully observe young children's lives, we realize that they do not naturally struggle with power issues. Even when a power struggle exists, children's meaningful social interaction tends to undo or prevent further power struggles. Young children construct fairly equal perceptions of one another. When they learn new knowledge, they tend to gather information without a value judgment (e.g., chopsticks are not funny or strange things, but simply different tools for the same purpose of eating food). Even when children seem to hold unfair social perceptions of others (e.g., Jake's case: They look different and I don't know about them; therefore, I don't play with them.), they have an intellectual capacity of undoing their preexisting unfair perceptions through personally meaningful experiences with others. Early childhood teachers must recognize that many contemporary young children

- experience multidirectional, multidimensional, multilingual, multiethnic developmental growth and change;
- construct unique ways of knowing based on the ways they perceive the world within the cultures they encounter;
- face continuous, new sociocultural changes as they grow; and
- live in dynamic and changeable family structures, cycles, and environments.

From this vantage point teachers see that classrooms are always filled with students representing multiple/multiethnic perspectives reflecting their individual dynamic ecological and biological changes as well as their unique multiethnic daily experiences. In order to provide an equal, fair, developmentally meaningful, and culturally congruent learning environment for these students, early childhood curriculum must become multidimensional responding to the multiple forms of realities that keep evolving.

Observing these young children's evolving learning experiences, we see that we have created complex conflicts and sociocultural discomfort for them by excessively and inappropriately imposing narrow child development theory, social rules, and sociocultural values wrapped within a kind of ethnically singular multiculturalism in schools. In the name of education, we limit and perhaps damage their human potential. Thus, how we come to understand multiculturalism becomes an ethical issue when we talk about schooling for all young children.

The time has come to push beyond the popular group orientation to education that is multicultural (ETM) and search for what is critically missing in our ever-changing, multiple understandings of human dynamics within the self (individual) as an ecological organism (see, for example, Diamond & Hopson, 1998; Gardner, 1999; Pearce, 1977; Shore, 1996, 1997). We need to respond to the multicultural/ multiethnic perspectives that exist in every moment in every classroom when it comes to young individual children's developmental growth and change. We need to recognize the numerous cultural identities shaped by everything from broad sociocultural influences to unique family influences.

Research has shown that the human brain changes physiologically as a result of experiences (Diamond & Hopson, 1998; Shore, 1996, 1997; Wolfe & Brandt, 1998). Shore (1996) discussed this phenomenon as an evolution that equips human species with an "ecological brain" dependent throughout its life on sociocultural environmental input. Because of its plasticity, the brain constantly changes its structure and function in response to external experiences. This natural human condition allows both micro and macro sociocultural environments to affect individuals' multidirectional growth and developmental change, equipping people with diversified sense-making capabilities in terms of living, learning, and constructing knowledge during their entire life span. Especially during the early childhood period (ages 0–8), this ecological human brain is more responsive to sociocultural influences than in later years (Hyun, 2005a; Pearce, 1977; Shore, 1997). As illustrated in the foregoing vignettes, because of diverse sociocultural environments, the nature of young children's developmental growth, change, and learning is multidirectional (eight-month-old Yoko viewed things from multiple directions; Jane, Tony, and their friends used multiple resources for a specific purpose), multidimensional (Syler saw directions from the multiple dimensions), multiethnic (Newly learned diverse ethnic linguistic codes as naturalistic human interaction), and everlasting (Jake found himself changing through interaction with other children).

To create equal, fair, developmentally meaningful, and culturally congruent schooling for all learners, curriculum must have multidirectional, multidimensional, and multiethnic capacities. The past several decades have produced in educators a keen awareness of social and cultural pluralism, emancipatory knowledge, and critical pedagogy, which combine to form a foundation for that kind of curriculum construction (see, for example, Delpit, 1995; Giroux, 1997; Lather, 1986; Slattery, 1995); yet few have attempted to relate that foundation to early childhood education. In order to move closer to equal, fair, developmentally meaningful, and culturally congruent curriculum construction for young children from their points of view, we must realize cultural complexities starting at the personal level.

Engaging in cultural pluralism begins with one's autobiographical realization of self and family identities (Baker, 1994; Banks, 1994; Hyun, 1998; Kincheloe, 1993; Kumabe, Nishida, & Hepworth, 1985; McAdoo, 1993; Nieto, 1992; Sleeter & Grant, 1999; Stewart & Bennett, 1991). Lacking awareness and acceptance of one's own identities, individuals risk failing to perceive and respect the equally genuine and complex cultural differences between oneself and others, a failure that prevents the development of multiple/multiethnic perspective-taking abilities (Hyun & Marshall, 1997). The resulting cultural myopia severely diminishes democratic practices for pluralistic schooling and curriculum (examples are illustrated in the images of teachers' curricula practices presented in Chapters 5, 6, & 7).

Appreciating cultural pluralism leads to the realization that all knowledge results from interpretation derived from one's own identities, backgrounds, and experiences. This realization, basic to the pluralistic orientation, leads teachers to value emancipatory knowledge constructed by individual learners in the process of locating themselves (while being located by others) within their world, on their own terms as they act to change their worlds (like Syler). The desire to promote pluralistic emancipatory knowledge like this guides teachers' critical pedagogy (Giroux, 1997; Lather, 1986; O'Loughlin, 1992). Critical pedagogy refers to teaching that proceeds from a consideration of diverse students' everyday lives and experiences (Giroux & Simon, 1989) instead of an imposed cultural canon (Nieto, 1992). Critical pedagogy reflects teachers' thinking and action that goes beyond those commonsense assumptions shaped by one's own singular worldview. Because mere commonsense assumptions cannot lead to congruent schooling experiences for all children (e.g., not all children maintain eye contact when they talk to the teacher; not all children agree on only four directions when they look at a map), critical pedagogy demands an ethical questioning of the teacher's own practices with respect to how she or he may best serve every student. Teachers practicing critical pedagogy continuously try to learn about and question their own beliefs and practices and to escape from the cultural myopia that society promotes, understanding that "you become what you are in the context of what others made of you" (Giroux, 1997, p. 27). This critical recognition serves to guide all decisions about what to teach, how to teach, and how to interpret learners' self-growth.

An early childhood teacher who strives to infuse critical pedagogy into his or her curriculum practice believes that learning depends on children's using what they already know in the service of creating new ideas, skills, and dispositions. When unwilling or unable to evoke what children already know to inform their work, teachers imperil teaching and learning processes, making developmentally and culturally congruent equal and fair schooling and curriculum experiences impossible. When teachers assume that mainstream behavior is "normal" and that the behavior of other groups is deviant or deficient, they are apt to ignore the cognitive structures children already have, to misread children's abilities, to misdesign or maintain a limiting curriculum. Thus, a power struggle between teachers and learners remains intact within curriculum practice (Bowman, 1994) unless they decide to solve (negotiate) the conflict by being socially and intellectually proactive about their limits.

## Connection Toward Curriculum

Developmentally meaningful and culturally congruent practice is pertinent not simply to specific ethnic groups but to all young children who by definition experience new cultures as they grow and as their family structures, cycles, and environments change. Depending on how the teacher defines what curriculum "*is*" and "*does*" to and for the learner, the quality and effectiveness of developmentally meaningful and culturally congruent practice may be different. Thus, it is very important that each teacher explore and contemplate from her or his own perspective what curriculum *is* and *does* to and for the learner (see Chapter 2). At the same time, within the notion of developmentally meaningful and culturally congruent practice, teachers ought to construct an intellectual curriculum framework with multiple capacities for responding to young children's multidirectional, multidimensional, and thus multiethnic needs in their developmental growth and change as well as in their formal learning experiences. Teachers strive to learn about and understand each child's unique family influences, which immediately affect the child's development, learning, and problem-solving skills. This effort leads the teacher to reflect on how she or he can use the child's personal knowledge and family background as powerful pedagogical elements within the classroom. This kind of fundamental reflective thinking used with the teacher's actual everyday practice is essential to curriculum construction. Such reflection helps to ensure that teachers consider multiple and diverse viewpoints as well as the long-term social and moral consequences of their decisions. Teaching in this fashion will likely result in education that is meaningfully multicultural—that is, for all children.

Within the formal educational environment, curriculum for developmentally meaningful and culturally congruent practice becomes a shared, organic, mutually created, or lived experience blending elements of teachable moments (see Chapter 5), emergent curriculum (see Chapter 6), and curriculum negotiation (see Chapter 7). As teachers and prospective teachers are exposed to and become familiar with the notions of teachable moment-, emergent-, and negotiation-oriented curriculum, it is hoped that they will freely borrow from these three curricular traditions while attempting to become critical thinkers, ethical caregivers, careful listeners, and active learners themselves. Moreover, teachers, parents, and learners all share the power and responsibilities inherent in the process of making decisions for lived curricula experiences that its process promises.

## Chapter Ending Question

- How have I explored the cultural complexity of young children's lives as a rich teaching and learning experience in my daily practice as teacher?

## Note

[1] Ordinary people's real life stories are presented throughout this book to convey the contemporary cultures of young children and families. From 1988 to 2002, people's stories (vignettes) were collected from naturalistic observations at variety settings in different states (California, Nevada, Louisiana, Illinois, New York, New Hampshire, Pennsylvania, and Florida). The settings include people's homes, public libraries, buses, trains, airplanes, restaurants, bookstores, post offices, malls, parks, movie theaters, museums, streets, day care centers, play grounds, public schools, a gas station, and college classes, and so on. Pseudonyms are used in each vignette.

# Chapter Two

# Curriculum Understanding: Its Relationship to Teaching

## Initial Inquiries

- How are curriculum and teaching related?
- What *is* curriculum? What is curriculum expected to accomplish or *do*?
- How do instruction-oriented teaching and pedagogy-based teaching differ in a teacher's curriculum work?

Because twenty-first-century U.S. education policy, particularly the NCLBA (2001), supports positivist "proctoristic" teacher responsibility, instruction-oriented teaching has again become prevalent (Hyun, 2003). We have an ethical responsibility to examine critically the difference between instruction and pedagogy in field-based curriculum studies.

## Instruction Versus Pedagogy in the Relations Between Curriculum and Teaching

How do curriculum scholars (workers) define instruction? Bruce and Weil (1972), for example, viewed instruction as a teaching effort to lead the learner in a certain direction to achieve planned goals and objectives. Sowell (2005) perceived instruction as the imparting of knowledge or skill: Instruction entails the manner in which curriculum is delivered to learners. Sowell defined instruction as the delivery of curriculum to students through teaching agents (e.g., teachers, school staff, other learners, instructional materials, programmed instruction). Passing preexisting contents on to learners is the essence of instruction.

The word *pedagogy*, however, derives from the Greek *paidagōgia,* meaning the "duties of a pedagogue/educator/school teacher." *Pedagogy* denotes "the principles and methods of instruction or the activities of educating or teaching learners." According to Best (1988), in Europe the term *pedagogy* symbolizes the controversy between those who believe schools should exclusively concern instruction and those who believe schools should also play an educative role, one that includes not only instruction but also the civil, social, and moral aspects of education. Pedagogy is a human and social science albeit geared toward action. Pedagogy is concerned with taking part in a process of social evolution leading to progress in the educational system and for the people involved in it in order that children and adolescents can shape their own future. Thus, pedagogy exceeds instruction, hints at the necessity of power-sharing, particularly with regard to processes of democratization, and simultaneously articulates the limitations of instruction. In some European languages other than English, *pedagogy* is understood as the teacher's interpersonal competencies and is thus used to refer to the moral and ethical—as opposed to the technical instructional—aspects of the teacher's work.

Even though *instruction* has been one of the most prevalent terms in curriculum studies, few curriculum scholars discuss the distinction between instruction and pedagogy. Here, I discuss the perspectives of J. Dewey, E. Eisner, and critical pedagogy (e.g, Freire, 1971; Giroux, 1988, 1992, 1997).

*Dewey's perspective*: In *The Child and the Curriculum* Dewey (1902) discussed problems inherent in instruction:

> Problems of instruction are problems of procuring texts giving logical parts and sequences and of presenting these portions in class in a similar definite and graded way. Subject matter furnishes the end, and it determines method. The child is simply the immature being who is to be matured; he is the superficial being who is to be deepened; his is narrow experience which is to be widened. It is his to receive, to accept. His part is fulfilled when he is ductile and docile (p. 8). . . . Abandon the notion of subject matter as something fixed and readymade in itself, outside the child's experience; cease thinking of the child's experience as also something hard and fast; see it as something fluent, embryonic, vital; and we realize that the child and the curriculum are simply two limits which define a single process. Just as two points define a straight line, so the present standpoint of the child and the facts and truths of studies define instruction. (p. 11)

Dewey argued that instruction harms the learner because it assumes the child's passivity and submissiveness in obtaining subject matter knowledge. Through instruction, Dewey further argued, "the subject matter does not appeal [to the child]; it cannot appeal; it lacks origin and bearing in a growing experience" (p. 29). Dewey viewed instruction as subject matter-driven teaching that underestimates the child's experience-based learner capability, separating the child from the curriculum.

To connect the child and the curriculum, subject matter-driven instruction involving facts and truths needs to be, in Dewey's term, psychologized by the child; that is, he or she needs to translate or reconstruct such instruction into immediate and individual experience. Here, the teacher practices pedagogy to make the subject matter appeal to the learner. Only then will subject matter-driven instruction have significance for the child (p. 22). Through the child's psychologized interests, facts and truths become meaningful facts and meaningful truth to her or him. Dewey recognized the importance of pedagogy in the child's individualized meaning-making of (subject matter-driven) facts and truth (p. 29); pedagogy promotes the transformation of subject matter-driven instruction into the child's self-producing meaningful facts and meaningful truth. In sum, in Dewey's world, instruction creates a single process of "teaching to the learner to receive and accept," and it does not have enough capacity to connect the learner and the curriculum. Used to overcome the limitation of instruction, pedagogy is the medium that interconnects the child and the curriculum (see Figure 2.1).

**Figure 2.1. Dewey's View on Instruction and Pedagogy**

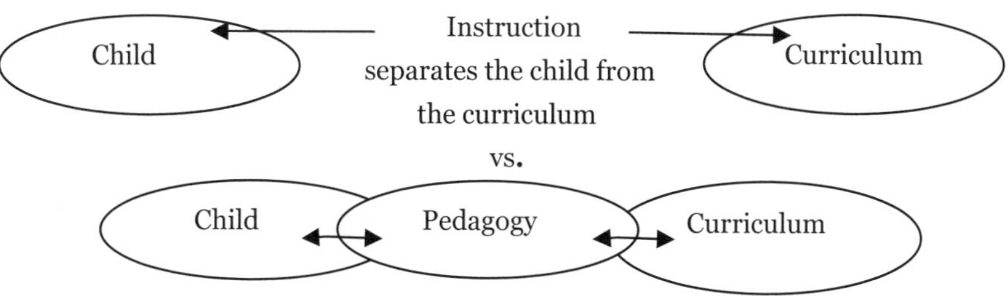


Pedagogy is the medium that interconnects the child and the curriculum.

For Dewey (1938a, 1938b) curricula are educational practices that provide experiences enabling individual learners' continuous reconstruction of the experience that adds to the meaning of experience and increases their individual ability to direct the course of subsequent experience (Pinar & Grumet, 1976; Schubert, 2004). Curriculum is viewed as continuous reinterpretation by the learner, aptly derived from the Latin infinitive *currere*, meaning "to run." *Currere* is to experience the self ("I am experience") with each breath regardless of the context. The self runs a course of experience that is curriculum. Hence, the learner runs (and should run) the curriculum (Pinar & Grumet, 1976). Thus, passing the existing knowledge such as instruction-based teaching or simply commanding "what is appropriate" or "what is not appropriate" may hinder each learner's *currere*. By contrast, explicitly supporting continuous reconstruction of the learner's learning experience such as pedagogy-based teaching illuminates curriculum as *currere*.

*Eisner's perspective*: In *The Educational Imagination* Eisner (1994) differentiated between instruction and pedagogical adaptation in lieu of pedagogy (pp. 160–162). According to Eisner instruction is harsher, less organic, and more mechanical than pedagogical teaching (p. 160). Often overlooked, even by teachers who provide it regularly in instruction is pedagogical adaptation with a difference of degree. Instruction is the effort to maximize the possibility that learners will learn what the instruction intends by interacting with a predetermined educational arrangement. From the standpoint of instruction, educationally desirable practice individualizes instruction when the teacher alters the teaching method, content, and goal to fit well with particular children's needs. In this act of altering, several forms of pedagogical adaptations can easily be ignored, such as: (a) the use of different kinds of explanations for different children; (b) the variety of questions and types of examples teachers provide; (c) the different ways in which motivation is created; and (d) the intonation and tempo of the teacher's voice to suit individual children. Eisner (1994) asserted that these forms of pedagogical adaptations do not employ mechanical means such as workbooks, standardized tests, or color-coded boxes of reading materials; thus, at the heart of individualization or individualized instruction is the teacher's effort to communicate with the learner. Eisner called these pedagogical adaptations *elements of the artistry of teaching*, and they reflect pedagogy, which welcomes the act of engaging exploration, trusting unknowns (i.e., the child's hidden capability), risk-taking, and cultivating the disposition to do so. The notion of pedagogy or pedagogical adaptation entails the teacher's intention of reaching out to the learner to make the instruction meaningful to the students.

What is teaching? How do instruction and pedagogy shape teaching? To state it simply (although to do so implies inherent pitfalls), teaching is the practice or act of being a teacher. Instruction-oriented practice shapes teaching most concerned with preplanned movements through topics by a teacher. This approach is embodied in the phenomenon of the linear lesson plan, a structure developed more around a topic, a given standard, and a teacher's interests—you teach who you are—than around a group of learners (Davis, 2004).

From the perspective of the critical theorist, teaching, as Davis (2004) articulated, is possibly explained as an approach oriented toward "making the familiar strange" (see also Gordon, 1972) and challenging what tends to be taken for granted as normal. Aligned with the critical theorists' perspective, pedagogy-based practice provides the foundation for teaching that is most concerned with uncovering normative structures and developing counternormative knowledge co-construction.

*Toward critical pedagogy*: Paulo Freire (1921–1997) argued from a poststructuralist perspective that in pedagogy-based teaching teachers and learners ought to transgress one another's boundaries: Teachers become learners and learners become teachers in a shared and dialectical learning experience of overturning old structures and inventing new ones that are more democratic (Freire, 1971).

Influenced by Freire's work many postmodern curriculum scholars have interpreted pedagogy as practices that are opposed to teacher-driven instruction. They have articulated pedagogy in conjunction with relationship-building and power-sharing with learners in the context of teaching. For example, Max van Manen (1977, 1991, 1996) and Davis and Sumara (2004) articulated pedagogy as grounded in action and relationship and concerned with the individual's lived experiences of learning anchored in the ethical and moral awareness that promotes further learning. According to Giroux (1988, 1992, 1997), pedagogy refers to the production and complex relationship among knowledge, texts, desire, and identity; it signals how questions of audience, voice, power, and evaluation and assessment actively engage and work to construct particular relations between teachers and students, institutions and society, and classrooms and communities. Pedagogy illuminates the relationship among knowledge, authority, and power. It draws attention to questions concerning who has control over the conditions for the production of knowledge. In this particular matter, Giroux advanced the notion of critical pedagogy (1992), which refers to classroom teaching that proceeds from a consideration of students' everyday lives and experiences (Giroux & Simon, 1989). It begins with several fundamental questions that can be raised by reflective teachers, such as: (a) What relationship do my students see between the activity or the work we do in class and the lives they live outside of our classroom? (b) Is it possible to incorporate aspects of students' lived culture into the work of schooling without simply confirming what they already know? (c) Can this incorporation be practiced without devaluing the objects and relationships important to students? and (d) Can this practice succeed without ignoring particular groups of students as "other" within a "dominant" culture? As evidenced through such questions, the notion of critical pedagogy is fundamental to education that is multicultural (ETM) (e.g., Grant, 1981) because critical pedagogy is based on the experiences and viewpoints of students instead of an imposed culture (Hyun, 1998; Nieto, 1992).

Figure 2.2 briefly summarizes and illustrates instruction versus pedagogy leading to curriculum negotiation. Instruction favors the teacher's passing content knowledge to the learners and students' mastery of obtaining the existing content knowledge. Passing (pre)existing contents on to learners is the essence of instruction-oriented curriculum practice. Pedagogy, however, stresses the building of relationships among teacher, learner, learning experiences by their meaning-making, curiosity, negotiation, and questioning that lead to more than repeating existing content knowledge and skills. By sharing the power between teacher and learners through negotiation, pedagogy (or pedagogy-based teaching) brings learners' voices and the possibility of uncovering learners' unknown capabilities leading to new knowledge construction that empowers learners, teachers, and others: In that regard Davis (2004) and Gordon (1972) asserted that pedagogy-based practice provides the foundation for teaching that is most concerned with uncovering normative structures and developing counternormative knowledge coconstruction (for example, see Lynn's story in Chapter 6 and Syler's story in Chapter 7).

Instruction is a technicist's mechanic way of maintaining the relation between curriculum and teaching. Pedagogy is an awakened educator's "organic" way of promoting the relationship among the learners, curriculum and teaching, where *organic* means "living, acting, and practicing with an awakened mind that maintains an honest consciousness of oneself, others, society, and content." Thus, it is a moral and ethical phenomenon.

**Figure 2.2. Instruction Versus Pedagogy**

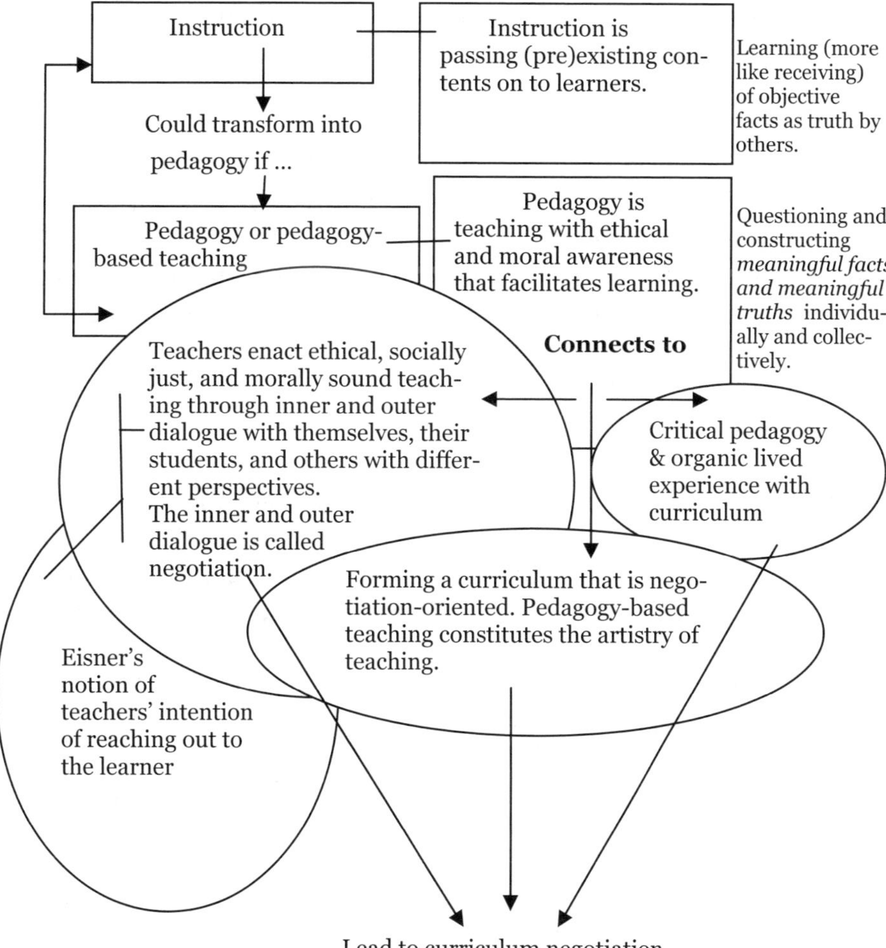

### Instruction Versus Pedagogy in Relation to What Curriculum *Is* and *Does*

Should teaching be instruction-oriented or pedagogy-based? The answer may lie in what kind of curriculum enactment the teacher is striving for in the act of teaching. Before considering whether curriculum should be instruction-oriented or pedagogy-based, the following fundamental question might be considered: What does curriculum do to and for the learners?

The term *curriculum* means different things to different people, each with its own form and purpose. In other words, every representation of what curriculum *is* and *does* represents a choice as to how to approach the education of learners (Posner, 1995). Educators who engage in curriculum discussions too often fail to define curriculum as much more than content knowledge to be taught and learned (Stark & Lattuca, 1997). What is curriculum? What is it supposed to do or accomplish? What does curriculum have to do with schooling? Is it a scope and sequenced-based academic plan? Is it a representation of our cumulative wisdom that some authorities believe all students should acquire (Bennett, 1984, 1995, 1997; Cheney, 1989; Hirsch, 1987)? Is it a set or series of intended learning outcomes (Goodlad 1966; Tyler, 1949)? Is it a collective expression of what is important for students to know and experience (Johnson, 1967, 1977)? Is it a set of courses offered to students? Is it the content of specific disciplines? Is it a contextualized time frame within which teachers provide education? Is it a series of experiences that will lead to the healthy growth of an individual (Dewey, 1938a, 1938b)? Is it an institutional condition, capacity, or sociocultural intention to prepare the next generation's performance? Is it a personal journey of autobiographical learning experiences in a holistic context (Greene, 1975, 1978, 1995; Hyun, 1998; Noddings, 1992, 1995a, 1995b, 1995c; Kincheloe, Slattery, & Steinberg, 2000; Pinar & Grumet, 1976; Pinar, Reynolds, Slattery, & Taubman, 1995; Slattery, 1995)?

Formal school curriculum in particular represents certain beliefs, theories, and assumptions of those who create it: philosophy (goodness, truth, beauty, the good life, and so on); sociology and anthropology (democratic society, equality, culture, hermeneutic meaning-making, personal journey, aliveness, wide-awakeness, spirituality, and so on); psychology (what makes people be, act, feel, know, and believe, and so on); biology (brain research, physiology, etc.); and so on. Ultimately, curriculum work involves careful attention to the interactions among the following: (a) content/subject matter, that is, knowledge, typically disciplinary, or what to know; skills or how to do; and dispositions or why to know and do; (b) people/self, that is teachers, students, parents—who they are, why they do what they do, what they know and believe; and (c) context/social, that is, where everything takes place and how all of these environmental elements—physical, social, cultural—work relative to content and people (e.g., Posner, 1995; Henderson & Hawthorne, 2000). Understanding curriculum involves critically questioning one's own knowledge, beliefs, and practices when answering the following questions (Apple, 1979, 1985, 1999): What or whose knowledge, skills, dispositions, and experiences are most worthwhile? Why? For whom? Under what circumstances? Toward what ends? In whose interests?

Most typically, curriculum understandings stem from the following premeditated inquiries: What educational purposes should we seek to attain? What knowledge and experiences will serve to attain these purposes? How can this knowledge and experience be effectively organized? How can we determine the achievement of these purposes? These conventional questions used in developing curriculum serve to illustrate what it is and what it does (see Figure 2.3 and Figure 2.4).

Historically, understandings of what curriculum *is* and *does*, as they pertain to institutional instructional curricula, have ignored—or at least interfered with—the broader sociopolitical, ethnohistorical, and socioeconomic intentions behind schooling, resulting in a perpetual power struggle between the institution and its representatives as well as a growing segment of diverse beneficiaries. Thus, instruction-oriented teaching has been prevalent and has not transformed into pedagogy-based teaching.

A power struggle between teacher and learner is inherent in a curriculum delivered mainly by instruction-oriented teaching. This power struggle can be understood best in regard to what curricularists call the hidden (unstated) and null (left-out) curriculum (Giroux, 1988, 1992, 1997; Apple, 1979; 1985; 1999; Kincheloe, Slattery, & Steinberg, 2000). Furthermore, what curriculum has generally focused on learners resulted in neglecting what curriculum is and does for teachers. In every case the teacher is the primary agent operating within the neo-conservative understanding of curriculum.

**Figure 2.3. Various Views Used in Understanding Curriculum Definitions**

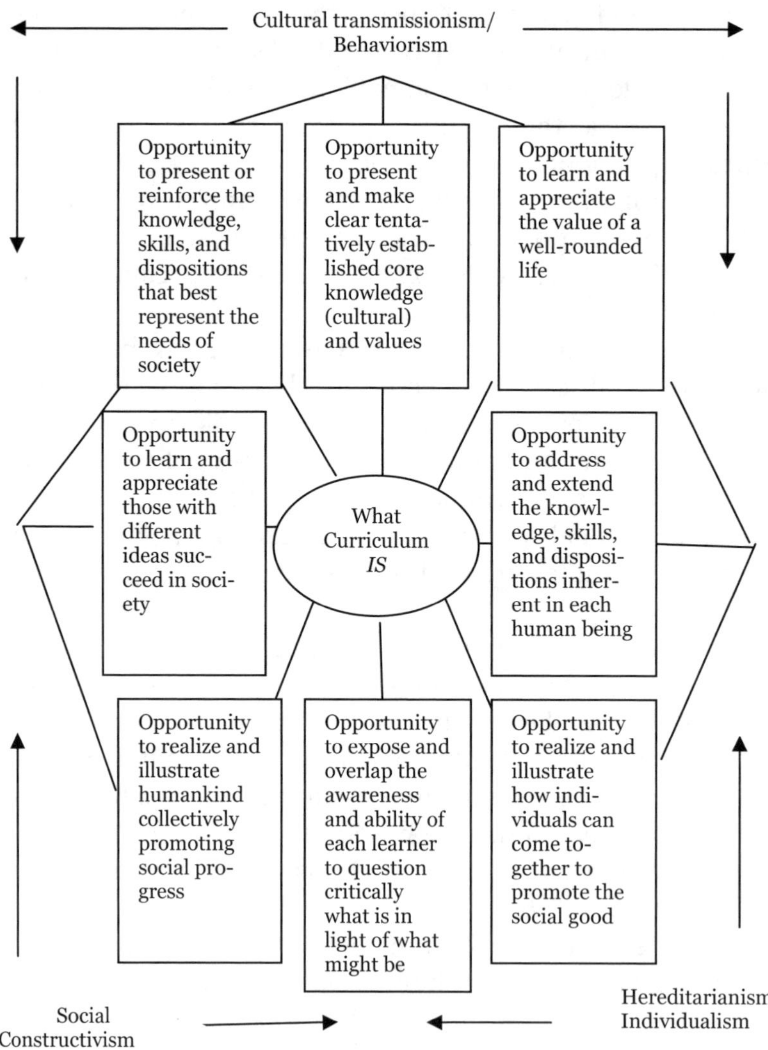

**Figure 2.4. Various Views Used in Understanding Curriculum Purposes**

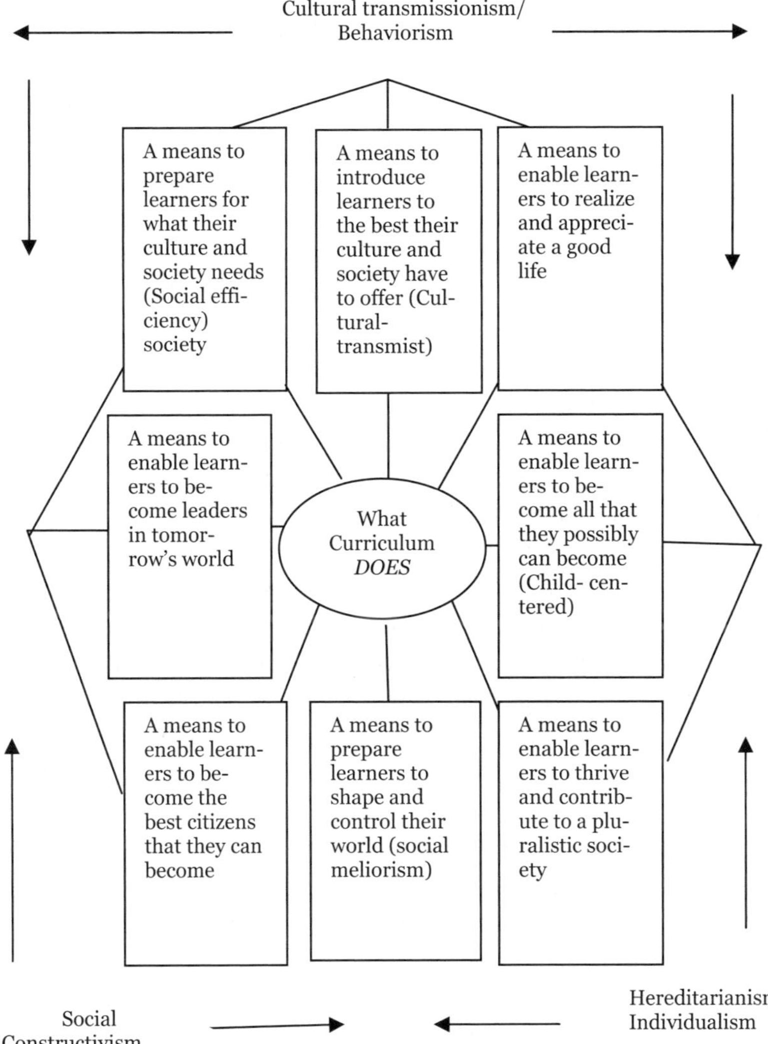


In the neoconservative understanding of curriculum, particularly under the NCLBA as exemplified in the twenty-first-century United States, the teacher functions as a proctor who focuses on the parts of teaching: test scores, seating arrangements, discipline plans, state- and district-mandated lesson plans, regulating times, distributing materials, monitoring for cheating. All of these "proctoristic" teacher images were framed by positivism, which basically insists that all knowledge is scientific in nature (i.e., verified and proven), thus measurable and quantifiable. Knowledge, therefore, is transmitted through an instruction-oriented curriculum (a packaged, scope and sequence-based curriculum) to the students, and the success of transmitting the knowledge is determined by testing them. From this perspective teachers are perceived as institutionally trained information deliverers (Held, 1980; Kincheloe, Slattery, & Steinberg, 2000; Kneller, 1984; Smith, 1983). Thus, prescribed instruction-oriented teaching is expected. Teachers are not perceived as knowledge coconstructors with learners in the processes of uncovering unknown knowledge within their social and individual journeys of teaching and learning. Dewey's notion of learning to be psychologized (internalized) by the learner and Eisner's notion of pedagogical adaptations are not recognized or valued and are usually perceived as additional things to do. Historically, politically, economically, and socially, the voices of marginalized learners are further muted in the classroom discourse under the political scrutiny of public education law driven by neoconservatives' interest and power (NCLBA, Hyun, 2003). Thus, advanced pedagogical practices like critical pedagogy (Giroux, 1992) stay within a limited capacity of the teacher. Within this type of instruction-oriented teaching, what does the curriculum do to the learner and the teacher? This type of curriculum takes empowerment away from the learner as well as the teacher. The continuation of power struggle is inevitable and inherent: In the name of education, limitation of individual growth is prevalent in the democratic society, and hence the act of education becomes ethically and morally questionable.

Instruction-oriented teaching is composed of parts (e.g., prescribed content, objectives, testing, and assessment) that eventually combine to educate the learner as a whole. Those who practice pedagogy-based teaching understand these parts only in the context of the whole. Instruction-oriented teaching focuses on identifying and delivering knowledge as timeless truths, social rules and laws, and a fixed-core curriculum mostly within the Western paradigm and values. Pedagogy-based teaching, however, is less structured and less predetermined, its artistry representing context-specific processes sensitive to the evolving needs of individuals, the learning community, and the society. Instruction-oriented teaching reflects an objective knowledge base (scientific, measurable, and quantifiable). Pedagogy-based teaching values subjective interpretation of meaningful facts and meaningful truths as well as epistemologically varied ways of knowing that are logical but holistic, interconnected, intuitive, emotional, and empathetic within and among the learners including teacher as learner (Hyun & Marshall, 2003a, 2003b). Within pedagogy-based teaching, what does the curriculum do to the learner and the teacher? The curriculum empowers the learner and the teacher as well as promotes transforming the teacher into learner and the learner into teacher. In the process of transforming identity in pedagogy-based teaching, the teacher in particular must adapt reflective questioning that illuminates Giroux's critical pedagogy and engage in an inner and outer dialogue—negotiation (Hyun, 2006).

**The Movement from Instruction to Pedagogy to Study-Based Pedagogy in Teachers' Curriculum Work**

Influenced by Freire's (1971) notion of pedagogy, Pinar, Reynolds, Slattery, and Taubman (1995) indicated that pedagogy is a teacher's act, one that requires transformation, that is, transforming teacher into learner and learner into teacher; it is the teacher's responsibility. Pinar (2004a), however, later argued that

> pedagogy is a subsidiary concept in contemporary curriculum studies. . . We have unwittingly contributed to our victimization by overemphasizing pedagogy, especially in its technicist forms, i.e. "instruction." Because we have inhabited a world of instruction, not study, we have positioned ourselves to be set up. . . . (pp. 22–23)

By adapting McClintock's (1971) theory of the sustained teacher (p. 167), Pinar (2004b) argued that not pedagogy or learning but study constitutes the process of education grounded in human individuality, autonomy, and creativity (p. 4). Teachers, Pinar and McClintock argued, should question what opportunities for study ought to be offered, what agencies should be used, and what help should be available for learners. Thus, curriculum should be paired with study, not pedagogy, because in Pinar's view the teacher's job should not be to instruct, not to transform, but to provide and oversee the continuous exercise of each student's power of communication (Pinar, 2004b, pp. 8–9). Pinar further advanced his advocacy of "curriculum and study" by introducing Block's (2004) notion of study, a spiritual discipline rooted in the Yeshiva, the Judaic tradition of pedagogical methods:

> study is institutionalized as a performative act carried out by the students' participation, and the learning space is shaped by the intensity and quality of the ongoing exchange of its students. Such complicated conversation is simultaneously intellectual and spiritual. . . . Study must be related to the practical . . . that can be realized in our daily lives in this world. (Pinar, 2004b, pp. 5–6)

Even though Pinar used the expression "not pedagogy, not learning, but study," his notion of study represents a disciplined teacher's professional inquiry that employs a doubled inquiry logic, that is, a disciplined study of study as learning (Henderson, 2005). Since the 1980s in the United States a similar idea has been reflected in Giroux's (1988, 1992, 1997) critical pedagogy and Eisner's (1994) notion of thoughtful teachers' pedagogical adaptation to strengthening curriculum practice, one requiring a real-life based dialogue to make the learning meaningful to learners.

Pinar has emphasized the importance of teachers always remaining in a study mode, using reflective questioning, such as asking what opportunities for study ought to be offered to the learners, what agencies should be used for the learners, and what assistance should be available to the learners. In this kind of study mode, however, it is extremely important for teachers to engage in power-sharing with learners and in transforming the identity of teacher as learner as it happened in LD's story (Chapter 5), Lynn's story (Chapter 6) and Syler's story (Chapter 7). "You teach who you are," and if you are not consciously aware of learners' reality from their perspectives or do not exercise multiple perspective-takings by aligning your thoughts with their multicultural, multiethnic, and multilinguistic realities, you will subconsciously impose your own values upon their realities and will find yourself limited in the degree to which you can provide developmentally meaningful and culturally congruent assistance for learners from diverse backgrounds. Thus, democratic educational practices may suffer.

In reality teachers continue to be responsible for multiple aspects, such as demonstrating "knowledge and facts" to cover basics (e.g., reading from left to right in Western print culture vs. reading from right to left in Eastern print culture); transforming identities to create developmentally meaningful and culturally congruent learning opportunities from the learners' points of view; and making learning meaningful and powerful by listening to learners' individual voices and explicitly supporting their continuous re-construction of learning experiences. We take a risk if we separate the act of study built into curriculum practice from pedagogy. Instead, we can look at teachers' pedagogy and study as interdependent acts shaping the curriculum. Pedagogy is strengthened by one's own study of self when the teacher simultaneously engages as learner in a teaching process that welcomes negotiation. Curriculum and study align with study-based pedagogy, calling for the teacher's awakened, careful, ethical, socially just, and morally sound practice through inner and outer negotiation with self and others to communicate effectively with the learners. Study-based pedagogy is based on the beliefs of human interconnectedness and interdependency among themselves as well as individuality, autonomy, and creativity.

No longer exclusively practice-oriented (i.e, instruction-oriented), curriculum studies have become more theoretical, historical, political, cultural, research-oriented, and study-based (Pinar, 1988; 2004a). Much will depend, however, on how the teacher perceives "what curriculum *is*" and "what curriculum *does*." The way teachers make sense of curriculum largely determines whether their teaching becomes instruction-oriented or pedagogy-based.

## Chapter Ending Questions

- What relationship do you see between pedagogy-based teaching and developmentally meaningful and culturally congruent curriculum practice?
- Define what curriculum *is (or should be)* as you see it. Based on your definition, imagine and articulate "what the curriculum *does*" to the learners from diverse backgrounds. What *does* the curriculum do to you as a teacher? What kinds of limitations do you see

in your definition of curriculum? How would you reconstruct your definition of "what curriculum *is*" to bring a different reality of what curriculum *does* to the learners and you (the teacher)?

# Chapter Three

# Influences in Modern Early Childhood: Curriculum and Teaching

## Initial Inquiry

- What historical influences have affected modern early childhood curriculum and teaching in the U.S.?

## Tylerian Curriculum Influence in ECE

Early childhood educators have been slow in critically articulating its understanding of what curriculum *is* and *does*. Generally, the term *curriculum* has been simply used to suggest the teacher's general sense of how she or he operates within the learning context relative to the kinds of learning experiences, physical arrangements, and materials at hand (Bredekamp 1987; Bredekamp & Copple, 1997; Epstein, Schweinhart, & McAdoo, 1996; Seefeldt, 1999). In many cases when early childhood educators talk about curriculum work, they recognize the importance of observation and assessment; however, without a critical awareness of contextual relationships between child studies and cultural studies[1] (Cannella & Viruru, 1999), observation and assessment focus mainly on children's cognitive functions and developmental progress (Martin, 1994).

In the field of early childhood education (ECE), the term *curriculum* has become synonymous with *program, model, approach, framework, practices,* and *guidelines* (Bredekamp & Rosegrant, 1992, 1995; Epstein, Schweinhart, & McAdoo, 1996; Hohmann & Weikart, 1995). In other words, the distinction between what curriculum *is* and *does* remains unclear. The relationship between neither curriculum and teaching nor instruction-oriented teaching and pedagogy-based teaching has ever been clearly articulated in ECE curriculum work. Instead, references to early childhood curriculum typically allude to a pedagogical model or approach that combines theory with practice relative to a series of national, subject-based standards (e.g., Bredekamp & Rosegrant, 1992, 1995). Each ECE curriculum model or approach derives from a theory and knowledge base reflecting certain sociopolitical and philosophical orientations supported in varying degrees by developmental child psychology-based research and educational evaluation (Cannella, 1998). These models and approaches include either explicit directions or general guidelines on how to set up the physical environment, structure the activities, interact with children and their families, and support staff members in their initial training and ongoing implementation of the model. Ironically, curriculum seems to be the unexamined center of any discussion of early childhood education (Epstein, Schweinhart, & McAdoo, 1996).

According to the NAEYC, *curriculum* is defined as

> an organized framework that delineates the contents that children are to learn, the processes through which children achieve the identified curricular goals, what teachers do to help children achieve their goals, and the context in which teaching and learning occur. Assessment is the process of observing, recording, and otherwise documenting the work children do and how they do it as a basis for a variety of educational decisions that affect the child, including planning for groups and individual children and communicating with parents. (Bredekamp & Rosegrant, 1995, p. 16; Bredekamp & Rosegrant, 1992, p. 10)

Here, according to the NAEYC, curriculum is a context-bound organized framework of contents and processes designed so that children produce work that can be assessed within this framework.

In many cases the most popular ECE curricula come complete with specific goals and objectives, strategies to accomplish goals and objectives, specific assessment tools and frameworks for measuring goals and objectives, and teacher training programs for mastering all of the above (Epstein, Schweinhart, & McAdoo, 1996). In short, popular modern U.S. early childhood curricula adhere to a certain degree to the Tyler Rationale (Tyler, 1949) that teacher prepared, instruction-oriented teaching and curriculum practices are somewhat inherent.

Although the Tyler Rationale has long since fallen out of favor within the field of curriculum studies (see, for example, Pinar, Reynolds, Slattery, & Taubman, 1995; Marshall, Sears, & Schubert, 2000), a certain degree of early childhood education curriculum practice continues to embrace its utility. We have not yet come to realize how its seemingly straightforward questions serve to mask the basic importance of the screens through which we sift our decisions (see Tyler, 1949, pp. 33–43). Furthermore, although Tyler himself recognized the need to employ philosophical and psychological screens, he was not willing or able to expand on this point, nor was he able to predict (in 1949) the undeniably crucial autobiographical (*currere*) screen. In other words, those who simplistically employ the modernistic Tyler Rationale can address questions regarding instruction-oriented *what to teach* and *how to approach that.* They, however, have little postmodern pedagogy-based guidance when it comes to their own autobiographical complicity in this process, not to mention that of learners' own autobiographical journeys. The absence of such basic awareness works against the creation of critical thinking and inquiries related to assumptions of human learning and democratic life. Without this sort of careful, honest reflection, educators are unlikely to wonder about what ECE curriculum *is* and *does* in any real sense. They may be less sensitive to considering questions like, for example, the following:

- Does the curriculum directly care for and continuously nurture a personal journey of autobiographical learning experiences within a holistic context?
- Does the curriculum directly promote children's individual and social meaning-making without a teacher's (adult's) pre-programmed intentions?
- Can human beings learn only one specific way? Should they?
- Does a universally "good" or effective way of facilitating learning exist?
- Can uniform objectives (e.g., DAP-based objectives) be worthwhile for all young children?
- Can all learners recognize and accept the same content as important to learn? Should they?
- Can prescribed, universal content appropriately benefit all children's multidirectional, multidimensional, and multiethnic life experiences and learning relative to their futures?
- Does any one curriculum tradition, approach, or model have an inherent and pervasive capacity to celebrate and promote *all* children's unique identities and backgrounds while recognizing their unique qualities as fundamental to understanding curriculum resources and components?

If we revisit the stories of Syler and Newly as examples discussed in Chapter One, we see that these questions lie at the heart of critical inquiry necessary to construct a meaningful (thus lived) curriculum for children. In the field of early childhood education, deconstructing the Tyler Rational, is long overdue, as is re-conceptualizing our understandings of curriculum work in general (Kessler & Swadener, 1992).

## Historical Traditions in U.S. Early Childhood Curriculum

When we review the historical influences that have affected the U.S. early childhood curriculum, we find three major curriculum traditions: cultural transmission (behaviorism), hereditarianism (maturationism), and constructivist interactionism (Piagetian constructivism) (e.g., Morrison, 2000; Seefeldt, 1999).

*The cultural transmission tradition:* Formal education within this tradition is designed to reflect what is most important to those people and institutions representing the dominant or controlling culture. Thus, in typical teaching and learning contexts, those in charge translate predetermined knowledge, skills, and dispositions into learner expectations. In other words, the conditioners' culture is transmitted into the learners'. At its core this tradition grows from a behaviorist understanding of learning; its proponents view learning and development as a continuous set of changing behaviors (representing learning) governed by the principles of conditioned learning instead of a series of maturationists' "age-bound" behaviors (Morrison, 2000). Thus, through conditionally arranged external reinforcements (stickers, progress reports, grades, and so on), children learn information, acquire certain attitudes and dispositions, and accumulate specific skills. Said differently, the external environment or dominant culture shapes the child's overall development and learning. We can see this below with Susan:

Story of Susan

Twelve-month-old Susan likes to touch her mother's coffee cup, which is decorated with colorful balloons. Each time Susan's hand moves toward the cup, her mother lightly raps Susan' s hand while saying, "No, no, no. It's hot. Don't touch it!" Eventually, Susan learns to look at her mother when reaching for the colorful cup. When she sees her mother's face change and hand begin to move, Susan stops. Her mother responds with "Good! Please don't touch it again. Here's a cookie. This is your cup (a pink plastic one) with milk

> in it. It is not hot. You can touch your cup. Hold your cup like this" (mother shows Susan how to hold the cup). (Ruston, LA, 1989)

Here, Susan's knowledge (hot/cold, right/wrong, and so on), skills (cup usage, "reading her mother's face," and so forth), and dispositions (curiosity, acceptance) are entirely shaped by her mother's control of this situation.

This particular curriculum tradition calls for a direct instructional model for ECE, the most popular of which is DISTAR. Within this tradition (as briefly presented in the Table 3.1), the teacher transmits preexisting cultural, value bounded, culturally acceptable knowledge by creating a learning environment that is highly structured, work-oriented, and fully focused on academics. Regardless of their differences, young children are always—to one degree or another—influenced by an external force to learn culturally sanctioned knowledge, skills, and dispositions. Moreover, the primary emphasis of the DISTAR curriculum is on target language (English) acquisition and skills since these skills are deemed to be essential to school success by its proponents (Becker, Engelmann, Carnine & Rhine, 1981; Bereiter & Engelmann, 1966). Clearly, a high degree of hidden and null curricula practices prevails in this curriculum, including the message that using languages other than English is not appropriate in schools, and that bilingual children's linguistic code-switching to support one's own meaningful learning is not acknowledged as a powerful social and cognitive learning tool for problem-solving skills and divergent mental flexibility. Consequently, social and political power struggles were inevitable—starting with young children as early as three years of age and sometimes earlier.

In a behaviorist learning theory-based curriculum like DISTAR (a typical orientation for teacher-directed practice and instruction-oriented teaching), curriculum *is* an opportunity to present and reinforce previously determined and sanctioned knowledge, skills, and dispositions to learners; curriculum *does* enable learners to behave in certain expected ways.

*The hereditarian tradition:* This curriculum tradition within ECE represents a belief that human learning and development are based on biologically preprogrammed sequences as readiness or maturation.

Maturationists believe that each human organism contains a biologically coded schedule of development. For example,

> once infants can reach, they start to modify their grasp. When the grasp reflex of the newborn period weakens at 3 to 4 months, it is replaced by the ulnar grasp, a clumsy motion in which the fingers close against the palm. Around 4 to 5 months, when infants begin to master sitting, they no longer need their arms to maintain body balance. This frees both hands to become coordinated in exploring objects. Babies of this age can hold an object in one hand while the other scans it with the tips of the fingers, and they frequently transfer objects from hand to hand. By the latter part of the first year, infants use the thumb and index finger opposably in a well-coordinated pincer grasp. Then the ability to manipulate objects greatly expands. The one-year-old can pick up grains and blades of grass, turn knobs, and open and close small boxes (Berk, 2000, p. 149).

These developmental movements lead to further and other kinds of learning, and while learning, each individual simultaneously affects her or his environment. To illustrate the point, we visit Kato:

> Story of Kato
>
> Kato is a 12-month-old boy. Kato's mother observes that he does not understand the danger of touching "hot" cups, nor can he use his own cup independently yet; so his mother places her "hot" coffee cup far enough away from Kato that he cannot reach out and touch it. She also holds Kato's cup for him when he drinks his milk. Kato's mother continues to give him his milk bottle until he is capable of holding the cup alone. (Portsmouth, NH, 1996)

In the hereditarian tradition teachers and parents are encouraged to wait until the child's biological development indicates a readiness for taking advantage of the environment as a component of his or her learning. Once nature permits growth without undue harm, interference, or restrictions, the child will develop further. From this maturationist perspective, teachers and parents should carefully observe the child's growth and provide relevant experiences at suitable times.

The hereditarian curriculum tradition is consistent with what we call age-appropriateness—a concept rooted in Gesell's (Gesell, 1940; Gesell & Ilg, 1940) developmental theory. Unfortunately, when a child's growth doesn't follow "universal" (linearly progressive) patterns, her or his uniqueness is often understood as developmental delay (Lubeck, 1996). The maturational orientation to school learning has spawned numerous culturally incongruent, virtually meaningless readiness tests (e.g., Gesell School Readiness Test) and screening tests used for curriculum planning (Wortham, 1998). One unfortunate result of our use of such measures is that retention has become a popular concern of ECE professionals despite evidence (e.g., Shepard & Smith, 1989) that kindergarten retention does nothing to boost subsequent academic achievement. Regardless of what the extra year may be called, these children are socially stigmatized. Moreover, retention actually fosters inappropriate academic demands in first grade (Wortham, 1998).

In the maturationists' child-centered curriculum or age-appropriate curriculum tradition, curriculum *is* an opportunity to offer a safe environment for learners to undergo their own developmental readiness and maturity albeit according to a pace determined to be normal, and curriculum *does* provide learners with the resources to promote healthy growth in terms of established patterns of readiness and interests.

*The constructivist interactionist tradition:* Influenced by Jean Piaget's (1952) cognition-driven theory of child development, constructivist traditionalists within early childhood education maintain that environments and human organisms interact with each other. Constructivists believe that a person's development, while greatly influenced by biology, will adapt in ways that fit her or his environment. During childhood the structures of the mind (cognition, schema) construct ways to better fit within or represent the external world. Having accomplished suitable constructions, the external world is thus altered as far as the organism is concerned, resulting in new and different needs for re-construction. This simultaneous interaction between environment and an organism's biology leads to the organism's development and learning. Here, Isa provides an example:

Story of Isa

Isa is 12-month-old girl. Isa's mother gives her a plastic sippy cup with a safety top with a hole in it. Since Isa seems interested in cups, maybe colorful cups, the mother buys more colorful plastic cups, some with colorful balloons on them. All of the cups have safety tops on them so that even if Isa topples the cup, her milk will not spill. Isa's mother believes that by using the colorful cups, Isa will be able to learn colors while learning how to use regular cups. Initiated by Isa's interests and her mother's careful observation and proper environmental arrangements (more resources in this case), Isa experiences a safe way to use cups and learn colors. (Clarion, PA, 1995)

Piagetian constructivists clearly value the importance of rich environmental resources. According to the Piagetian perspective, interacting with various materials that are appropriate to the child's age and interests will promote her or his development and learning; conversely, certain children, especially those living in poverty, risk labeling as disadvantaged learners, that is, learning delayed because of their lack of experiences with multiple and varied concrete materials. Critical analysis of the Piagetian constructivist perspective and illustrations of its limitation appear in Mrs. Englishwill's case in Chapter 5 and in Lynn's case in Chapter 6.

**Figure 3.1. Example of Isa**

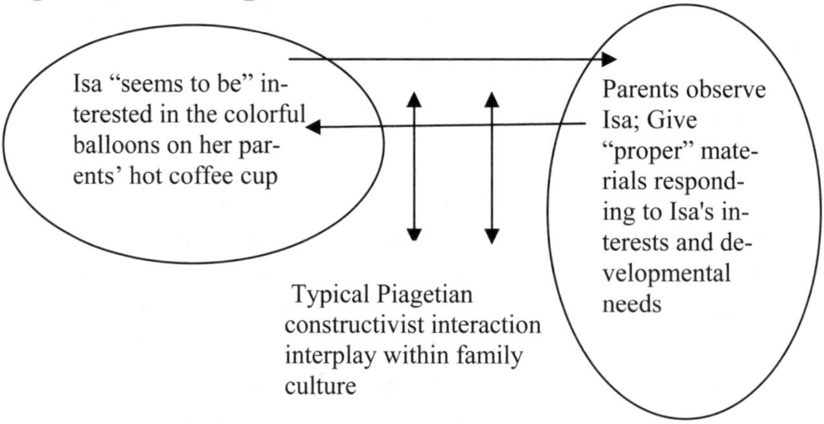

Isa "seems to be" interested in the colorful balloons on her parents' hot coffee cup

Parents observe Isa; Give "proper" materials responding to Isa's interests and developmental needs

Typical Piagetian constructivist interaction interplay within family culture

Since the late 1970s (Vygotsky, 1930/1978, original work published in 1930, 1933, 1935) U.S. early childhood educators have paid more attention to a Vygotskian constructivist orientation, finding Piaget's cognitive constructivist understanding too narrow and individualistic for appreciating how children's learning takes place. Lev Vygotsky (1896–1934) theorized that children's cognitive, language, and social development results primarily from social and cultural influences. This Vygotskian sociocultural view differs from the Piagetian perspective, which portrayed children more as solitary learners and constructors of their own intelligence. Today, many early childhood educators attempt to promote a more socially cognitive constructivist curriculum based on Vygotsky's theory of how children construct knowledge, which suggests that learning and development cannot be separated from social context, learning can lead development, language plays a central role in mental development, and social interaction with and assistance from adults or mature peers influence children's learning and development (Bodrova & Leong, 1996), as illustrated in Isa's story.

Although Vygotsky's social constructivist orientation has introduced the important domain of sociocultural influences into the early childhood constructivist curriculum, neither his theory nor current curriculum practices based on his theory have successfully articulated how to respond to contemporary young children's cultural complexity in conjunction with developing a curriculum framework that is multiethnic, multidirectional, and multidimensional. Vygotsky's belief that, beginning at birth, children seek out adults for social interaction and that children's development occurs through these interactions lends more power to teachers (adults) than it does to young learners. Thus, Vygotsky's sociocultural constructivist orientation lies the possibility of knowledge transmission-based curriculum construction depending on *who is the teacher* believing what curriculum *is* and *does*—a concern that merits further investigation, including a careful epistemological exploration.

In the constructivist child-centered or individual-appropriate tradition, curriculum *is* an opportunity to create environments rich in materials and resources, especially knowledgeable human resources, for learners' self-exploratory learning and development; curriculum *does* promote individuals' self-discovery, independent learning, and social consciousness.

In sum, to the extent that ECE curriculum has progressed from cultural transmission to constructivism, we have moved closer to its capacity to promote diverse children's voices, multidirectional and multidimensional ways of looking at and assessing young children's potential, particularly children from unique family structures and different ethnic and socioeconomic backgrounds as well as children with unique learning styles and conditions identified as special needs. However, all of these traditions remain prominent despite the obvious drawbacks inherent in the cultural transmission and developmental traditions, and significant issues pertaining to power, group orientation, and teacher utilization remain inherent in them all. Based on these three traditions that have affected contemporary U.S. early childhood curriculum discourse, Figure 3.2 and Figure 3.3 present a brief theoretical comparison.

**Figure 3.2. Three Major Theoretical Traditions Influencing U.S. Early Childhood Curriculum**

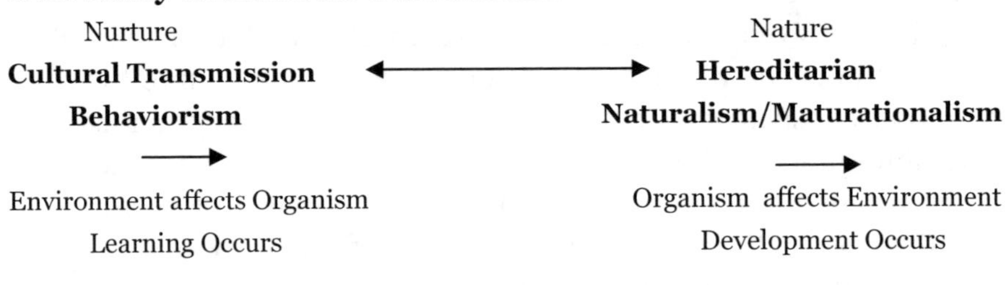


**Constructivism**

Environment and Organism Interact

Learning and Development Interdependently Occur

Theoretical and educational contributors

Comenius (1592–1670) Piaget (1896–1980) Rousseau (1712–1778)
Locke (1632–1704) Bruner (1915– ) Freud (1856–1939) Pestalozzi (1746–1827)
Watson (1878–1958) Vygotsky (1896–1934) Dewey (1859–1952)Froebel (1782–1852)
Skinner (1904–1990) Montessori (1870–1952) Erikson (1902–1994)Hall(1844–1924)
Gesell(1880–1961)

Example programs, curricula, and approaches

| | | |
|---|---|---|
| DISTAR Curriculum | Head Start Curriculum | Naturalism or |
| Content specific | Bank Street Approach | Romantic Approach |
| standardized | Montessori Curriculum | A.S. Neil's *Summer hill* |
| curriculum & | High-Scope Curriculum | |
| assessment | Kamii-DeVries Curriculum | |
| | Creative Curriculum | |
| | DAP-based curriculum | |
| | Project Approach | |
| | Reggio Emilia Approach | |

**Figure 3.3. A Brief Comparison for Curricula Understanding**

Behaviorists' learning theory-based curriculum (Typical orientation for teacher-directed practice)

Curriculum *is* an opportunity to present and reinforce the knowledge, skills, and dispositions to learners to learn

Curriculum *does* enable learners to behave in certain expected ways

Instruction-oriented teaching is a dominant form in curriculum practice

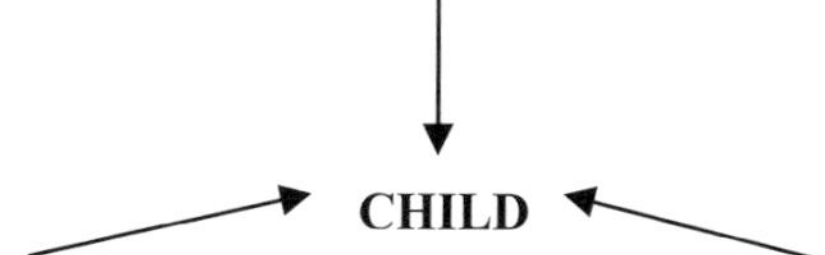


Maturationists' child-centered curriculum (Typical orientation for age-appropriateness)

Curriculum *is* an opportunity to offer a safe environment for learners to practice their own developmental readiness and maturity

Curriculum *does* promote a safe learning environment and learners' healthy growth in responding to learners' readiness and interests

Instruction-oriented teaching can be a dominant form in the curriculum practice

Constructivists' child-centered curriculum (Typical orientation for individual appropriateness)

Curriculum *is* an opportunity to create an environment that has rich materials and resources for learners' self-exploratory learning and development

Curriculum *does* promote individual processes of self-discovery and independent learning

Pedagogy-based teaching may be a dominant form in the curriculum practice

## Current Concerns in Reshaping ECE Curriculum

Table 3.1 briefly presents characteristics of the most well-known U.S. early childhood curriculum models and approaches as they pertain to each of these traditional orientations. Reviewing these, we see that all are driven by European-generated, psychology-based learning theory—bases that by definition have an inherent bias toward behavior and cognition (i.e., intelligence). In short, in formal education, particularly early childhood education, cognition is the center of the universe when it comes to questions of learning and teaching.

### Table 3.1. Main Characteristics of Existing ECE Curriculum Models/Approaches

| Curriculum Model/ Approach | Characteristics |
|---|---|
| DISTAR (Direct Instruction Curriculum Model) | This model relies upon principles of behaviorist psychology and learning theory, not a theory of child development. Behaviors are learned after being reinforced by arranged conditions. The teacher creates an early childhood learning environment that is highly structured, work-oriented, and fully focused on academics. The primary emphasis is on target language (English) acquisition and skills since these are believed to be essential to school success (Becker, Engelmann, Carnine, & Rhine, 1981; Bereiter & Engelmann, 1966). |
| Nursery school: Naturalism or Romantic Approach | Rooted in J. J. Rousseau (1712–1778). "God makes all things good" according to Rousseau's philosophy. Rousseau advocated a return to nature, which would take care of the child's development and learning. This approach to educating children is called "naturalism." To Rousseau, naturalism meant abandoning society's artificiality and pretentiousness. A naturalist education permits growth without undue interference or restrictions. We should observe the child's growth and provide experiences at fitting times. This idea is consistent with what we call "age-appropriateness." |

| | |
|---|---|
| Bank Street Approach | Influenced by J. Dewey, J. Piaget, and L. S. Mitchell, this curriculum is intended to promote the development of the whole child. Its goals for children include competence, individuality, socialization, and integration. Children are seen as active learners who encounter the world by interacting with and transforming it. The curriculum relies heavily on the teacher's understanding of child development. The teacher guides children through planned activities to reach goals. The teacher's primary role is to observe and respond to activities initiated by the children. The classroom has a well-defined structure with specific areas and clear rules. Children can work individually or in groups. The setting allows for freedom of movement and choices as well as easy access to materials (Biber, 1984; Biber, Shapiro, & Wickens, 1977; Mitchell, 1950; Zimiles, 1987, 1993). |
| Montessori Curriculum | Montessori's philosophical idea is that "children teach themselves through their own experiences—autoeducation." The curriculum provides a carefully prepared and ordered environment in which children naturally pursue their developmental ascent. Included in this environment are didactic and sequenced materials geared toward promoting children's education in four areas: development of the five senses, conceptual or academic development, competence in practical life activities, and character development. The materials, like children's development, proceed from the simple to the complex and from the concrete to the abstract. The teacher's role is primarily that of facilitator, introducing children to the materials and demonstrating their proper use with a minimum of verbal instruction. Children generally work individually instead of in groups, although they are encouraged to interact as they engage in activities. The goal is to help children become competent, socially conscious citizens of the world who respect themselves and others (Lindauer, 1987, 1993; Montessori, 1964, 1973). |
| Head Start | Head Start is a child development program that has served low-income children and their families since 1965. Head Start |

and Early Head Start are comprehensive child development programs, which serve children from birth to age 5, pregnant women, and their families. They are child-focused programs with the overall goal of increasing the school readiness of young children in low-income families. The Head Start program is administered by the Head Start Bureau, the Administration on Children, Youth and Families (ACYF), Administration for Children and Families (ACF), Department of Health and Human Services (DHHS). Grants are awarded by the ACF Regional Offices and the Head Start Bureau's American Indian and Migrant Program Branches directly to local public agencies, private organizations, Indian tribes and school systems for the purpose of operating Head Start programs at the community level. The Head Start program has a long tradition of delivering comprehensive and high-quality services designed to foster healthy development in low-income children. Head Start grantee and delegate agencies provide a range of individualized services in the areas of education and early childhood development; medical, dental, and mental health; nutrition; and parent involvement. In addition, the entire range of Head Start services are responsive and appropriate to each child's and family's developmental, ethnic, cultural, and linguistic heritage and experience.

High/Scope Curriculum

Based on Piaget's constructivist theory of child development, this curriculum was originally developed for use with economically disadvantaged preschool children in the High/Scope Perry Preschool program. The curriculum rests on the fundamental premise that children are active learners who learn best from activities that they plan, carry out, and reflect on. An important part of the curriculum is the Plan-Do-Review sequence of the daily routine, in which children make choices about what they will do, carry out their own ideas, and then reflect on their activities with teachers and peers. Teachers use a series of "key experiences" as a conceptual framework to help them plan activities, observe children, think about the day, and encourage a variety of experiences that are essential to young children's healthy physical, intellectual, social, and emotional growth. The teacher's role is to observe children's activities carefully and provide appropriate support and guidance. The teacher also extends children's learning by listening, asking open-ended questions, and providing a variety of materials and experiences for exploration. In this way, the teachers and children are viewed as active partners in the educational process (Hohmann, Banet, & Weikart, 1979; Hohmann & Weikart, 1995; Weikart & Schweinhart, 1987, 1993).

**Kamii-DeVries Curriculum** Proponents of this model, based on Piaget's theory, view children as constructors of their own system of knowledge, intelligence, morality, and personality. Curriculum emphasis is on learning through mental action. Young children are most active mentally when they are physically engaged in figuring out how to do something. The curriculum stresses active learning: Children learn by inferring from what they do and creating a system of knowledge from their inferences. The overall objective of the curriculum is for the child to come up with interesting ideas, problems, and questions, and for the child to put things into relationships and notice similarities and differences (Kamii & DeVries, 1977, 1978, 1980, 1993).

**Creative Curriculum** This curriculum relies on Piaget's cognitive theory, Erikson's stages of socioemotional development, and general developmental principles of children's physical growth. Teachers emphasize social competence by focusing on 10 interest areas or activities in the program environment: blocks, house corner, table toys, art, sand and water play, library corner, music and movement, cooking, computers, and outdoors. The curriculum includes description of how to set up interest areas, how children can learn in each area, and the teacher's role in promoting learning and growth (Dodge, 1988; Dodge & Colker, 1990, 1992; Dodge & Phinney, 1990).

**DAP-based Curriculum** Since 1987, the field of early childhood education has had a guide known as Developmentally Appropriate Practice (DAP) based on Piaget's constructivist orientation and Gesell's developmental theory. This guide is used by the National Association for the Education of Young Children (NAEYC) (Bredekamp, 1987; Bredekamp & Copple, 1997). DAP-based curriculum emphasizes age appropriateness, individual appropriateness, and sociocultural appropriateness. As a major mode for meeting the individual child's needs, child-initiated, child-directed, teacher-supported play are essential components (Bredekamp & Coople, 1997; Bredekamp, 1987).

| | |
|---|---|
| Project (or Project-Based) Approach | This approach, originally adapted by Anna Freud in the 1920s, was prominent in English infant education and became part of the open education movement in the United States during the 1960s and 1970s. Based on children's learning (Kandel & Hawkins, 1992), it represents the current trend toward integrating the curriculum and group projects conducted by the preschool children of Reggio Emilia. The project is an in-depth investigation of a topic usually undertaken by a small group of children within a class, sometimes by a whole class, and occasionally by an individual child. The key feature of the project-based curriculum is that it is inquiry-driven and deliberately focused on finding answers to questions about a topic posed either by the children, the teacher, or the teacher working with the children. The goal of project-based curriculum is to learn more about the topic rather than to find correct answers to questions posed by the teacher. The approach is suggested as a complementary or informal part of any existing curriculum. It provides children with contexts for applying the skills they learn in the more formal parts of the curriculum and for group cooperation. It also supports children's natural impulse to investigate things around them (Katz, & Chard, 1993; Katz, 1994b). |
| Reggio Emilia Curriculum | This curriculum reflects a theoretical relationship with Dewey, Piaget, Vygotsky, and Bruner. It was initiated by the municipal early childhood program in Reggio Emilia, Italy. The community has a long history of supporting families with young children. Parents are expected to take part in discussions about school policy, child development concerns, and |

curriculum planning and evaluation. The curriculum emphasizes the concept of teachers as learners, environmental importance, long-term projects with small groups of children, and children's symbolic languages in the context of a project-oriented activity. The major teaching strategy is to purposefully allow for mistakes to happen or to begin a project with no clear sense of where it might end and to promote children's ability to negotiate in the peer group, thereby rendering teacher intervention in children's conflicts minimal. One of the most important aspects of this curriculum is the solicitation of multiple points of view regarding children's needs, interests, and abilities, and the concurrent faith in parents, teachers, and children to contribute in meaningful ways to the determination of school experiences. Trust is another important part of the curriculum. Teachers trust themselves to respond appropriately to children's ideas and interests, they trust children to be interested in things worth knowing about, and they trust parents to be informed and productive members of a cooperative educational team (Edwards, Gandini, & Forman, 1993; Hendrick, 1997; New, 1993) .

Note: According to the 1996 High/Scope Educational Research Foundation's research report (Epstein, Schweinhart, & McAdoo, 1996), 78% of the nation's early childhood educators use one or more curriculum models as a resource in forming their educational programs. Forty-five percent said that they prefer using a variety of curriculum models; 21% reported using no curriculum model at all. According to the survey the early childhood curriculum models most widely known and examined, that is, where respondents have studied or received training in the model, are Montessori and High/Scope, followed by the Creative Curriculum, Kamii-DeVries, and Direct Instruction; the Bank Street model is more widely known but less widely examined than the latter three models (Epstein, Schweinhart, & McAdoo, 1996).

Ever since the sociopolitical shock the United States suffered after the Soviet Union's launching of Sputnik in 1957, schooling, including education for young children, has been cognitively driven, focused on mainly linguistic and logical-mathematical achievements for students. Furthermore, the No Child Left Behind Act (NCLBA) of 2001 requires U.S. public schools (K-12) to describe their success and effectiveness based only on students' attainment of prescribed academic standards and performance on mostly standardized linguistic (English language only) and logical-mathematical tests (Hyun 2003). This focus has made educators look for and advocate other kinds of human potential (e.g., Gardner, 1983, 1999, 2000).

The NCLBA has forced teachers to engage in instruction-oriented teaching and curriculum delivery instead of pedagogy-based teaching and curriculum practice (Hyun, 2006). As a result, many young children exhibiting preferences and strengths related to different types of intelligences for example, an ability to read and respond to others' nonverbal emotions and feelings, to create something new out of nothing, and to express themselves through physical and multidimensional mediums rather than one-dimensional school worksheets, (see Chapter 4, Sara's two daughters story and Kevin's story as examples), experience trouble in school because even the constructivist orientation to curriculum has a seriously limited capacity for promoting and assessing diverse children's various intelligences that are not linguistic and logical-mathematical.

What is missing in most of our ECE models and approaches and absent from the center of any of them is the *social necessity of needing others who are different*. In the United States of tomorrow, the varieties of knowledge, skills, and dispositions necessary to sustain a justly equitable and democratically functioning society will rest largely upon this need. As such, the field of ECE must move toward a more complex set of curricula understandings and practices.

Our inability to produce such change becomes a serious issue when we consider the real and immediate challenges presented by the sociocultural context and political scrutiny (i.e., NCLBA). Today, more and more young children enter day care, preschool, and formal schools identified as suffering from one form or another of developmental delay, deficiency, or disability. These situations reflect a growing set of situations and economic, social, personal, and cultural circumstances related to the difficult work of raising children in the contemporary United States. Moreover, the nation's increasingly multiethnic population with its different child-rearing beliefs and practices provides contemporary early childhood educators with learners whose intelligences are more likely to be multidimensional and multidirectional than cognitively unidirectional (e.g., McAdoo, 1993). Constructivist curricula have improved understanding and practicing appropriate ECE curricula, yet because of their heavy focus on linguistic and logical-mathematical cognitive development, they simply cannot provide a developmentally meaningful and culturally congruent curriculum for all young children.

The three traditions of early childhood curriculum represent a well-nourished European-oriented, male-dominated positivistic scientific cultural paradigm still mired in modernism. What we need today are theoretical orientations that enable us to create curriculum frameworks for educating young children that provide multiple ways of understanding how children learn differently alone and together and how ever-changing sociocultural environments affect every child's multidimensional development and learning. The following chapter contains a discussion of one such contemporary postmodern early childhood curriculum framework in terms of what that curriculum *is* and *does*. This framework is intended to enable and promote developmentally meaningful and culturally congruent curriculum practices from the learner's point of view that illuminate pedagogy-based teaching.

## Chapter Ending Question

- If there were no mandated standards for you to cover in your teaching, how would you create a curriculum for young children that would fully support individual children's developmentally meaningful and culturally congruent learning experiences?

## Note

[1] Cultural studies implies examination of (a) multiple constructions of childhood in diverse cultural settings; (b) how these constructions have changed over time and in different contexts; (c) the extent to which the constructions are actually related to the lives of the young children; (d) the public policy that has been and is being created

based on these constructions, whether through education, human services, or other forms of institutionalization; and (e) the influence of "child-based" public policy on individuals, families, and societal groups (Cannella & Viruru, 1999, p. 19).

# Chapter Four

# Curricula Understandings

## Initial Inquiry

- How do we engage in a postmodern curriculum understanding for developmentally meaningful and culturally congruent practice in light of diverse learners?

## Incongruence and Misunderstandings

Based on Chapters Two and Three, this chapter questions whether the typical teacher-owned curriculum understanding is relevant to the complexity of children's lives. Let's start with Ken's story.

> Story of Ken and His Family
>
> Ken, a 12-month-old boy, lives in a poor rural Pennsylvania community with his birth mother and father, who adopted Ken as his son. Ken's grandmother lives two houses down from Ken's family, and his uncle and aunt live about 300 yards (about 274 meters) from Ken's backyard. Ken sees his grandmother and aunt almost every day because his grandmother baby-sits Ken and his cousin (his aunt's daughter, who is 7 years old).
>
> Ken's mother prevents him from touching hot coffee cups by reinforcing him (like Susan's mother), saying, "If you don't touch the cup, I'll give you Ka Ka (meaning cookie or goodies, an example of conditioned learning). In contrast, Ken's father (using a behaviorist approach) holds Ken's hands and together they touch the hot cup very quickly, his father saying; "It's hot! Don't touch it. You'll get hurt. You don't want a boo- boo." With a more naturalistic approach, Ken's grandmother never puts her "hot" coffee cup anywhere near Ken's cup and always helps him hold his milk or juice cup. She wipes his mouth each time he finishes drinking his milk or juice, then she gives him a kiss, a big hug, and says "Oh! You are growing every day!"
>
> Ken's aunt, a second-grade elementary school teacher, bought three sets of colorful sippy cups, which have the Sesame Street characters on them (blue Cookie Monster, yellow Big Bird, and red Oscar). More of a constructivist when it comes to Ken's learning about cups and drinking, she talks with Ken by asking about each cup ("Where is your blue Cookie Monster cup?") or asking him to hold the cup ("Show me how to use this cup"), or pretending to drink milk using one of the cups ("This is how I use this cup. Look at this hole. I sip milk from this hole. Would you like to try what I did?"). (Leeper, PA, 1996)

As described in this vignette, Ken experiences conditional as well as naturalistic and constructivist cognitive-oriented interactions within his extended family culture. The various interactions affect his social learning context as well as his learning style. What would constitute a developmentally meaningful and culturally congruent classroom culture that might extend Ken's meaningful learning experiences when he begins preschool in three years? What kind of curriculum would be appropriate for him? How about for Susan (illustrated in Chapter 3), who may experience conditional learning most of the time; for Kato (illustrated in Chapter 3), who may experience naturalistic learning most of the time; or for Isa (illustrated in Chapter 3), who may be experiencing constructivist cognitive-oriented learning most of the time? These children have experienced somewhat distinctively different home environments and cultural dynamics that have influenced their learning styles and modes of interaction with others during their childhood.

What happens to children who enter formal education environments different from those of their home culture? The stories of Sara's two daughters and Kevin's family are cases in point:

Story of Sara's Two Daughters, Jenny and Rara

Thirty-eight-year-old Sara, who is still trying to get her G.E.D. (high school equivalency diploma), has two children (9-year-old Jenny in 3rd grade, and 3-year-old Rara, a biracial preschooler). Sara and her two daughters live in a subsidized housing community, consisting mainly of poor single mothers with children in Southwest Florida. Sara has been married and divorced three times. Below, she and her two daughters explain their life at home, in the community, and in school.

*Sara*: Jenny loves to come up with crazy charades she thinks we'll never get the answer for. It gives her a chance to act and have people actually watch her. Jenny likes to make me laugh, so she will use things around the house to pretend she is Jim [an ex-boyfriend] or Adam [an ex-husband] or her teacher or one of her friends. She likes to draw a lot, so we are playing Pictionary even more than regular charades now. Plus, Rara likes to guess what the pictures are and can never guess charades right. . . . Rara made a picture for me out of an old cereal box label. She colored it with crayons and wrapped a shoelace around it to make it a necklace. Jenny . . . is making a whole city practically out of old popsicle sticks. . . . She has a barn, a stable, an outhouse, and a regular house and she made a stop sign. . . . There is not enough room or money for toys and stuff here, so they just come up with stuff that is lying around the house. Jenny plays outside a lot and hangs out with her friends, and I think she learns some ideas from them. She [Jenny] is always helping Rara, and I think that Rara uses her mind a lot to keep up with Jenny. If they do something that I wouldn't think of, that's creative learning in my opinion.

*Cindy* (Sara's older sister): My sister Sara has a home that is decorated very creatively on a budget. Most of what she has displayed in the interior of her home is furnishings from antique shops, garage sales, flea markets, and hand-outs from the rich people. An old parachute hangs from her living room ceiling, and the children's stuffed animals hang from the parachute. One of her walls neatly displays antique hats; she has strewn them together in a romantic pattern with lace. The rest of the apartment appears drab, but she is continually improving the apartment and regards it as work in progresses.
*Sara* (responds to Cindy): Yeah, I furnish it, but the ideas I come up with are to excite the kids. I wouldn't have all this stuff otherwise.

*Cindy* (asks Jenny): What do you do at school?
*Jenny* (3$^{rd}$ grader): We do spelling, reading, and math every day.
*Cindy*: Do you get into centers?
*Jenny*: No. No centers. Miss Max's third-grade class [a full-time gifted class] is creative. They do centers, go outside, and do experiments. [In my class] we put heads down for a long time.
*Cindy*: Every day?
*Jenny*: Every day for about 20 minutes, 'cause we're not following the rules.
*Cindy*: Can you tell me what you do from the time you get to school?
*Jenny*: We do chores. First, we take all our stuff out of the backpacks and hang up our backpacks. We have to stay at the door until he [the teacher] says we can come in, then we put down chairs, sharpen pencils, open up our assignment books, and wait for him to come around and make sure our parent signed it. If they did, we get a check. If not, we have to write something like, "I will come to class with a parent signature."
*Cindy*: What do you do that is fun in class?
*Jenny*: We made a card for Mother's Day, and a paper tree at Christmas.
*Cindy*: So, on holidays you do fun things. What about fun activities, like playing games in class. Math games?
*Jenny*: No. We sit in our desks and do reading, then spelling, then math, then we go to a special [e.g., P.E.], then we put our heads down, then we do science or read at our desks, and then we write our homework in our homework folder and get ready to go home. (N. Ft. Myers, FL, 1999)

The story above conveys so many issues. One of them pertains to the striking discontinuity or mismatch between home culture (a creativity-driven environment that invites divergent learning and living) and classroom culture (a teacher-driven environment that requires convergent learning and living) as they pertain to children's learning styles and problem-solving skills. The teacher's teacher-driven, instruction-oriented curriculum is unable to acknowledge and enrich Jenny's rich and creative home culture and learning curriculum. Kevin's case promotes further discussion:

> Story of Kevin and His family
>
> Kevin's parents were shocked when the teacher sent them a note saying that Kevin had been disturbing his kindergarten class for two weeks. During the teacher-parent conference, they learned that Kevin was moving around and acting out instead of quietly sitting and listening each time the teacher read a story.
>
> *Teacher*: Listening quietly and being able to comprehend and understand stories are important skills for kindergartners to develop. When I finish reading a book with the children, we talk about the story before each child engages in further activities, such as creating his or her own book using sound spelling or drawing a picture of his or her favorite part of the story. To conclude the activity, each child explains what he or she did. Kevin is always physically acting out the story as I read and is bothering the other children who are listening to the story. I am not sure whether he really understands the story because he is always so busy pretending to be one of the characters. . . . Did you ever consider testing him to find out whether he is some type of special needs child, such as ADD or ADHD?
> *Father*: Can you also consider allowing the children to physically act out or pretend the story as a follow-up activity, not just table sitting-oriented activities? They are all good ones that you are doing with the other children, but these activities may not be attractive to my son. . . . At home we used to pretend to be characters in stories each time we read children's books. . . . We have been doing this since he started to talk at about age 2. It makes him interested in reading books. He keeps bringing new books to me to read for him. . . . In fact, we still do this type of reading at home with our son. . . . By the way what is ADHD anyway? (Shippenville, PA, 1995)

Clearly, Kevin and his father are facing a dilemma: whether their style of reading activity at home has negatively affected Kevin's kindergarten learning experiences. The teacher is well-regarded and respected among parents. The teacher is genuinely concerned that because Kevin's behavior is inappropriate and disturbing, he and his classmates are not fully benefiting from her well-planned and well-prepared curriculum. She values constructive teaching presented through instruction-oriented, teacher-led and teacher-orchestrated teaching (Chapter 8 contains a discussion of various forms of constructive teaching approaches).

What sort of curriculum framework could help Jenny's and Kevin's teachers become more fluent and flexible in readjusting and changing their preplanned lessons in ways that might make the curriculum more responsive to children's imaginations, interests, and learning styles? What kinds of curriculum understandings should we promote during teacher preparation? How can future teachers develop a wide-awake mind that will help them to analyze critically, re-create, and promote a lived curriculum that is always flexible and fluently responsive to diverse learners' voices and needs? What sort of curriculum framework could allow each one of the diverse children introduced thus far to feel comfortable with their own style of learning and challenged to explore new forms of meaning-making?

## Who Owns the Curriculum?

Today, too many children and families suffer from narrow, teacher-driven, instruction-oriented, and socioculturally insensitive approaches to early childhood curriculum. This is especially true for those families and children with unique physical, emotional, and intellectual special needs, those who are socioeconomically disadvantaged, poor, and those with different sociocultural, ethnic and linguistic backgrounds (Delpit, 1995). When traditional orientations to curriculum and the curricula representing those orientations cannot provide diverse children with equal, fair, and congruent educational experiences, these children come to be seen as disturbed, problematic or limited learners suffering from "disabilities" or "delays," sometimes even by so-called well-informed teachers.

Notions like critical pedagogy, emancipatory knowledge, multiple forms of intelligences, and ecological brain functioning may provide opportunities for rethinking and re-conceptualizing early childhood curriculum in more multidimensional and multidirectional ways; however, we are mistaken if we think of these notions as additional components or angles that we might bring to existing ECE curricula. This is the error we see in early childhood curriculum understandings and practices that have added multicultural curriculum, inclusive curriculum, or anti-bias curriculum components to their frameworks. When this occurs, teachers feel that they need to infuse (or add) specific activities and content into their daily curriculum practices to reflect those issues. In most cases, however, tacking on some multicultural or anti-bias curriculum component does not change our functional understanding of the curriculum or our association with it: The dominant belief is that teachers still have the responsibility of curriculum delivery and children still have the responsibility of receiving it.

The central issue here is curriculum ownership. Teachers need a framework to transform themselves into colearners, coproducers, coconstructors, codiscoverers, or coinquirers with learners in conventional curriculum traditions; however, the idea of shared ownership with learners is hindered by commercialized materials and politically influenced standardized curriculum guidebooks. For example, to support teachers responsible for infusing multiculturalism into their integrated curriculum for young children, many major organizations and publishers have created curriculum materials to make teachers' work less demanding. These activity manuals and lesson plan packages include "what to do" and "how to do it" materials and guides. Efforts such as these only reinforce teachers' understandings of themselves as deliverers of curriculum understood as prepackaged experiences for children. Teachers' intuitive, critical, autonomous, and ethical thought processes manifested through their engagement with children's thoughts, interests, questions, imaginations, and needs remain unexplored and sometimes uninvited.

We cannot educate all young children by adding into a curriculum each newly popularized idea or strategy that reflects a unidimensional understanding of children, teaching, and learning. The time has come to stop adding new components and begin removing problematic and outdated ones that have been damaging diverse children's learning and growth while perpetuating teachers' overwhelming operational responsibilities (Brown & Moffett, 1999). One way to bring focus to this particular problem is to examine the teacher's role in any curriculum framework. In most conventional curriculum orientations, the teacher serves as proctor, information deliverer, planner for supposedly appropriate learning, and a careful observer and facilitator guided by Western developmental psychology and typical learning theories. Conventional ECE curriculum workers have not clearly articulated what curriculum *is* and *does* to and for the teachers. Teachers are seen as representatives of the curriculum in use whose job it is to see that the curriculum works with students. They are less viewed as life-long knowledge coconstructors with the children in their mutual journey toward meaningful moments of learning (i.e., *currere* in Pinar & Grumet, 1976; Schubert, 2004*)*. Most ECE curriculum models and approaches are presented as guides for teachers to be employed so that their students will follow them and receive some educational benefit.

What early childhood educators need instead are curriculum frameworks that help teachers to seek teachable moments that reflect genuine learnable moments, to be more sensitive and willing to negotiate and explore children's emergent interests in a prolonged learning engagement, and to negotiate continuously the curriculum with their students. Together, these teachable moment-, emergent-, and negotiation-oriented learning experiences form a lived curriculum for both learners and teachers. In this framework of lived curriculum, children and teachers see themselves as interdependent learners and counternormative knowledge coconstructors, codiscoverers, coinvestigators, and codecision-makers of all meaningful and thus important learning experiences. Children's and teachers' unique linguistic characteristics, ethnic perspectives, physical and intellectual characteristics, emotional, spiritual, and aesthetic sensitivities are all considered as equally powerful resources and meaningful tools in forming a lived curriculum for all. Such a re-conceptualized contemporary curriculum framework will highlight teachers' conscious and critical awareness of their practice and increase the likelihood that all children will experience developmentally meaningful, culturally congruent, fair, and equal learning opportunities.

## Understanding Contemporary Postmodern Curricula for Young Children

Can curriculum become a conscious framework that guides teachers' ethical, critical, and reflective thinking and action for all young children's formal educational experience? Can curriculum be a conscious framework that requires teachers to deal carefully and continuously with and go beyond the preexisting orientation toward a knowledge base which curriculum frameworks have the capacity continuously to promote teachers' "wide-awakeness" (Greene, 1978) and self-monitoring of their decision-making in order to provide diverse opportunities for all children to explore? How can teachers engage in their curriculum work as their own curriculum studies (Pinar, 2004a, 2004b)?

Curriculum can and should be a conscious framework that allows teachers to be awakened and be caring multiple perspective-takers when it comes to educating young children. At the same time, this conscious curriculum can provide safe boundaries within which all young children explore their personal and social journeys of meaning-making and celebrate their unique socioemotional, spiritual, physical, ethnic, intellectual, and linguistic characteristics as young human beings (i.e., *currere*). Within these boundaries children can and should continuously explore their curiosities as they expand their multidirectional, multidimensional, and multiethnic developmental growth, change, and learning alone and with others (see Figures 4.1 and 4.2).

**Figure 4.1. What Curriculum *Is*, What It *Does*, Thus, the Lived Curriculum**

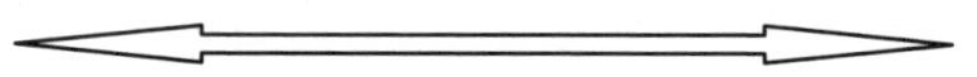

| | | |
|---|---|---|
| Curriculum *is* a conscious framework that allows teachers to be wide-awake professionals through critical thinking and multiple perspective-taking; and it *is* an ever-changing conscious institutional capacity and sociocultural intention designed to pro- | Practitioners of lived curriculum are always conscious of teachable moments, emergent moments, and negotiated moments. | Curriculum *does* provide a safe boundary for all children's personal and social meaning-making journeys (i.e., *currere)*, and in the meaning-making process curriculum *does* not only cover a subject, but also uncover unknown know edge/ |

vide diverse opportunities to ALL individual children to explore their lives both individually and socially.

counternomative knowledge; therefore, chidren's multidimensional, multidirectional, and multiethnic developmental growth and change continue.

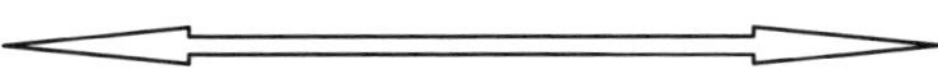

As described in the stories of Syler, Newly, Jane, Kevin, and Tony in the previous chapters, teachers always face unexpected situations initiated by learners. In order to maintain a developmentally meaningful and culturally congruent (i.e., responsive) curriculum for young children, teachers must have a conscious awareness of their own multiple identities—ethnic, linguistic, cultural, gender, and socioeconomic—along with a willingness and ability to step back and critically reexamine their own interpretations of the identities of the children they teach. Examples and stories presented in Chapters 5, 6, and 7 explore this particular matter in depth.

Teachers who encourage and permit children to change the curriculum always nurture students' learning and meaning-making (Greene, 1978; Kincheloe, Slattery, & Steinberg, 2000). This form of lived curriculum requires teachers' conscious awareness and willingness to change in an effort to promote learners' active and relevant personal and social meaning-making experiences. Within a lived curriculum teachers continuously realize that their knowledge is always incomplete and that they, too, are participating in a constant journey of learning with the children (i.e., *currere*). A preplanned, teacher-driven, instruction-oriented curriculum representing a set of intended learning outcomes produced by others can never be a fully lived curriculum for young children representing a multidirectional, multidimensional, and multiethnic sociocultural world.

From a contemporary postmodern standpoint, we cannot continue to hold tight to such simplistic curriculum ideas and practices (Lather, 1991; Constas, 1998; Giroux, 1997). The key question that we share in postmodernism is this: What are the contemporary social, political, and cultural conditions under which a human act takes place that supports a person's capability to de-construct, re-construct, and interpret new meanings in a recursive manner? Postmodernism rejects the ethnocentrism of so-called Western or dominant culture. Postmodernism not only challenges the form and content of dominant models of knowledge and curriculum but also produces new forms of interdisciplinary knowledge by taking up objects of study that were simply and literally unrepresentable in the dominant paradigm (Giroux, 1997).

These postmodern sensibilities influence people to revisit and question critically the historical and political influences on curriculum and open doors for more contemporary curriculum understandings. Clearly, we can no longer depend upon notions of curriculum as what is to be learned or a structured series of intended learning outcomes or accumulated wisdom to be transmitted to new generations (see, for example, Johnson, 1967; Goodlad 1966; Hirsch, 1987; Tyler, 1949). In addition, we can no longer expect curriculum to attend only to the development or healthy growth of individual experience (i.e., Dewey, 1938a). Instead, the postmodern perspective portrays contemporary curriculum as an ever-changing conscious framework developed within and for a pluralistic and interdependent learning community (e.g., Giroux, 1997; Marshall, Sears, & Schubert, 2000; Pinar, 2004a, 2004b; Pinar & Grumet, 1976; Schubert, 2004; Slattery, 1995).

Curricula understandings for developmentally meaningful and culturally congruent practice respond to this postmodern perspective. Curriculum should be perceived as an ever-changing and conscious institutional capacity or sociocultural intention designed to provide diverse opportunities for all children to explore the following:

- their own unique human potentials (individual);
- what they want to learn; why they want to learn specific things in their own specific ways; how they want to share their own knowledge (including counternormative knowledge), interests, interpretations, and meaning-making with others (individual and social);
- how they want to learn; how they create meaning-making by themselves as well as with others (individual and social);

- how they can use personal qualities as powerful learning resources for themselves as well as for others (individual and social); and
- how they can use personal knowing and knowledge for the benefit of others in an interdependent learning community (social).

Developmentally meaningful and culturally congruent practice emphasizes inquiry-centered approaches to conscious individual and collective curriculum constructions in order to be responsive to the multiple perspectives in a pluralistic human learning community. Alone and together, teachers ask:

- What is purposeful action (ethical, moral, democratic, humanistic) in curriculum decision-making?
- How can this particular purposeful action be achieved?
- How do autobiographical influences interfere with decision-making? What are the critical limits to anyone's personal beliefs?
- What opportunities for study ought to be offered to the learners, what agencies should be used for the learners, and what assistance should be available to the learners?
- How can I be sure that my way of doing things will also be appropriate to ALL diverse individual children? What relationships do my students see between what we do in class and the lives they live outside of the class? How can I make more congruent connections as well as help them to expand their multidimensional experiences for new (counternormative) knowledge and learning?
- What should I reconsider and change in my plans for "appropriate" practice to make them more meaningful and relevant to the individual children's learning experiences while encouraging genuine social meaning-making for ALL children?
- How do we construct, deconstruct, and reconstruct our role of teacher as a wide-awake practitioner to create a lived curriculum?

These types of consciousness and deliberative inquiries have much to do with teachers' critical and reflective examinations of their own practice in the classroom. Teachers' reflective and critical examination of their own teaching is the powerful driving force in maintaining and promoting a lived curriculum.

## Toward a Lived Curriculum

Teachers' conscious curriculum considerations start with recognizing individual differences as unique learner qualities while simultaneously questioning preexisting notions of good practice. In many cases teachers' personal beliefs of good practices do not always hold for diverse learners (Delpit, 1995; Hyun, 1998). Teachers ought to be perpetual skeptics, not only about others' knowledge and formulas but also about their own beliefs and practices. They are always somewhat uncertain and, as such, always open to change when such change will ultimately serve children and society. In addition, teachers ought to be ever-curious in their search for different and more defensible ways to understand and construct curricula that will support diverse individual learners' unique developmental change and growth within the context of others. Teachers continuously (a) examine the multiple constructions of childhood in diverse cultural settings; (b) try to understand how these constructions have changed over time and in various contexts; and (c) search for the extent to which the constructions are actually related to the lives of the individual child (Cannella & Viruru, 1999).

In short, teachers who consciously construct curriculum are in the habit of asking situational questions in the service of *lived curriculum* practice. These questions might include the following:

- How can I know whether the teachable moment is a real (or equally) learnable moment for the children? (teachable moment-oriented curriculum, see Chapter 5)
- How can I know that the teachable moment represents a genuine interest of the children that might lead them to move further toward related meaningful experiences? (emergent-oriented curriculum, see Chapter 6)
- How can I know that the way I negotiate what I want to (or have to) teach these children and what they actually want to learn is honestly apparent in my daily practices? How can I be sure that my teaching itself will also come from negotiating with the children's personal/social and critical meaning-making processes? (negotiation-oriented curriculum, see Chapter 7)

For such teachers critical self-monitoring (wide-awakeness) that will move them toward a lived curriculum is ongoing and inherent. Teachers' sense-making of what to teach and how to teach for appropriate practice is not uniform or formulaic. Instead, it becomes a lived curriculum that reflects (a) spontaneous phenomena, which hold immediate importance for learners; (b) children's situated self-expressions and various forms of intellectual cultures, which suggest relevant ideas and experiences to be pursued; and (c) shared-power between children and their teacher (see Figure 4.2).

Teachers integrate these three notions of curriculum by using multiple/multiethnic perspective-taking manifested by their reflectivity (reflection-in-action, reflection-on-action, reflection-for-practice, see Chapter 9). In doing so, they are no longer the ultimate powerholders in any conscious curriculum decision-making. Instead, teachers recognize and situate themselves as members of true learning communities who contribute their voices and experiences as learning resources and who appreciate and promote individual qualities as ever-lasting learning resources for all. This lived curriculum allows them to go beyond limited prescribed curriculum practices.

As more and more states mandate uniform standards for public school accountability under NCLBA, the U.S. has faced the serious danger of prescribed instruction-oriented teaching and curriculum practice (e.g., core-knowledge curriculum) that is extremely limited in meaningful learning and emphasizes Western developmental psychology-driven high-stakes standardized assessment, which easily fail to assess children's multiple forms of intelligence and potential. We need to educate our prospective teachers to be aware of the given condition that they will face but be able to critically see and overcome the limits of that condition by implementing a lived curriculum framework in their everyday practice with children.

## Chapter Ending Questions

- If you were a teacher of Jenny or Kevin, how could you have become more fluent and flexible in readjusting and changing your preplanned lessons in ways that might make the curriculum more responsive to the two children's imaginations, interests, and learning styles? How can you make the curriculum practice culturally congruent between home culture and classroom learning culture?

- What kind of curriculum framework would be helpful in facilitating a teacher's (your) autonomous decision-making for young children's meaningful, thus high-quality learning experiences?

**Figure 4.2. Elements of Developmentally Meaningful and Culturally Congruent Curriculum Understanding**

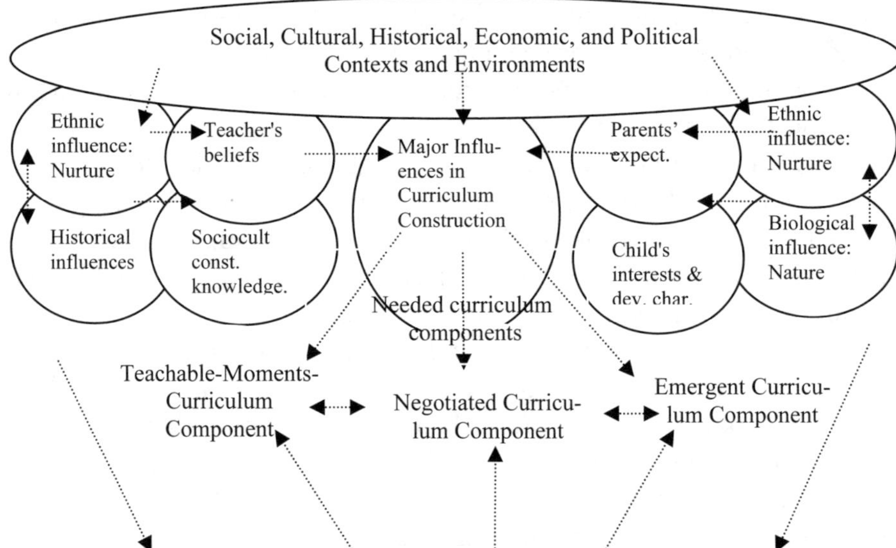


Developmentally meaningful and culturally congruent curricula understanding: Curriculum *is* a conscious framework that allows teachers to be wide-awake practitioners with critical thinking and multiple perspective-taking. It *is* an ever-changing conscious pedagogical capacity and a sociocultural intention that is designed to provide diverse opportunities to all individual learners to explore their lives. Curriculum *does* provide a safe boundary for all children's personal and social journey of meaning-making. In the meaning-making process, it *does* not only cover a subject but also uncover unknown knowledge; thus, their multidimensional, multidirectional, and multiethnic developmental growth and change continue. Lived curriculum has a conscious framework of

- Teachable moment-orientation (maintaining teachable moments that belong to learners' learnable moment-oriented experiences)
- Emergent-orientation (responding to ALL individual children's emerging and prolonged interests)
- Negotiation-orientation (promoting shared-power decisions and negotiations in learning and teaching).

# Section II: Re-conceptualizing Curricular Practices

# Chapter Five

# Teachable Moment-Oriented Curriculum

## Initial Inquiries

- How do teachers make sense of a teachable moment-oriented curriculum in their daily practice?
- What are the critical aspects of teachers' teachable moment-oriented curriculum practice?
- Is the teachable moment the same as the learner's learnable moment?
- How does a teachable moment-oriented curriculum serve a developmentally meaningful and culturally congruent curriculum?

How do teachers make sense of teachable moment-oriented teaching? What are the critical aspects of teachers' teachable moment-oriented curriculum practice? What kind of teacher consciousness and consistent practices promote teachable moment-oriented curriculum practice with young children? What does a teachable moment-oriented curriculum mean to ECE teachers? How does the teachable moment-oriented curriculum support developmentally meaningful and culturally congruent practice for all learners? This chapter explores the answers to these and other questions regarding teachable moment-oriented curriculum practice.

## Perspectives

Even though no single authoritative definition of *teachable moment* appears in the literature of early childhood education, the notion of the teachable moment is typically expressed in terms of the teacher's role. For example, in Jean Jacques Rousseau's (1712–1778) *Émile* (1933), teachable moments take the form of a teacher's response to the learner's natural growth and interests. Johann Pestalozzi (1746–1827) suggested that teachers use teachable moments to guide, not distort, the natural development of the individual child. Friedrich Froebel (1782–1852) emphasized teachable moments by describing the adult role in children's learning and development: to observe children's natural unfolding and provide activities that will enable them to learn what they are ready to learn when they are ready to learn it. Arnold Gesell (1880–1961) posited that the teachers are obligated to use careful observation and to wait until they can help children develop their inherent qualities and readiness for learning. John Dewey (1859–1952) believed that the teacher's responsibility was to observe carefully children's thoughts, feelings, interests, curiosities, and impulses and to use them as the foundation of a plan and method of teaching. Jean Piaget (1896–1980) believed that learners construct knowledge through their own actions and that they must derive personal meaning from experiences in order to learn. When a teacher provides appropriate manipulative materials for those moments that are based on his or her observation of students' interests, development, and learning can follow. Lev Vygotsky (1896–1934) also believed that children construct knowledge, but its development cannot be separated from its social context. For Vygotsky cognitive construction is always socially mediated. When a teacher reads moments of child-initiated learning or development, he or she can in turn provide the appropriate curriculum needed to build upon the child's interests, strengths, and developments within the child's zone of proximal development.

Prospective teacher Karen McGreevy[1] stated: "Teachable moments are fortuitous opportunities provided by the learners that are recognized, interpreted, evaluated, and acted upon by the teacher (knowledgeable other)" (Hyun & Marshall, 2003a). Contemporary researchers interpret the teachable moment variously such as: (a) the interwoven nature of learning lived through experiences (Eeds & Wells, 1989; Sipe, 2000); (b) those times when the flexibility of the teacher allows her or him to value children's thinking and to change plans (Pourdavood & Fleener, 1997); (c) prompted by something that was said by a student (Schnur-Laughlin, 1999); and (d) a type of learning particularly memorable and dramatic because learners learn what they need to know when they need to know it (Freeman, 1994).

Some scholars have left the teachable moment undefined but recommend it as an important pedagogical approach: Yvonna Lincoln (1998) used the teachable moment in the process of sensitizing students to the special ethical concerns of fieldwork in qualitative study, and Marie Pagliaro (1991) provided examples of how a crisis can be used as a teachable moment to lead students through an active interdisciplinary approach to learning. A review of current literature reveals no single in-depth exploration of teachers' sense-making of teachable moment-oriented teaching that shapes their curriculum practice.

William Ayers (1989) portrayed good teachers as always on the alert for teachable moments, tentatively understood as opportunities that may arise when students are excited, engaged, and primed to learn. Teachers use the phrase *teachable moment* when they reflect on their, "appropriate," memorable, or effective teaching experiences; however, no current scholars directly discuss what it is, who has the real power in that kind of pedagogical practice, or how teachers construct teachable moment-oriented curriculum practice through their interaction with young children.

## Images of a Teachable Moment-Oriented Curriculum

Let's explore prospective ECE teachers' field-based examples of teachable moment-oriented teaching. Those appearing below were collected by a team of six collaborating ECE professors working in California, Florida, Minnesota, Oklahoma, Pennsylvania, and Texas to explore the way prospective ECE teachers make developmentally meaningful and culturally congruent curriculum connections during their field experiences. In the following excerpts, prospective early childhood teachers offer their examples of teachable moments (Hyun, DiPento, Duarte, Matthews, Morales & Smrekar, 2000).

> Topic: Teachable moment-oriented curriculum practice
> Conf: DCAP and Curriculum
> Date: Saturday, October 16, 1999 03:38 p.m.
> Well, I had a teachable moment in the classroom I have been observing for the past 5 weeks. The second grade class has many centers, [but] I encountered the teachable moment in the science center. The children started with caterpillars and watched them as they [the caterpillars] formed their cocoons, hatched, and turned into butterflies. One of the insects had difficulty hatching from its cocoon, so both the head teacher and the student teacher stopped what they were doing and discussed what was occurring, asking what students felt they should do. Ultimately, the student teacher did "surgery" on the cocoon to help the butterfly escape. The problem was that the butterfly had not detached itself from the cocoon, and its wings began to dry out while trying to hatch. The children expressed many ideas to help the butterfly and great concern about whether the butterfly would live. The head teacher, the student teacher, and I [a pre-service student teacher] were

> thrilled to be able to take the time to answer questions and discuss concerns the children had. Great experience! (Reflection of a prospective ECE teacher in Pennsylvania, posted on Internet WebBoard for field experience-sharing, Sept., 1999)

In this example, the prospective ECE teacher perceived a teachable moment initiated by the classroom teachers' observation of the children in the science center, and they purposefully conducted teachable moment-oriented teaching by responding to the children's concerns and questions.

> Topic: Teachable moment-oriented curriculum practice
> Conf: DCAP and Curriculum
> Date: Thursday, September 30, 1999 01:48 a.m.
> Monday, I was teaching a lesson on a story entitled "Help, Help!" I asked the children what they would do if they heard someone calling for help. They replied, "Call 911." One began to elaborate, using an example of a person who was bleeding. . . . I intercepted and said that if a person is bleeding, we should not touch him or her. We should just call 911 because it is not good to touch someone who is bleeding. I instantly thought about this as a teachable moment. (Reflection of a prospective ECE teacher in Florida, posted on Internet WebBoard for field experience-sharing, Sept., 1999)

In this example, the prospective ECE teacher explained that her teachable moment occurred during a prepared lesson. Within this context she found that one child's understanding of handling a medical emergency was somewhat unexpected but still focused on the topic. The student teacher identified a teachable moment to instill an important concept—don't touch a bleeding person—one that she understood as an important health and safety issue to teach to the children.

> Topic: Teachable moment-oriented curriculum practice
> Conf: DCAP and Curriculum
> Date: Sunday, June 18, 2000, 10:58 a.m.
> Teachable moments happen many times a week. The teacher always walks around and often comes across a frustrated child. The teacher usually sits with the child and helps by allowing the child to discuss a problem out loud with her. Then together, they think of strategies to solve the problem. I began to do this also, and I believe I really made a difference with one child

> and his writing skills. I let him tell me about the problem he was having, which was writing letters of the alphabet. He could sound out the word and knew its letters but would forget how to write the letter. So after talking about what to do, we decided to go on a letter hunt throughout the room. Together, we counted all the places that the alphabet could be found in the classroom. This gave him a place to refer to when looking for a letter. When I left, he didn't have to use the posted alphabet cues as much. This type of teachable moment promotes self-help skills. (Reflection of a prospective ECE teacher in Florida, posted on Internet WebBoard for field experience-sharing, Spring 2000).

In this case, the prospective ECE teacher saw teachable moment-oriented curriculum practice occurring through the teacher's intentional, ongoing observations, naturalistic assessments, and interactions with individual learners. Based on such observations of each child, a teacher-initiated constructivist approach developed into teachable moment-oriented practice.

*Teachable moment* is a phrase frequently used by early childhood teachers when they reflect on their most memorable and effective teaching experiences, but no scholars to date have directly discussed what it is, how teachers construct the notion in their practice, or what it means to learners. Prospective ECE teacher Karen McGreevy formulated her own concept of teachable moment-oriented curriculum in Vygotskian terms during her field experience:

> Teachable moments are fortuitous opportunities provided by the learners and recognized, interpreted, evaluated, and acted upon by the teacher (knowledgeable other). Through the teacher's understanding of the various theories of child development and knowledge of developmentally and culturally appropriate pedagogical practices, these opportunities are transformed into meaningful learning experiences for the students. When a student denotes a specific interest, displays a particular type of engagement, or interacts with materials in a way that is different from previously exhibited behavior, these become indicators that a teachable moment is about to happen. A teachable moment may occur during one-on-one interaction between the teacher and the student, or the teacher may observe it while a student is working alone, interacting within a small group or with a whole-class activity. A teachable moment presents itself when the student expresses an interest and readiness, a window of opportunity, to move to another level of learning and development.

> Therefore, teachable moments-oriented curriculum results from the teacher's ability to read the student's teachable moments (indicative behaviors and natural interests) in order to prepare and provide an individually, developmentally, and culturally appropriate curriculum for each student's cognitive, social, emotional, and physical progress. (KM's reflection, 1999)

Karen saw that a teachable moment-oriented curriculum depends on the teacher's knowledge of child development and ability to read learners' emerging learnable moments; however, she also articulated some constraints that may limit teachable moment-oriented curriculum practice:

> In the process of implementing a teachable moment-oriented curriculum, it would be unrealistic and inappropriate to believe that the teacher would simply wait for the students to provide teachable moments, determining the direction of the curriculum. It would also be unrealistic to believe that there would not be state and local mandates and requirements that must be met. The key is to find that individually, developmentally, and culturally appropriate balance that provides for an interesting, challenging and thought-provoking environment while helping all to meet the requirements.
>
> Students must have time and opportunity during the daily class schedule to express their thoughts, to ask questions, to interact and interject, and especially to play. Play (activities initiated and directed by children) is the natural business of children, and during play the student exhibits natural developmental levels. Many early childhood and primary schedules include center or station time, when students are involved in activities and control their learning experiences, providing many opportunities for teachers to capture teachable moments.
>
> Students have innumerable ideas, interests, and questions; and they need opportunities to interject these into the program in order to facilitate and promote their own personal learning experiences. Students must be actively involved in the process in order for learning to be meaningful and personal; learning is a two-way street. Much of the school day consists of maintaining a schedule in the classroom as well as during the activities outside the classroom, but time can still be found to allow the students to express the directions they wish to go. Unfortunately, many teachable moments are lost because schedules must be met. (KM's reflection, 1999)

Karen realized that teachable moment-oriented curriculum practice requires adequate time for children to be engaged fully in active learning within a play-based environment. It also requires the teacher to juggle state-mandated requirements, his or her knowledge of child development, learning initiated by the children, all the while creating a stimulating learning environment for young children.

Regarding the time-consuming nature of teachable moment-oriented curriculum practice, Karen believed that to bring learnable moments to life, teachers need to appreciate teachable moment-oriented practice through multiple perspective-taking:

> During whole-class lessons a student may raise a question that appears on the surface to be irrelevant to the topic at hand, but the teacher needs to take the time to engage in *a few seconds of thought* [second-person perspective-taking] to evaluate the particular student and why she or he raised the question. If it is important and appropriate to one student, it could possibly be important to many. Then, the teacher needs to take the time to decide [using second-person perspective-taking] whether or not addressing this question will plant a seed for later cultivation in developing the student's knowledge base. If straying from a preplanned course for several minutes provides for a later quality learning experience to occur, then those few minutes work to guarantee a genuine educational experience. (KM's reflection, 1999)

So what is a true picture of teachable moment-oriented teaching and curriculum practice? Is it totally dependent on each teacher's ability to read children's initiations? Is it truly a learner initiative and learner-oriented curriculum practice? What kind of teacher consciousness and consistent practices promote teachable moment-oriented curriculum practice for young children? What does a teachable moment-oriented curriculum mean to teachers? What does a teachable moment-oriented curriculum mean to learners? How does a teachable moment-oriented curriculum support developmentally meaningful and culturally congruent practice?

## Making Sense of a Teachable Moment-Oriented Curriculum

Teachable moment-oriented curriculum practice combines teachers' emerging purposeful action with those of the learners in their charge. Teachable moments arise when teachers observe, recognize, and interpret the spontaneously occurring interests of diverse learners. These spontaneous moments represent a confluence of unique cultural identities and developmental growth and change patterns as well as students' particular needs, interests, and curiosities. Teachers' recognition, careful observation, and interpretation of teachable moments from the students' perspective help to form emerging purposeful instructional or pedagogical action. Once this kind of emerging and purposeful instructional or pedagogical action becomes an inherent and pervasive daily practice within teachers' continuous consciousness of what they are doing, teachable moment-oriented curriculum practice is established. Let's explore three ECE teachers' personal reflections on their journey toward constructing a teachable moment-oriented curriculum. Each voice represents a teacher reflecting on his or her own experience during a regular ECE teacher education class. Their voices are reconstructed, here, using pseudonyms:

Soya's Story

> Soya, a certified CDA (Child Development Associate), a $4^{th}$-year preschool teacher and a day care provider, reflects on her teachable moments:
> My curriculum is always evolving with teachable moments based on my daily observations of the children. For example, when I was supervising children during their free playtime on the playground, I saw Brian, who was wearing a hearing aid and eyeglasses, passing near the swing set Akiko was on. When the swing almost hit Brian's face and arm, I rushed to check whether he was O.K. At the same time I was thinking, this is a teachable moment to teach about playground safety. These children need to know Brian's uniqueness as well as the needs of maintaining a safe environment for all. Of course, we talked about this the first day of preschool, but this incident led me to repeat it, because safety is so important, especially for a child like Brian who needs special attention because of his vision and hearing problems. Safety is also important for me to keep my license! (S.K.'s reflection based on academic journal and class discussion, State College, PA, 1993)

Soya made sense of her teachable moment-oriented curriculum in relation to ongoing observations guided by what she believed were important matters, safety in this case, for young children's learning and her professional life as an early childhood educator. Considering Brian's unique conditions worked to strengthen Soya's teachable moment-oriented curriculum practice.

Story of Tony and Jane's Kindergarten Teacher Steven

Steven, who has an elementary teaching certification and has worked as an early childhood teacher for 3 years, is one of Tony and Jane's (see Chapter 1) private kindergarten teachers.

Steven explained: After deciding to give children a choice of using either chopsticks or a fork when they eat lunch, once in a while I see children using the chopsticks in a sword fight at the lunch table. I am a firm believer of keeping a peaceful environment for young children and staying free from any kind of school violence; therefore, I always take full advantage of these children's dangerous pretend play as moments to teach the importance of maintaining a nonviolent learning environment and a safe classroom. I guess, when it comes to issues of school violence, I have pretty much established a teachable moment-oriented curriculum in daily practice. Sometimes, it is tricky, though, such as when the children play in the block area, pretending to go hunting and using a block as a rifle. I know from child development theory that imagination and imaginative play like this is very important for these young children's learning, so times like this are always confusing to me and to the children. I want them to engage fully in imaginative play, yet I don't want them to engage in that kind of violent play. You know what I mean? I am still working on this part. I guess my teachable moment-oriented curriculum for school safety, peace-keeping, a caring environment, etc., is still under construction. I also believe that my kind of teachable moment-oriented curriculum represents not only developmentally but also culturally appropriate practice these days. The issue of school violence seems to be on the front page of most newspapers. Don't you think? (S.M.'s reflection based on academic journal and class discussion, State College, PA, 1994)

Here, Steven expressed his personal beliefs about promoting a nonviolent learning environment for young children through his teachable moment-oriented curriculum. His careful observation of children's violent pretend play guided him purposefully toward teachable moment-oriented curriculum practice. His knowledge of child development and play-based learning also served as guiding principles in his teachable moment-oriented curriculum, yet his knowledge of child development and his personal beliefs about nonviolent learning environments are at odds in his curriculum-making process.

Story of Kindergarten Teacher Mrs. Englishwill

Mrs. Englishwill, who has taught preschool and kindergarten for 32 years in both private and public settings, reflects on her understanding of teachable moments:

I do not know whether this is what you call a teachable moment, but I think it is; and I have been doing this type of teaching for 32 years. I believe that my style of teaching constitutes my real curriculum. Forget about DAP. That is too vague for me to depend upon. No, I would rather say DAP is too clear-cut (appropriate vs. inappropriate) to follow, especially when you are always working with children with special needs and culturally and linguistically diverse children and families. DAP is too political. Here's my example of teachable moment-oriented curriculum practice: In my kindergarten, the learning of letters and numbers is very important because of the children's first-grade school readiness. Let me tell you about my Angelo. He is a Hispanic child who used to use a mixture of English and Spanish when he spoke. I was concerned about his language limits. He could not say one full, clear sentence in English. One day, I observed Angelo pointing at all the alphabet letters one-by-one and saying the name of each letter in English, not only in the order of the alphabet but also randomly. He did the same with the numbers from 1 to 10, which were displayed on the poster board in my classroom. From that observation, I knew that Angelo knew all the letters and numbers we were learning in class. He used to say them in Spanish, but not anymore! That's a good sign because he has to learn and use English in order for him to learn at school. Now he knows letters and numbers [in English]; however, each time he writes his name on a sheet of paper, he always seems to have a difficulty writing the letters. Not all of his letters show the correct shapes; it almost looks like 3-year-old scribble. His ways of holding pencils, crayons, and thick markers are very clumsy. Since his family is very poor, he may not have enough materials like pencils, crayons, markers, and paper to play with at home. Thus, a limited opportunity with proper materials may have been a cause of Angelo's developmental delay. We know from Piagetian theory how important playing with manipulatives is for young children's development. That was apparently missing in Angelo's home setting, I think. Based on this observation, I concluded that Angelo had very limited eye-hand coordination and a lack of small muscle development. As soon as I knew that his developmental delay was not an intellectual but a physical matter, I needed to consider providing some play-oriented activity for him to exercise his coordination and small muscle development. The next day during morning free playtime, I saw Angelo playing with Play-doh and building a very detailed truck. He said to me, "It's my truck!" At that moment I saw that his fine motor skills seemed very well adjusted, so I decided to take advantage of that moment and showed him ways to make other kinds of cars. I also modeled ways to build alphabet letters to make the word *truck*. Afterward, each time he attempted to write his name, I reminded him of the way we built the letters of *truck* using Play-doh—carefully and slowly by looking at each alphabet letter on the chart. That teachable moment helped Angelo to practice his nice, neat, and correct handwriting skills, I think.

(M.E.'s reflection based on academic journal and class discussion, Fort Myers, FL, 1997)

Mrs. Englishwill's observation and interpretation of Angelo's growth and learning behavior were based purely on her limited knowledge of child development and monolingual—in this case English—dominant school culture. Mrs. Englishwill's Piagetian orientation to developmental psychology prompted her to see Angelo as developmentally delayed: She thought that his materially deprived home environment, about which she actually knows little, lacked play-oriented learning experiences with proper materials. In her imagination this deprived home context must have led to his lack of eye-hand coordination and fine motor skills in his writing. Furthermore, her acceptance of monolingual dominant school culture led to her interpreting of Angelo's emerging bilingual capability as a language deficiency. Based on this type of observation and interpretation and guided by specific subject matters that she believed to be important learning experiences for kindergartners, Mrs. Englishwill's teachable moment-oriented curriculum was constructed in ways that reinforced her routine daily practices.

Each of these teachers' sense-making of their own emerging purposeful instructional action is different, yet each constitutes a form of teachable moment-oriented curriculum practice. What they all share is a practice based on careful observation in interaction with children, an ability to recognize and interpret their observations according to their understandings of child development theory, and a strong set of what each believes about what is important to teach. From such thoughtful and purposeful teachers learners receive clear messages about what is important and necessary for their safety and future well-being as children and learners.

At the same time, all these teachers seem limited by their own first-person perspective-taking; that is, their teachable moment-oriented curriculum seems driven by a premise illustrated in the following monologue: "I believe it is important for children to learn (safety, nonviolent interaction, or letters and numbers); thus, I purposefully pursue the matter each time it arises or when the children initiate an interest or exhibit readiness through their play-oriented learning. This approach ensures that children will learn what they need to learn. It also makes me an effective teacher since I am responding appropriately to their needs."

A teachable moment-oriented curriculum for developmentally meaningful and culturally congruent practice represents, however, a purposeful practice that evolves from teachers' careful and ongoing observations, their ability to recognize the unique essence of the situation, and most importantly, their ability to make sense of the moment from *the child's point of view*, not from the teacher's point of view. In other words, the practice of teachable moment-oriented curriculum for developmentally meaningful and culturally congruent practice goes well beyond the good intentions of seemingly responsive teaching. It empowers teachers in their professional lives because it pushes them to engage in second-person perspective-taking, that is, to put themselves in the place of the very students who initiate those spontaneous events. It requires early childhood professionals to employ empathy.

Clearly, learners' interests, readiness, or spontaneous situations initially indicate these teachable moments to teachers. In that sense the teacher moves toward learner-centered, as opposed to content-oriented, curriculum practice. Purposeful actions resulting from these teachable moments, however, too often seem controlled by teachers. In this type of practice, teachers remain the primary definers of purposeful learning. Ironically, children are the main source of the teachable moment-oriented curriculum, but their interests and voices are recognized only from teachers' first-person perspectives, which establish understandings and intentions: Children remain passive, and what they learn is predetermined by adults, their teachers. Here, the teachable moment-oriented curriculum becomes a pure reflection of how most ECE teachers understand conventional child developmental psychology.

As a human science, developmental psychology has a long tradition of describing how children learn and grow from the perspective of Western, male-dominated thought—a perspective that has created normative and pathological views of childhood and individualistic interpretations of human beings, for example, Gesellian and Piagetian orientations. Within mainstream developmental theory, children are understood as social, cultural, political, context-free, and independent of time, situation, or condition; furthermore, they are classified into stage-oriented hierarchies based on notions of "normality." This mainstream developmental orientation has profoundly influenced the construction of modern early childhood professionals' images of children and their education. For example, in the early stage of "normal" human development, children are socially, emotionally, and intellectually understood as separate, not yet matured, distinct from adults, who are at higher developmental stages than children. Children depend on adults not only for the fulfillment of physiological needs, such as food, nurturing, and care, but also to learn how to function like adults in an adult world (Cannella, 1998). These principles have supported adults' intervention into the lives of children as important and serve as the basis for ECE's "appropriate practice." This perspective has bestowed a kind of ultimate power to the adult, teacher, and expert to determine what children need to learn and how to educate children according to universal developmental behaviors and outcomes within the dominant culture (Cannella, 1998; Silin, 1995; Takanishi, 1987; Woodhead, 1990). The teachable moment has its roots in perspective-representing practice that both child-centered and, ironically, adult-controlled beliefs based on a dominant culture and each teacher's individual beliefs of "good" practice. Obviously, such practice will seldom be developmentally meaningful and culturally congruent from the learner's point of view.

## Critical Aspects of a Teachable Moment-Oriented Curriculum

In many cases teachable moment-oriented curriculum practice stems from teachers' knowledge of developmental readiness derived from Western developmental psychology as well as their own personal beliefs about effective teaching and important matters. As illustrated in Figure 5.1, teachers' personal beliefs, sociopolitical constraints, and conventional knowledge of child development guide their observations of a child's growth, play, and learning. The learner indicates a readiness or interests through play, action, or expression. The teacher, in turn, captures the moment, observes, recognizes, and interprets it by filtering the moment through his or her own personality, knowledge, and beliefs, then considers, creates, and presents some spontaneous purposeful learning experience accordingly. On a continuum of responses, the teacher observes the child's response and interacts with or intervenes in the child's learning moment.

In this dynamic, the teacher must grasp, observe, recognize, and interpret a teachable moment and transform it into meaningful, sometimes unexpected, curriculum practice that will have a positive effect on the child's learning and developmental experiences. If the teacher misses, ignores, or cannot appreciate the moment, the child loses a learnable moment. As such, the teacher maintains a great deal of control over learning and teaching in this type of practice. Even in teachable moment-oriented curriculum practice, this control, which is both conscious and unconscious, is the key to our understanding of the explicit or readily apparent curriculum and the implicit or hidden curriculum.

A hidden curriculum is the unstated curriculum that lies behind the explicit or apparent curriculum. This hidden curriculum can be far more influential in the learning process than the explicit one. In these cases, the hidden curriculum becomes what learners really remember, learn, and act upon (Apple, 1979; Eisner, 1994). For example, when Angelo was reading the alphabet in both English and Spanish, his emerging bilingualism was not appreciated; in fact, Mrs. Englishwill ignored it because she believed that all children need to learn English in order to succeed in the monolingual school culture. This belief, coupled with a Pigetian interpretation of child development that cast Angelo as a deprived learner, created a hidden curriculum implying that speaking a language other than English is not good, being poor exerts a negative influence on high academic performance, and only adults and teachers are wise and powerful enough to steer young children through schooling toward a successful life.

A teachable moment-oriented curriculum for developmentally meaningful and culturally congruent practice requires that we understand the continued presence of our hidden curriculum. With this conscious understanding we can embrace the power of teachable moments through continuous critical self-reflection and inquiry:

**Figure 5.1. Conventional Dynamics of Teachable Moment-Oriented Curriculum**

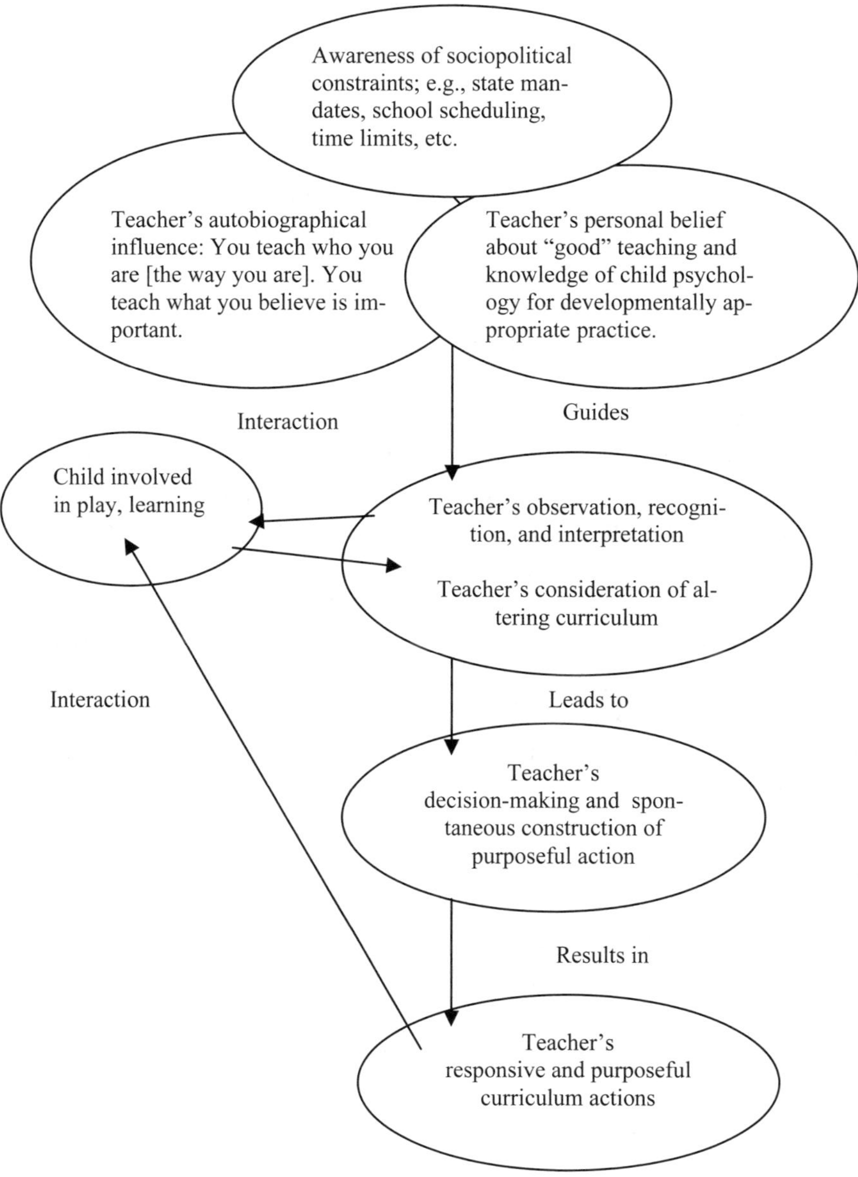

- How do I capture, observe, recognize, and interpret learnable moments so that they can become powerful teachable moments?
- How can I be sure that my knowledge of child development is fair to all the culturally, linguistically, ethnically, emotionally, physically, intellectually unique and diverse children whom I teach?
- How can I be sure that my personal beliefs about what to teach as important knowledge does not limit culturally, linguistically, ethnically, emotionally, physically, intellectually diverse children's self-initiated and autonomous learning experience?

In the best case a responsive teacher is a keen observer of individual children's teachable moments and acts accordingly. This kind of pedagogy has been historically identified and is still valued as powerful, good practice for young children. In every case, however, appropriate practice depends on the teacher's belief system, personal knowledge of child development, personal values based on his or her own sociocultural backgrounds, various pedagogical constraints, both real and perceived, and what she or he knows and feels about each child. All of these (see Figure 5.1) serve as filters when the teacher conducts teachable moment experiences—curriculum—for individual learners.

However, while teachers' keen observations of teachable moments work for some, perhaps most, young children, this does not guarantee that teachable moments will present themselves for all children because their success depends entirely upon whether the teacher can capture the teachable moment or not. If a teacher misses, does not recognize, or misinterprets a young child's learnable moment, both the learner and the teacher lose a meaningful learning experience. Said differently, the teacher remains, paradoxically, the ultimate power-holder within this learner-generated curriculum, leaving the risk that both teacher and learner become losers within their own cultural paradigms. Thus, while teachable moment-oriented curriculum practice is important—especially when the teachable moment pertains to young children's physical health and safety or basic social, emotional, and physical skill development—it cannot alone fully guarantee equal, fair, and congruent empowering learning experiences for all children. Angelo's case makes this abundantly clear.

How should teachers consider the teachable moment-oriented curriculum so that they can engage in truly developmentally meaningful and culturally congruent practice? The case below provides an example offered by another prospective ECE teacher taken from the study that was conducted by six ECE professors in six different states (Hyun et al., 2000). In this example, we see the teacher effectively learning how to make a teachable moment equally empowering for both the child and the teacher (see Figure 5.2):

> Topic: Teachable moment-oriented curriculum practice
> Conf: DCAP and Curriculum
> Date: Wednesday, September 15, 1999, 07:55 a.m.
> As the children in the kindergarten class where I am interning colored the letter "B" page of their "Letter People Alphabet Books"—not DCAP, but hold on—a Mexican American child was counting the buttons around Mr. B, which he had colored many different colors. He counted, for example "Uno, dos, tres butones verde." Forgive my Spanish! When I noticed what he was doing, I knelt beside his table and repeated whatever sequence he said. He instantly became the "Spanish teacher," and I soon realized the frustration [second-person perspective-taking] of learning a new language, especially when learning the word for *purple*. He said it over and over again to help me learn it. Once, I said a series of words correctly, and he patted me on the back and said, "Muy Bueno," which means very nice in English. The child took a typical worksheet, and turned it into a wonderful teachable moment. I was the learner in the child's meaningful learning process. (Reflection of L.D., prospective ECE teacher in Florida, posted on Internet WebBoard for field experience-sharing, Sept. 1999)

Here, the lesson opened as a typical, teacher-driven worksheet experience. There was no rich context the child could engage in, no play-based learning experience to construct the concept of the letter B; however, the child's connection-making between what he was learning (the letter "B") and what he already knew (the concept of buttons and counting numbers in his own language) converting the worksheet activity into fully self-initiated, self-directed, self-engaged learning experience. At that moment, it was L.D., the prospective teacher, who was able to exercise her multiple perspective-taking and transform herself into a learner. Allowing the child to be a teacher created emotionally as well as cognitively meaningful learning experiences for both of them.

**Figure 5.2. Dynamics of a Developmentally Meaningful and Culturally Congruent Teachable Moment-Oriented Curriculum Practice**

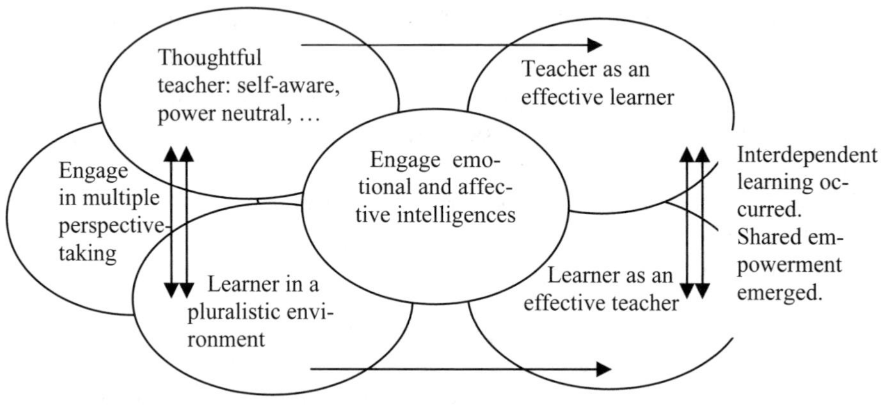


## Conclusion

Anna Freud stated, "Teaching is learning twice: first, one learns as one prepares for one's students, and then one learns from them, as one works with them" (Coles, 1992, p. 53; Britzman & Pitt, 1996, p. 117). L.D.'s developmentally meaningful and culturally congruent teachable moment-oriented practice is a powerful example of how a teacher transforms herself into an effective learner by using her second-person perspective-taking to make the teachable moment equal to a learnable moment for both the teacher and the learner. In that transformation teacher and child had engaged their emotional and affective domains in a cognitive-driven learning process. An equally shared sense of empowerment emerged as they cocreated a valuable and interdependent learning experience.

John Dewey (1859–1952) explained the importance of the social dimension of education that underlies the healthy growth of all individuals. He believed that curriculum could no longer be justified as solely academic and intellectual or solely vocational and social. Any subject or activity chosen for or recommended to individual students should contribute to their intellectual and social development as well as their personal development. The importance of each learner's personal internal reactions—thoughts, feelings, interests, curiosity, and impulse—and desire should be used as springboards; furthermore, the teacher's responsibility is to observe carefully and use that occasion for the formation of a plan and method of activity. He emphasized the importance of establishing continuity between the learner's world of experiences and a curriculum that arises from and further develops those experiences.

In order for us to create truly meaningful, fair, congruent, and equally empowering learning environments for all diverse children in a pluralistic learning community that celebrate emancipatory knowledge construction, Dewey's notion of an effective teacher—one who follows teachable moment-oriented curriculum practice exclusively in the service of transmitting a culture and in relation to so-called educational experience—must change. In developmentally meaningful and culturally congruent teachable moment-oriented curriculum practice we reconstruct teacher and learner images as transformative identities to allow young and old alike to explore new, emerging meanings. We do this not to try to ensure or perpetuate preexisting knowledge and power but instead to empower us to be who we are in the process of becoming. From this perspective teachable moments represent new, emerging ways for us to learn from one another by temporarily ignoring our institutional identities of teacher and learner in order to become a participating member of an interdependent learning community.

## Chapter Ending Questions

- What drives teachable moment-oriented curriculum practice?
- What is the key to teachable moment-oriented curriculum for developmentally meaningful and culturally congruent practice?
- Does teachable moment-oriented curriculum practice fully depend upon child-initiated and learner-centered learning? Why? How? Why not?
- Based on your field experience (teaching or observation) in Pre-K-third-grade classroom contexts, share an example of teachable moment-oriented teaching. In what ways does the teachable moment-oriented teaching support curriculum

practice for developmentally meaningful and culturally congruent practice from the children's perspective?

## Note

[1] Karen McGreevy was one of my students who was most interested in the notion of teachable moment during her ECE teacher preparation program, and quite willing to write and share her understanding of teachable moment-oriented curriculum practice in-depth. I had a year-long dialogue about teachable moments with Karen based on her field experiences. As a result, Karen defines teachable moments quite differently from the way her peers do.

# Chapter Six

# Emergent-Oriented Curriculum

## Initial Inquiries

- How is emergent learning understood? How does it appear?
- How do teachers and children create and shape an emergent-oriented curriculum?
- How is emergent-oriented curriculum practice similar to and different from teachable moment-oriented curriculum practice?
- What are the critical aspects of emergent-oriented curriculum from the perspective of developmentally meaningful and culturally congruent practice?

## Perspectives

Emergent-oriented curriculum is a notion used by many educators (e.g., Booth, 1997; Sheerer, Dettore, & Cyphers, 1996; Jones & Nimmo, 1994), but these popular notions seem to reflect mixed or varied conceptual understandings. Some early childhood educators, for example, define emergent-oriented curriculum as learning experiences and activities generated by the interests of children and teachers in a given context (Sheerer, Dettore, & Cyphers, 1996). In many cases authors *relate* emergent-oriented curriculum practices with developmentally appropriate practice (DAP)-oriented curriculum (e.g., Cassidy & Lancaster, 1993; Bredekamp, 1987; Bredekamp & Copple, 1997; Jones, Evans, Rencken, Stringer, & Williams, 2001; Jones & Nimmo, 1994). Other educators perceive the emergent-oriented curriculum as formed by certain pedagogical practices, for example, a thematic approach with subject integration (Beans, 1997; Peters & Schubeck, 1995); northern Italy's Reggio Emilia approach (Edwards, Gandini, & Forman, 1993; Malaguzzi, 1993; New, 1993); the Octopus Project, Australia's replication of the Reggio Emilia approach; or curriculum practices that use a project approach (Chard, 1992; Helm & Katz, 2001; Katz, 1990; Katz, 1994a; Katz & Chard, 1989; Katz & Chard, 1993; Katz & Chard, 2000). According to Jones, Evans, Rencken, Stringer, and Williams (2001),

> emergent curriculum . . . is the most sensible approach to teaching young children. . . . Preselected, presequenced lesson plans cannot possibly offer a

> goodfit in guiding the interactions of one classroom's unique group of people. . . . The teacher's agenda is not static; it is dynamic, based in part on her or his evolving goals for the children, individually and collectively. All good teachers have goals for children's learning—both content goals and process goals. This agenda also reflects the teacher's personal values, survival concerns, educational theory, and habit. It may or may not closely match the school's agenda. (p. 3)

This chapter characterizes and explores emergent-oriented curriculum practice through the experiences of Lynn, a prospective ECE teacher from the United States, as she coconstructs the meaning of emergent-oriented curriculum with culturally diverse pre-K (four- to five-year-old) children during her field experience. The chapter contains an examination of the way Lynn understood emergent learning, how she and the children created and shaped their curriculum, and what critical aspects pertain to emergent-oriented curriculum work from the perspective of developmentally meaningful and culturally responsive practice. Pseudonyms are used in the following vignettes that summarize a 12-week period.

## Preparing the Lesson

> *University supervisor*: Lynn, what will you be doing next week with the preschoolers?
>
> *Intern:* This is my lesson plan. It's for the Valentine's Day activity. It is rough, but I want you to see. I already shared the lesson idea with the cooperating teacher. She said it would be good since the children are already excited about Valentine's Day. They know what that is, so it will be easy for me to plan and teach the lesson like this compared to other lessons that have a subject the children may not be familiar with.
>
> *University supervisor*: How would you know whether the children are interested in a topic like this?
>
> *Intern*: [Silence]
>
> *University supervisor*: What kinds of observation or documentation of the children have led you into this kind of planning?
>
> *Intern*: Oh, now I know what you are talking about! Emergent curriculum! Project approach! Reggio Emilia approach! Trusting children's idea, child-

initiated teaching and learning, inquiry and research-based, family involvement, all that!

*University supervisor*: I hear you are making connections between what you have learned from the courses and your teaching experience.

*Intern*: Yes! As you know, next week we have Valentine's Day. The teacher decorated the classroom with the theme of Valentine's Day, and the entire center is already filled with Valentine symbols. The children are talking about the pictures, pointing out the signs and symbols; some of them drew their pictures of it, so I guess those are my observations of the children that indicate their interest in the lesson.

*University supervisor*: How would you facilitate the children's interests, such as promoting their thinking and many other possibilities within their interests?

*Intern*: By asking lots of questions to them, I guess.

*University supervisor*: I wonder what kinds of experiences you and the children might be coconstructing or engaging in?

*Intern*: It's a project. They will create and decorate their own heart-shaped Valentine's card for their parents or friends. I am not going to help them. They will do it all by themselves, but since they cannot make the exact shape of a heart symbol, the only thing I will do is prepare heart-shaped paper for them. I will use pink and red paper for that.

*University supervisor*: Why heart-shaped only? Why do you have to make the shape for them? Why only pink and red colors?

*Intern*: It's Valentine's Day card making! Heart, red, and pink, don't you know? What do you mean "Why only heart shaped and red and pink? I don't understand your questions." The children had already seen red or pink heart-shaped Valentine symbols in the decorations in their classroom. For three- to five-year-olds, drawing or cutting a heart shape is developmentally a very difficult task. They are still working on drawing a closed-circle shape as I learned from child development class, so I am going to make the shape for them prior to the activity.

*University supervisor*: I am just wondering whether all the children will be O.K. with the heart shape or only the two colors for making their own card. What do you think?

*Intern*: Now, I understand what you are suggesting: giving them choices! I am going to provide many different colors of markers and crayons and white paper too. Oh, I will also be doing a cooking project; it's making Valentine cupcakes for their snack. It's going to be a heart-shaped cupcake. Children will decorate the cake in as many different ways as they want to. All of their emerging creative ideas will be presented on each cup cake, so in this lesson I will have two projects: card- and cupcake-making. As the project approach says, I will ask lots of questions as we make the cake so that the children will think about the measuring, problem-solving, mathematical thinking, sharing, all of which will be integrated. I will also prepare a cupcake-making sequence chart using pictures and simple words so that the children will be able to read the chart as they make the cake. In doing so, logical-mathematical thinking, reading, and emerging literacy are also included in the project. I am going to assist the children only as they make the cake. I will be ready for responding to their emerging questions and their emergent interests as they make the cake. I will direct only when they need to put the cake into the oven for the safety reason, so it is really child-centered and inquiry-based problem-solving as they engage in the activity. Actually the idea of baking cake is from a parent. She will be bringing all the ingredients and cooking stuff, so parent involvement is also included in the project approach.

*University supervisor*: It sounds as if you are really excited about these two projects. How can I help you in terms of your self-evaluation for the teaching experience?

*Intern*: I don't know. Just see how smoothly the project goes and how I control the children since it is not a formal lesson but a project that has lots of freedom and emergent learning for the children. I am not sure how to control their behaviors. Give me any suggestion that you think might be helpful for my reflective self-assessment.

Lynn was a prospective teacher excited about her teaching and engaged in continuous dialogue with her cooperating teacher and university supervisor for the preparation of her lesson plans. Lynn had a very supportive cooperating teacher who was always willing to try new approaches with her intern, even though she was not familiar with all the new approaches the intern wanted to try. Lynn's supervisor practiced reflective clinical supervision (Hyun & Marshall, 1996), emphasizing her role as facilitator for the prospective teacher's explorative novice teaching experiences.

During the lesson preparation phase, Lynn clearly showed her intent of connection-making between theory and practice. She conceptually connected the notion of emergent-oriented curriculum practice with the thematic approach (Valentine's Day) and the project approach (creating cards) in light of child-initiated teaching and learning and subject integration.

At the beginning of her experience, the manifestation of Lynn's emergent-oriented curriculum practice seems identical to teacher-created learning experiences. She unnoticed diverse cultural awareness, assuming that all children know about Valentine's Day celebrations, and overlooked individual developmental considerations, assuming that children cannot create or draw shapes other than the circle at ages 3 to 5.

As Lynn engaged in implementation of the Valentine's Day project she prepared, she discovered unexpected emergent learning experiences as a teacher, and these led her to deconstruct some of her culturally bounded "teacher knowledge" to respond thoughtfully and promote the diverse learner's emergent learning. Let's continue our visit to Lynn's classroom.

## Presenting the Lesson/Project

> During the large-group time in the morning, Lynn and the cooperating teacher introduced four different center activities for the day. One of the centers was Lynn's project table. Children had their choice of visiting the four different centers during the small-group activity time.
>
> *Jeffery*: I am going to make my Valentine card for my mom.
>
> He looked around the project table, chose one pink heart shape from the activity box, looked at it for a couple of seconds, dropped it back into the box, went to the drawing table, and selected white paper. Using green markers and green and black crayons, he drew a diamond shape and tried to cut it out—he first used scissors, ignored the scissors, then tore it off with his hands. He made *a green diamond-shaped card* with three big happy smiles on it.
>
> *Jeffery*: It's for my mom!
> *Intern*: [Hearing Jeffery's voice, she looked at him and his card.] No, Jeffery, we are making a Valentine card. If you want to make a card for your mom, go to the project table, use the heart shape. You can pick either red or pink and make a Valentine card for your mom. You can decorate the card any way you want to using your own ideas.

> *Jeffery*: No! This is for my mom. I made it for my mom. She is my valentine. This is the card.
>
> *Intern*: [later, during the conversation with the university supervisor] In my mind, at first, I said no to Jeffery, but I knew I had to support what he made in his own way; so I simply redirected him to the Valentine card-making table. He said "No." It was totally outside my imagination; the original project was at risk because the child's creative meaning-making was extraordinary. I am beginning to realize that allowing children to have their own choices is an act of trusting children's unique ideas.
>
> Later, on the same day afternoon, Lynn had a brief chance to greet Jeffery's mother, who came to school to pick him up. Lynn showed the card to his mom. Jeffery's mom told Lynn that the green diamond-shaped Valentine card would make perfect sense to her.
>
> Lynn learned that Jeffery's single mother just became engaged. Her boyfriend, who happened to be Jeffery's best friend, gave his mom a diamond ring. This made Jeffery's mother very happy. So was Jeffery. Green was the favorite color of both Jeffrey and his mom. Jeffery had recently learned how to draw a diamond shape. He had practiced drawing diamond shapes and other shapes at home with his mom and Jerry (mom's fiancé) for a couple of weeks. He was very excited about the fact that he could draw a diamond shape all by himself!

By observing a child's unique approach to the teacher-originated project, discovering the child's compelling reason to do the project in his own way, and listening to the parent's perspective, the prospective teacher *unexpectedly has learned* how a child's current environment at home (a home culture) affects his growth, learning, and development. Cultural diversity goes well beyond what one might think it is: It is more than ethnicity, more than different languages, more than race. It originates in each and every one's contemporary home culture, environment, and situation. Home culture and environment also affect the child's developmental progress: Jeffery shows his interest in and ability to draw a diamond shape.

When the teacher prepared her lesson, she referred to U.S. commercialized images of Valentine's Day (e.g., red and pink colors, heart shapes), as well as to the children's supposed inability to draw shapes other than circles, guided by her teacher-driven knowledge of developmental psychology. During the actual implementation of her lesson, Lynn engaged in *deconstructing* a tenet of her traditional understanding of child development: The open-circle shape is usually understood as a first shape most young children attempt to draw, and shapes like squares and diamonds are more difficult for young children to execute (Cornett, 1999; Gesell, 1940; Kellogg, 1969; Lowenfeld & Brittain, 1987). Jeffery not only enjoys drawing diamond shapes, but the shape is also particularly meaningful for him and his family as he draws. Jeffery's use of green also put Lynn off her stride. He obviously understood and embraced both the theme and the project, but his interpretation of the project (as conceived by Lynn and the dominant culture) pushed her boundaries.

Lynn stated that trusting diverse learners' unknown and unique motivations and capabilities in their spontaneous choice-making, especially when they differ from the teacher's knowledge driven by a specific cultural paradigm, would challenge many novice teachers, presenting an opportunity for risk-taking if the teacher accepts the child's unique connection-making and initiation in a context of emergent-oriented curriculum practice. Sometimes, teachers and adults fail to see children's emerging capabilities, particularly when they are very different from the teacher's expectations or predictions as happened in Lynn's case. A child's unique capability could be perceived as inappropriate behavior or a misunderstanding, the teacher attempting to correct or redirect the learner's personally meaningful performing knowledge. In this instance the teacher might face *a risk-taking* that could lead to an inappropriate assessment and disempowering the learner.

As Lynn developed her experiential understanding of the unexpected journey toward the emergent-oriented curriculum, Jeffery's incident was not only the entrance to Lynn's emergent orientation to curriculum practice: She also discovered culturally diverse young children's unique ways of approaching the learning experience.

## Welcoming the Emerging Curriculum

> Other children in the classroom: Sixteen pre-K children were enrolled in the class: four African Americans; seven European Americans, including Jeffery;

three Asian Americans; and two Hispanic Americans. At first, they all made the Valentine card using the intern's materials. They were all the same. When the children saw a display of the greeting cards they had made (documentation), several of them pointed to the green diamond-shaped card and asked the teacher why Jeffery's card looked different and why he had made it in that way. A teachable moment emerged. Because of the children's interest in Jeffery's card and knowing Jeffery's mom's story, the next day Lynn and the cooperating teacher decided to give the children the opportunity to talk about the cards that they had made. After Jeffery talked about his special card, another child asked, "Can I make another card? A different one?" Other children agreed, "Yeh!" After the children heard the reason that Jeffery had made a green diamond-shaped card for his mom, they all decided to create their own unique cards with various shapes and colors, but the original idea of expressing their special feelings to a special person was much clearer to all the children in the classroom. Even one of the Korean children, who had absolutely no idea about what Valentine's Day meant, was able to create his own special cards for his mother and grandfather. It took longer than what Lynn and the classroom teacher expected, but the project was transformed.

That day Jin Min, a Korean child, said to the university supervisor, who was there watching their activities and could speak his home language, "Na umma rang hal-a-bu-gi sa rang hei. Ge le su, na e gu doo ke man del aus sae yo." English translation: "I love my mom and my grandfather, so I made these two." He had been living with his single mother since he was three months old. His grandfather took care of him when his mother was at work or at school.

*Intern's reflection*: I never thought about making a Valentine card using green diamond shapes. My way of thinking of "what to teach" and "how to teach" did not match with what was going on in the child's home setting that affected his thinking and learning. I did not know that the Korean kid had no idea what he was doing when he first made the card. He was very quiet, but I thought he knew what we were doing. He paid attention to the directions that I gave to the children. He simply made the first card without a problem; then he really understood the meaning of the card-making and made two more with very interesting shapes and multi colors for his mom and grandfather! I never thought that all the children would want to create different cards after they had seen Jeffery's unique card. I did not believe or trust that these young children could do anything like this. Jeffery's voice and creative expression had inspired an emergent interest and motivated a learning experience for the other children, not to mention the emergent learning experience for me!

> *One week later*: When the university supervisor visited the classroom, she saw a new table with a sign. The classroom had a new card-making table next to the art area. The children wanted to continue the card-making activity any time they wanted to or thought it was needed. For example, they made a "We love you, Goldfish" card for the new goldfish in their classroom. One of neighbors who lived near the school had donated three goldfish in a small fishbowl before he moved away. The children also made a card for the mother of a classmate who brought them snacks: "We like your cupcakes and the decorations." These demonstrate that what is being taught and learned had taken on a serious significance: New curriculum was formed by the children and existed in the classroom.

Observing and documenting the children's engagement in the teacher-created Valentine card-making project, becoming more knowledgeable about Jeffery's unique family experiences as demonstrated in his card-making, and learning about his mother's support of Jeffery's creation, the teachers reflected and made a pedagogical decision in response to the children's emerging interests. When the teachers heard the children question, "*Why does Jeffery's card look different from ours?*" it was a teachable moment during which teachers and learners together could allow purposeful action to emerge. A teachable moment arose when teachers observed, recognized, and interpreted the spontaneously emerging interests of diverse learners (see Chapter 5), hence the two teachers decided to give the children a chance to talk about their own cards.

Making and sharing his ideas in conjunction with the teachers' decisions to permit, explore, and exploit this event, Jeffery's voice invited other children to learn a deeper meaning-making than the previous card-making activity offered. Their newly emergent meaning-making led them to continue the project with some transformation of the original Valentine card-making project. Here, the children demonstrated self-assessment of their previous work by reviewing their own cards (documentation), and decided to proceed with more personally meaningful work. As the teacher observed and documented the children's work, she also discovered and learned what the children could do instead of what they could not do, and what they wanted to do rather than what she hoped they might do. The continuation of unexpected but profoundly powerful *dual learning* in both the teacher and the children shaped emergent-oriented curriculum practice. As the children continuously expanded the original project, giving it a new look, the teachers rearranged the classroom to support the children's serendipitous emerging expressions (i.e., adding a card-making table adjacent to the arts area).

Lynn's one-time event-oriented project transformed into an organic experience with lasting and socially meaningful implications. The children extended the project over time. The children wanted to make sure that the three goldfish did not feel sad because their previous owner had left them; they wanted to welcome them and make them feel loved. The children exercised empathy and used card-making to express their feelings. They also made cards to show their appreciation of other people's support of their learning. Underlying the transformation of Lynn's original theme-based project into an emergent-oriented curriculum is the premise that learning ultimately must be *organic and whole*. The project approach naturally and organically provides opportunities for collaborative work in many different areas and invites the exercise of many skills and dispositions. It also offers emergent opportunities for ongoing holistic social-emotional curriculum practices of early childhood (Booth, 1997).

> *Two weeks later*: One day Jin Min brought two books to school. They came from Seoul, South Korea, and were written in two different languages: English and Korean. Jin Min's mother and grandfather came to school and read the books to the children. Jin Min's mom read the book in English as his grandfather read it in Korean. Jin Min tried hard to explain in English how excited he was when he discovered the package containing the book in his home mailbox. Classmate Susan said, "Why don't we make a thank-you card for the person who sent the book to Jin Min? She will be also excited to find the mail in her mailbox. It will make her happy like Jin Min." A small group of children—Jin Min, Jeffery, Susan, and Asa—made a card during the activity time.

> As the children constructed their thoughts serendipitously but in socially powerful ways, another teachable moment emerged. Because the children had made the thank-you card for someone who could not come to the classroom to receive it, Lynn and the cooperating teacher thought that mailing the thank you card from the post office would be powerful. Heretofore the children had only delivered cards within their own classroom; so the two teachers asked the children how they could deliver the card to S. Korea. That thought-provoking question led the children to engage in unexpected new problem-solving. One child said, "We can give it to Jin Min so that he can

> give it to his aunt." Jin Min said, with the help of his mom translating his Korean into English, "We can go to the post office to mail the card to my eemo (aunt). I do that all the time with my mom and grandfather." They went to the neighborhood post office to mail their special thank-you card to Jin Min's aunt who had sent the children's book. Jin Min led the group to the post office and demonstrated how to mail an international letter with help from his grandfather. They mailed the card to Seoul, S. Korea.

As the children listened to Jin Min's story about the excitement he felt receiving mail, some children were able to make connections with the card-making table. When a small group of children continuously engages in the same project, applying increasingly complex reasoning and expanding the project into a new dimension, spontaneous emergent learning occurs (Katz, 1994a, 1994b; Katz & Chard, 1989).

"Children's emergent interests and experiences are implemented by an *observant teacher*; the teacher is then able to guide children to further inquiry and deeper understandings" (Schiller, 1995, p. 46). This was clearly in evidence when Lynn and her cooperating teacher decided to ask how they could deliver the card to S. Korea. That single thought-provoking question motivated the children to engage in new problem-solving.

Another teachable moment emerged when the teachers listened to the children's spontaneous and serendipitous but socially powerful new meaning-making. The two teachers engaged in deep and complex learning and discovery of each child's growth, change, and learning as well as assessing, reflecting, and expanding their own pedagogical practices. Thus, once again dual emergent learning occurred in which learners and adults were involved. The teachers' emergent learning about children's unexpected capabilities seemed simultaneously to accompany the teachers' emerging realization of teachable moments. Children's voices and inquiry in a social context occurring at the same time as teachers' continuous discovery of teachable moments seem to be the driving force in shaping an emergent-oriented curriculum practice.

> Lynn said, "I never knew that the children could understand the feelings of others on such a high level and suggest relevant ideas, such as Susan's knowing how exciting it was for Jin Min to find mail in his mail box and suggesting that we send a card to his aunt so she could share the excitement. My co-

> operating teacher and I were very surprised and happy to see what Jin Min could do when he suggested we go to the post office. This was his first time taking leadership of the group's learning experience."

As in Jin Min's case, if a culturally familiar topic or problem-solving task arises, a child can easily contribute to the group's learning process and even assume a leadership role that may have been previously out of reach because of the cultural incongruency built into the curriculum practice. Jin Min assumed leadership of the group learning process at a serendipitous moment, and the teachers discovered a child's unknown ability. Jin Min's voice allowed the children to experience new learning outside the classroom context in the community setting. Emergent-oriented curriculum practice has the capacity to overcome monocultural curriculum practice and offer much richer curriculum experiences if active parent, family, and community involvement and collaboration are a component.

> Right before the children left for the post office to mail the card, Jin Min's grandfather came to the classroom and showed how to write the address in Korean. One child asked Jin Min's grandfather, "Why do you have to write the address differently? Why not in English?" Jin Min's grandfather could not clearly understand the child's question because of his limited English speaking and listening skills. Lynn said, "I knew that was another pretty powerful emerging question, and I could relate it to their literacy experience with the bilingual Korean books. So many other new emerging interests and questions came up with the children; my cooperating teacher and I could not think of how to explore the question. Besides, my cooperating teacher and I had no idea how to explore the inquiry as deeply as we could other equally powerful questions that children brought."

All children's emerging interests cannot always be explored in depth in part because of the teacher's comfort level with the emerging topic. The truth of the famous expression "You teach who you are" is apparent even in the reflective teacher's emergent-oriented curriculum decision-making processes.

## Concluding the Lesson

By the end of Lynn's field experience, the project had expanded to incorporate many new ideas that the children, neighborhood, and families had brought to the classroom.

Lynn said, "After the visit to the post office, the children wanted to know how mail carriers know exactly where to deliver letters. They wanted to know how far away South Korea is and how long it would take for their letter to arrive. Where is Pennsylvania and where is South Korea on the map? How do people work together to deliver a card from one place to another, especially if the destination is very far away. They wanted to know why their moms' diamond rings are circular, not diamond shaped, but still called diamond rings. They wanted to see Jeffery's mom's diamond ring to see the shape. Children's learning never stops; it becomes more complex, unexpected. It's so exciting. I was so into listening to what they were wondering about. They asked powerful questions. I took their questions and went from there.

"Sometimes I feel as if I am taking an extreme risk because I do not have clearly written lesson plans to guide me as a prepared teacher. I never imagined that my culturally biased expectations or my culturally fixed ideas of Valentine card-making would take a turn and end up with mailing a thank-you card to South Korea. The children themselves expanded their experiences to world geography and postal system of communication! It's evolutionary.

"My cooperating teacher and I took a risk in letting the children express and explore their questions, even though we ran out of time to teach lessons that we had prepared. I think I finally got a sense of what emergent curriculum is. It's an evolving curriculum. It's a spiral curriculum driven by children's unique connection-making. Now, the written lesson plan does not make any sense to me. Listening and responding to the children's voices that take multiple directions are my living lesson plan! I must tell you that it is scary and difficult at the beginning. I still have those kinds of fears, but if I set my mind as an emergent learner like the children and with the children, I think I can enjoy that kind of curriculum practice. It is exploring unknown possibilities with the children, and we learn together!"

Uniquely powerful aspects that promote emergent-oriented curriculum include the following:

- purposefulness with which teachers (adults) become risk-takers as they allow mistakes to happen (Edwards, Gandini, & Forman, 1993);
- willingness to begin teaching and learning without a clear lesson plan, but initiating an open project;
- openness to serendipitous unexpected moments (teachable moments) and willingness to expand such moments for further and deeper exploration and to promote continuous learning moments with prolonged engagement;
- willingness to examine and continuously deconstruct one's own culturally bounded teacher knowledge and expectations, reconstructing the unknown possibilities of what diverse children can do and can bring into the exploratory learning process. Simultaneously, we practice trust and respect for children's ideas, trust in ourselves as teachers to respond and support children-led learning, and respect for parents as members of the collaborative education team.

These qualities represent aspects of the infrastructure of the emergent-oriented curriculum, the construction of which is an organically living, socially meaningful act.

**Dynamics of Emergent-Oriented Curriculum Practice**

Based on what we have observed in Lynn's experience, Figure 6.1 presents the dynamics of emergent-oriented curriculum. As seen in Figure 6.1, emergent-oriented curriculum can begin as a small-scale project created by children based on their emerging interests, or it can begin with the teacher's interpretation of his or her own observation and documentation of the children or simply as a project designed by the teacher. When the project is owned and shared in unanticipated ways by learners in *a social learning setting* (e.g., children looking at their own work and commenting and questioning about others' work in a display setting; children talking about their own work and sharing with others their own unique ideas in a group setting), and when the teacher simultaneously perceives *a teachable moment* within the context (e.g., when Lynn's students asked, *"Why does Jeffery's card look different from ours? Why don't we make a thank you card for the person who sent the mail to Jin Min? She will also be excited to find mail in her mailbox. Why do you have to write the address differently? Why not in English? How do people work together to deliver a card from one place to another, especially if it is too far to deliver? Why is Jeffery's mom's diamond ring a circle shape, not a diamond shape but still called a diamond ring?"*), then the project can transform and expand for a longer period than indicated in the original plan. Each child's personalized meaning-making in his or her approach to the project reflects the child's home culture and environment. The child demonstrates his or her ability to modify the project experience in ways unexpected by the teacher but culturally congruent with the child's cognitive and social growth, home culture, and learning experience (e.g., Jeffery's green diamond-shaped Valentine card for his mom).

Within the context of emergent-oriented curriculum, a reflective teacher experiences new and unexpected learning among the children by observing, interacting with, and documenting the emerging phenomena and communicating about the observations with family members. During that process, teachers also engage in deconstructing their teacher knowledge about what the children cannot do but reconstruct and newly construct their teacher knowledge of what the children can do, leading them to capture powerful teachable moments. At this point teachers perceive that serendipitous teachable moments are imminent, and thus they are mentally ready to capture the moments, as shown when Lynn said, "I was so into listening to what they were wondering about. They asked powerful questions. I took their questions and went from there."

> In social learning contexts teachers reflectively reassess their pedagogical practice and the physical classroom environment, making necessary changes in response to the children's emerging construction of the learning experiences. Guided by their own mental fluency in capturing teachable moments, teachers formulate and present thought-provoking questions, facilitating dialogue to extend the learning experiences to allow children to engage in a higher level of thinking and problem-solving. Teachers must be risk-takers, ready to entertain unknown possibilities and trust children's hidden capabilities; they must support those unknown possibilities and trust that the learners' hidden capabilities can coexist with their own pedagogy. Recall Lynn's comments:

"Sometimes I feel as if I am taking an extreme risk because I do not have clearly written lesson plans to guide me as a prepared teacher. . . . My cooperating teacher and I took a risk in letting the children express and explore their questions, even though we ran out of time to teach lessons that we had prepared. . . . I must tell you that it is scary and difficult at the beginning. I still have those kinds of fears, but if I set my mind as an emergent learner like the children and with the children, I think I can enjoy that kind of curriculum practice. It is exploring unknown possibilities with the children, and we learn together!"

In this dynamic, teacher and learner both engaged in the continuation of emerging new learning experiences. Active parents involvement and community members' contributions also enriched the children's serendipitous but socioculturally powerful emergent learning experiences. Consequently, learning experiences became collaborative, interdependent, organic, and holistic. The children's unique, emerging inquiry and the teachers' simultaneously capturing and using teachable moments transformed the project into emergent-oriented living curriculum.

## Emergent-Oriented Versus Teachable Moment-Oriented Curriculum Practices

Emergent-oriented curriculum appears to be an extension of teachable moment-oriented curriculum derived from learners' continuation of learnable moments because the teacher needs to capture children's moments of emerging interests based on his or her sensitive listening and careful observation and to preserve, nurture, and transform the moments into broader collaborative and theme-based or project-oriented teaching and learning while maintaining the core idea of "child initiation" (e.g., Coles & Nixon, 1998; Hyun & Marshall, 2003a, 2003b; Peterson, 2002). Figure 6.2 presents a brief comparison of teachable moment-oriented curriculum practices and emergent-oriented curriculum practices.

**Figure 6.1. Dynamics of Emergent-Oriented Curriculum Practice**

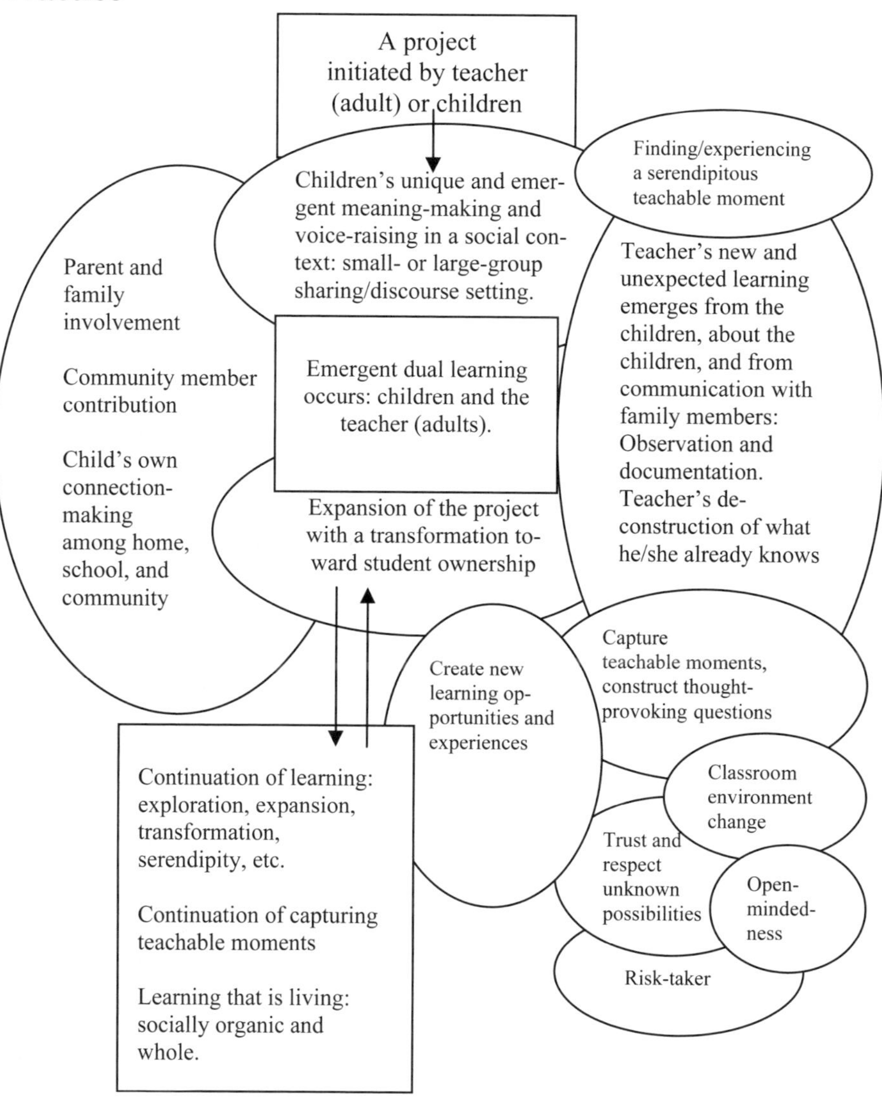

## Figure 6.2. Brief Comparison of Teachable Moment-Oriented Curriculum Practices and Emergent-Oriented Curriculum Practices

**Teachable moment-oriented curriculum practices:**

A short event focused on a child's interests or a teacher-interpreted readiness of child's capability is a fully teachable moment, but it may not be equal to a learner-motivated learnable moment. Even though the learner is the one who initiated the experience through his or her own interests, it is fully controlled by the teacher's emerging agenda.

May not or cannot extend the moment toward long-term learning or project experience.

It can have a purely individual base: one-to-one interaction between teacher and a child. Thus, it has the possibility of limiting the social learning context.

**Both**

Teacher recognizes teachable moments initiated by learners.

**Emergent-oriented curriculum practices:**

The teacher's mental fluency operates on a continuum of actions ranging from finding or experiencing a serendipitous teachable moment to intentionally expecting or believing in the possibility of serendipitous teachable moments occurring in a social learning context. Requires a longer period of intentionally exploring learners' interests and motivation, acculturating, and cultivating learners' process-oriented learning experiences to verify the continuum of learnable moments by providing stimulating and thought-provoking learning environments, where collaboration with parents and family members can occur. It creates a serendipitous moment to motivate new leadership by the children and new discovery of their unknown capabilities. To be an effective teacher in an emergent-oriented curriculum, the teacher must be a multiple/ multiethnic perspective-taker, risk-taker, and ongoing action researcher as well as trust and respect unknown and unexpected possibilities of diverse learners' capabilities and potential.

As presented in Figure 6.2, in comparison with teachable moment-oriented curriculum practice, emergent-oriented curriculum practice appears to exhibit more teacher intention to capture emerging interests and to use them as teachable moments within a social learning context: large- and small-group sharing and discourse of the topic or issue the learners engage in. It takes a longer period of teachers' reflective action research in which teachers intentionally explore learners' interests and acculturate learners' process-oriented learning experiences in order to make sure the emergent interests are part of the continuum of learnable moments as well as teachable moments. Trusting and respecting children's ideas and nurturing unknown or undiscovered possibilities, capabilities, and potential are important keys, requiring teachers to be multiple/multiethnic perspective-takers and risk-takers. Teachers continuously examine, assess, and rearrange the classroom environment as the children transform their emerging ideas into projects, so that the physical environment can also support their living act of learning. Active parents and family involvement and the individual teacher's effective and thoughtful communication with family members shape the pluralistic, living curriculum.

## Critical Aspects of Emergent-Oriented Curriculum Practice

One child's voice led to a learning experience that was more complex (in adults'/teacher's point of view) than the teacher-originated experience, but it became an individually meaningful experience to the children, which did not fully happen at the initial stage of the project when the teacher was the voice maker.

> *University supervisor*: (pondering) What would have happened if Jeffery had not voiced his ideas about his special green diamond-shaped Valentine card for his mom? What would have happened if Lynn had not shared her observation and documentation of Jeffery's unique card-making with his mother? What would have happened if the teachers had not given Jeffery a chance to talk about his special card to his large group of friends in the classroom? What would have happened to the other children? What would have happened if the teachers had not added the card-making table in the art section of the classroom? Would they have created such imaginative, divergent, and meaningful cards? Would they have questioned such conceptually sophisticated issues as why a diamond ring is circular, not diamond-shaped? What would have happened to Jin Min, whose family culture had no reference point for Valentine's Day card-making? Would he have been able to understand what he did at first and why he did more after Jeffery raised his concerns? Without the teacher's thought-provoking questions, would the children have expanded their learning experiences to world geography and the communication system, using their emergent higher-order thinking and inquiry skills? Without active family involvement, would culturally diverse children have had an equal, fair, and culturally congruent learning and leadership experience in the classroom as much as other children whose families represent the dominant cultural paradigm?

Emergent-oriented curriculum appears to depend upon learners' and teachers' open and expressive voice-raising to convey their interests and ideas emerging in the process of learning. Children who are socially proactive and free from cultural and language barriers may have greater opportunities to take advantage of, engage in, and take ownership of emergent-oriented curriculum experiences; they can also influence other children who do not have cultural and linguistic advantages. In Tinworth's (1997) study many of the emerging group-project ideas were generated by individuals, usually boys, who were socially powerful in the group. In such instances, we need to question whether emergent-oriented curricula promote learner leadership in those who exhibit oral linguistic intelligence in the target language or who are more externally expressive than others or who have loud voices when expressing their own ideas or who possess characteristics of the socially powerful group.

In the project approach, the initial stage is called *getting started* (Katz & Chard, 1989), when the children and teacher devote discussion time to selecting and refining the topic to be investigated. Katz and Chard have asserted that at least a few of the children should have enough familiarity with the topic to be able to raise relevant questions about it. If that is the case, will all students have fair opportunities to learn and contribute in the discussion-oriented curriculum decision-making process? What about those who come from language minorities, such as ESOL (English Speakers of Other Languages) or cultural minorities or those with hearing impairments or communication disorders? How about the children whose oral language expression is not easily heard in group brainstorming for an emergent project formation? Or children who have no sociocultural points of reference for the topic at the outset of the project? Will they be able to participate in equal and congruent ways in the emergent collaborative project and learning experience? Will they have an opportunity to become *empowered leaders* to the same extent as the children who have the advantage of language and culture? What would have happened if Jin Min or other language and cultural minority children had not had family members active in the school experience in the context of emergent-oriented curriculum where oral expression and dominant culture shapes learning experiences? What would have happened if the teacher would not have taken risks with the children's serendipitous and unexpected expressions to explore the unknown possibilities within the curriculum? Even when curriculum successfully emerges, it can still ultimately serve the status quo unless the teacher supports inclusivity and diversity.

How do we prepare future teachers when we introduce the notion of emergent-oriented curriculum practice like Reggio Emilia or the project approach? To what degree do we critically discuss and help them act responsively on behalf of children whose diverse voices may raise issues different from those prevalent in the dominant culture? The teacher's culturally responsive observation skills guided by his or her own multiple/multiethnic perspective-taking (Hyun & Marshall, 1997) (e.g., if I were Jeffery what would have made me create a card totally different from what my teacher wanted me to do? If I were Jin Min, what would I have thought about the Valentine card-making activity without knowing what that was for?), reflective communication, and collaboration with family members are critical keys in emergent-oriented curriculum practice with diverse children. Without teachers' critical awareness and recognition of diverse language and cultural paradigms in young children's real lives, an emergent-oriented curriculum may have a limited capacity for appreciation by the pluralistic learning community.

## Conclusion

We understand emergent learning as owned and shared social learning experiences in unexpected or unanticipated ways. It may appear in a social context when a learner raises his or her voice in a unique way that is of interest to others and creates a shared meaning among members of the learning community. This social phenomenon motivates new ideas found in serendipitous comments or insightful questions posed by members of the learning group. Planned lessons, projects, ideas, or inquiries transform into new entities in new physical environments that support the emerging interests. As a result, the unexpected learning phenomenon extends over a longer period of time during which the teacher welcomes unknown possibilities that may emerge from the diverse learners. Once the teacher practices reflective, thoughtful, and active communication with family and community members; is willing to deconstruct, reconstruct, and newly construct his or her understanding of what children can do; and is mentally fluent as a multiple/multiethnic perspective-taker and risk-taker, trusting and respecting diverse children's unknown capabilities, the possibility of bringing developmentally meaningful and culturally responsive practice increases. Consequently, emergent learning experiences prevail and evolve into emergent-oriented curriculum practice. A word of caution—we must make sure that every individual child has an equal, fair, developmentally meaningful, and culturally congruent shared balance of voice-raising that will help him or her to realize his or her leadership potential.

How do we prepare future teachers to learn to move away occasionally yet legitimately from the prescribed lesson planning while engaging in fluent "living" curriculum practice constructed during the process of exploring learners' emerging meaning-making and new discoveries? In many cases prospective teachers learn about curriculum practice like the thematic or project approach and the Reggio Emilia approach, but when they are placed in internships or field experience and are expected to transfer the conceptual learning into pedagogical action, the teacher education program supervisors usually require them to write a linear, teacher-driven first-person perspective-oriented lesson plan as occurred at the beginning of Lynn's story. As she coconstructed learning experiences with the children in her emergent-oriented curriculum, Lynn articulated the notion of a living lesson plan very different from what she was familiar. She also articulated her fear of lack of preparedness with written lesson plans in a bureaucratic school culture.

Regarding assessment in teacher education field experience, prospective teachers are evaluated in terms of how well they manage their classrooms and prepare lesson plans. Institutional structures do not always support future teachers' meaningful learning. Because of inconsistencies in what teacher educators preach and what and how they evaluate, future teachers remain confused and mistrustful of what they have learned in teacher education. Furthermore, few prospective teachers interact with cooperating teachers who fluently and freely practice this type of high risk-taking living curriculum with learners. In many cases prospective teachers cannot make meaningful connections between what they have learned and what they need to practice in the field during their field experience. They express their frustration or confusion and feel unprepared or inappropriately prepared. Once they realize that following statewide or districtwide standardized curriculum and testing procedures in primary grades is overwhelming, the main focus of their profession turns to what they perceive to be "politically correct" in order to survive and maintain their jobs. Situations like these put high-quality teachers in professional jeopardy, as shown in the following reflection: *"What I truly believe in to make the children's learning meaningful I cannot do because I have to make sure they are ready to perform on standardized tests. On top of that, I do not have the time and resources to use an ongoing project approach that I learned about like Reggio Emilia. Does that mean I am not a good teacher? Will I be? Am I really enjoying my occupation?"* (reflection posted on field-based ECE curriculum course Web board in 1997 by Nancy, who had gone through a teacher preparation program in Florida similar to Lynn's). Often, prospective teachers make similar comments when they learn about emergent-oriented curricula with a project approach or the Reggio Emilia approach. They say, *"Can I really do that in school with kindergartners? In the primary grades? What if the principal does not approve of what I do? What if I am fired because I try this? I have never seen teachers doing this kind of teaching in schools because they would be seen as unprepared, that is, without lesson plans"* (collective voices of field-based ECE curriculum students in Florida posted on course Web board, 1998).

Compared to other traditional scope and sequence-oriented standardized curriculum, emergent-oriented curriculum experiences can offer much room and support for children discovering and sharing unknown possibilities, capabilities, and potential in a socially constructive mode as learning occurs. Higher levels of teacher trust in children's exploration enrich curriculum possibilities. Furthermore, the possibility of a dual learning experience occurring between learner and teacher through reflective documentation and ongoing assessment is much higher: The teacher discovers or learns more about each child's unique capabilities and the approaches that enrich the reflective teacher's pedagogical decisions for improvement of the curriculum, and the child constructs his or her self-image as an active teacher and continues self-motivated learning. These kinds of dual learning experiences occurring because of trust and risk-taking are extremely important, particularly if the teacher is working with a child who is from a non-mainstream family culture or ethnicity, or linguistic cultural paradigm and uses a different cultural and linguistic code. Teachers' ways of knowing how children learn reflect their own pedagogical culture derived from their own paradigms. Teachers' trust in unknown possibilities of culturally diverse children's acts of learning that reflect their cultural paradigms can bring many possibilities into emergent learning that are unexpected and serendipitous but powerful for all, as happened in Lynn's case after all. Ironically, as the learner socially, intellectually, and emotionally matures in the process of schooling, curriculum may emphasize standards-driven or institution-driven decision-making in terms of contents and evaluation. Learners become more powerless as they grow older, more experienced, more mature, and more institutionalized. This conceptual understanding may also give us another interpretation of the reason that politically and economically disadvantaged minority students keep failing in the public school system: Children with diverse backgrounds who use different social, emotional, intellectual, cultural, linguistic codes may not be trusted in the narrowly defined learning approach and may have limited power in contributing their multiple perspectives and voices in the learning process. More critically, as the nation moves toward politics and economy-driven standardized curriculum and testing, starting with preschoolers (e.g., G.W. Bush's new education initiative on Jan 23, 2001 "No Child Left Behind." The bill passed on Dec. 2001 by the U.S. Senate) (Hyun, 2003; Karp, 2002), teachers will likely have extremely limited vision that will institutionally blind them to the possibility of trusting diverse children's unique learning approaches and processes.

Emergent-oriented curriculum practice is a powerful pedagogical act. In order that a theoretically well-articulated curriculum can be part of all learners' school experience, more rigorous collaboration, dialogue, and negotiation must occur in teacher education institutions, in school systems, and in political arenas where money and power exert heavy influence.

Considering the reality of teachers' professional struggle between what they know to be good and powerful curriculum practice and what they have to follow (even though they do not believe in standardized curriculum practice and assessment) under political scrutiny, we need to help them develop mental frameworks of critical pedagogical skills to help them become thoughtful curriculum negotiators as they work with diverse learners in a school culture driven by standardized curriculum and assessment.

As discussed in Chapter 5, a teachable moment-oriented curriculum is sensitive to the issues of ownership of the moment, but is this a moment equally learnable to the learner? Emergent-oriented curriculum, discussed in this chapter, is highly sensitive to individual's voice-raising, but whose voice is it? The next inquiry involves how we can construct a curriculum that promotes equally powerful learning experiences to all? In that regard, the next chapter discusses the negotiation-oriented curriculum.

### Chapter Ending Questions

- What drives emergent-oriented curriculum practice?
- What is a key in emergent-oriented curriculum practice for developmentally meaningful and culturally congruent practices?
- Does emergent-oriented curriculum practice fully depend upon child-initiated and learner-centered learning? Why? How? Why not?
- Based on your field (teaching or observation) experience in Pre-K–3rd grade classroom contexts, share an example of emergent-oriented teaching:
    a. What relationship have you seen between teachable moment-oriented teaching and emergent-oriented teaching?
    b. In what ways does the emergent-oriented teaching support curriculum practice for developmentally meaningful and culturally congruent practice from the children's perspective?

# Chapter Seven

# Negotiation-Oriented Curriculum

## Initial Inquiries

- What does negotiation-oriented teaching and learning look like? How does it occur?
- How can teachers transform instruction-oriented teaching into pedagogy-based teaching in negotiation-oriented curriculum practice?
- What are critical aspects in negotiation-oriented curriculum practice from the perspective of developmentally meaningful and culturally responsive practice?

Chapter 2 discusses pedagogy-based teaching opposed to instruction-oriented teaching. Pedagogy-based teaching shapes curriculum that entails study-based, ethical, socially just, and morally sound practice resulting from inner and outer negotiation among the teacher, students, and others. Chapter 7 discusses negotiation-oriented curriculum in conjunction with pedagogy-based teaching. In negotiation-oriented curriculum, teachers deliberately look for a particular kind of moment as a teachable moment that is equally a learnable moment.

## What Is Negotiation?

> If teachers set out to teach according to a planned curriculum, without engaging the interests of the students, the quality of learning will suffer. Student interest involves student investment and personal commitment. Negotiating the curriculum means deliberately planning to invite students to contribute to, and to modify, the educational program, so that they will have a real investment both in the learning journey and in the outcomes. Negotiation also means making explicit, and then confronting, the constraints of the learning context and the non-negotiable requirements that apply. Once teachers act upon the belief that students should share with them a commitment to the curriculum, negotiation will follow naturally, whether the set curriculum is traditional or progressive, and whether the classroom is architecturally open or closed. (Boomer, Lester, Onore, & Cook, 1992, p. 15)

What is negotiation? It is an acting knowledge of how to work with other people so as to achieve one's goals as well as shared collective goals in the process of agreement and disagreement (e.g, consensus) (Loewenstein & Thompson, 2000). Negotiation is reaching agreement: It resembles reaching provisional agreement until there is something new to question in the provisional agreement. It requires the individual's study-oriented critical thinking, critical reading, critical designing, and critical evaluation in the process of negotiation (Lester & Boomer, 1992). Negotiation is driven by reflective inquiry of one's own questions, interests, goals, desires, and subjective interpretation of the agenda. The reflective inquiry occurs in the middle of negotiation. Thus, the individual's reflection-*in*-action lies at the core of negotiation (Hyun, 2006; Hyun & Marshall, 1996).

Agreement and disagreement are both functions of the intersubjective meaning that emerges as people interact to negotiate. Negotiation is a systematic inquiry with people into the *why* of their needs and interests (Taylor, 1971). It is a dynamic process that helps to construct the *why* and reflectively shapes and transforms the needs and interests under discussion. The process focuses on the reflective inquiry (i.e., reflection-*in*-action, Hyun & Marshall, 1996; Schön, 1983; Beck & Kosnik, 2001) at the core of the negotiation with the presumption that negotiation is an emergent process (Cobb, 2000; Hyun & Marshall, 2003a). Negotiation, therefore, takes account of the unexpected interaction, accommodates emerging thoughts of the people, and constructs immediate goals to enhance achievement.

In the process of negotiation, individuals' ways of thinking manifested in their needs and interests are always reflected as acting knowledge influenced by the context of individuals' sociocultural paradigm (i.e., class, ethnicity, race, occupation, religion, region, and so on) (Avruch, 2000) as well as gender identity (i.e., men negotiate one way, and women negotiate another way) (Kolb, 2000). Hence, in order to understand and effectively and meaningfully engage in negotiation, people (teachers in particular) need to be aware of the cultural context of the individual's interests and perspectives (Avruch, 2000).

The language and notion of negotiation prevalent in business, law, and politics carries basically the same meaning in education as it does in other disciplines: For example, all the parties in a business come together, bring with their own perspectives, needs, interests, and desires, and together they work for the consensus or outcomes most satisfactory to all concerned matters. In education the outcome of negotiation may be the meshing of minds, an interlocking of intentions, an agreement about means and ends between teacher and students. The focus is on bringing about the best meaningful learning for the learners. If the act of teaching is negotiation-oriented or curriculum allows negotiation, it offers the best chance of maximizing the learning productivity of the students in the classroom (Cook, 1992). Negotiation-oriented curriculum, therefore, transforms teacher-driven instruction-oriented teaching into pedagogy-based teaching (see Chapter 2) that invites and infuses learners' voices and identities (Hyun, 2006).

### Pedagogy-Based Teaching Becomes a Negotiation-Oriented Curriculum Practice

Under the massive movement of standardized content standards requirements and assessments (testing) (e.g., NCLBA, 2001) teachers are set out to teach according to a planned curriculum via instruction-oriented teaching, without engaging the interests of the students, as a result the quality of learning suffers (Boomer, Lester, Onore, & Cook, 1992; Hyun, 2003). For some teachers bargaining or negotiating with students becomes necessary to achieve the learning goals along with facing conflicting reality and professional dilemma (Ennis, 1995). Cook (1992) argued:

> If teachers alone cannot do the kind of programming demanded by learners, help must be provided. Only learners can provide that help, since only they know their own minds, intentions, and experiences—or can work them out, given encouragement and talking and thinking time. So teachers must genuinely ask learners to tell what they know, think, and whole, so that teacher and learners may together plan for profitable work. That is, they must negotiate the curriculum. Teachers and learners must negotiate together because neither can go it alone, if optimum learning is the aim. (pp. 18–19)

Cook clearly articulated the inevitability of transforming instruction-oriented teaching into pedagogy-based teaching, and negotiation with the learners is the key in the teachers' teaching in order to make the meaningful transformation for developmentally meaningful and culturally congruent learning from the learners' point of view. The story of Syler (briefly introduced in Chapter 1) illustrates Cook's point of view. Let's re-visit Syler's case with an analysis of negotiation processes.

When Syler, who is African American, was five years old, he and his two fathers attended story time every Saturday at their local library. One day a storyteller read a book entitled *Between Earth and Sky: Legends of Native American Sacred Places* (Bruchac & Locker, 1996). Syler loved the story so much that after hearing it, he preferred to be called Little Bear like the main character in the story. From this story Syler and his fathers learned about the seven directions: north, south, east, west, earth, sky, and the seventh direction within us all, the place where we distinguish right from wrong and maintain balance in life by choosing to live in a good way. Two years later when Syler was in the second grade, his class learned about directions. When the teacher and the textbook referred only to four directions (north, south, east, and west, based on the Sunshine State [Florida] Social Studies Content Standards), Syler disagreed, explaining to his teacher and classmates that he knew about three other directions: earth, sky, and the judging of right and wrong. (At this point, Syler was the only one in the group who could provide this information because he knew his own mind and experience.) The teacher answered, "Syler, we are learning about north, south, east, and west. These are the main directions we need to learn." (The teacher maintained instruction-oriented teaching.) Puzzled, Syler went home at the end of the day and explained what had happened at school. He and his father Jeffray returned to the local library and checked out the book they remembered so well. The next day Syler took the book to school and asked the teacher whether he and his father Jeffray could read the book together to the class. Because there were some big words in the book that Syler couldn't yet read by himself, he needed his father's help (Syler's inner and outer dialogue in negotiation with the teacher). The teacher agreed, not to change the content but to support parental involvement in the classroom; however, she wanted to read the book before making a decision about letting Syler and his father read the book. (The teacher's inner and outer negotiation occurred.) The following day Syler and his father Jeffray read the book together to the class. Syler's classmates and the teacher listened to the story and learned of seven directions. When Syler and his father finished reading the book, the teacher captured a teachable moment and genuinely asked the children to tell what they knew about the new directions, how they were different from the first four directions, and what they thought about the other three directions. Wanting to add the three directions, the children asked the teacher about it (outer negotiation between the children and the teacher) and changed the bulletin board to reflect the three new directions along with the previous four. Later the children talked about not only which directions Christopher Columbus took to get to North America but also which direction they should take to make good decisions for building (not "keeping") peace on earth and in their classroom.

In Syler's story, the lesson had begun as a typical instruction-oriented teaching of objective facts about directions but gradually changed and transformed into pedagogy-based teaching that went beyond the mastery of factual knowledge. What motivated this transformation? Emerging inner and outer multilevel negotiations had occurred among the learner, parents, teacher, and other learners in this particular context. The teacher and learners negotiated together because neither could go it alone; consequently, optimal learning occurred.

In order to promote a pedagogy-based teaching that supports developmentally meaningful and culturally congruent learning experience for learners, teachers must have a conscious awareness of their own multiple identities (ethnic, linguistic, cultural, gender, socioeconomic, and so on) along with a willingness and ability to step back and critically reexamine (study) their own interpretation of the identity of the children they teach. Pedagogy-based teaching requires more than what Davis (2004) asked: "the teacher's interpersonal competencies for moral and ethical awareness as they work with learners." It also requires the teacher's own intrapersonal engagement to examine and reexamine his or her own thinking and act of teaching: this teacher's own intrapersonal engagement is the inner dialogue with inner negotiation. Figure 7.1 illustrates the relationship and interconnectedness among a teacher's pedagogical practice, inner and outer dialogue, negotiation, and teacher reflectivity.

## Inner and Outer Dialogue in Curriculum Negotiation

Pedagogy-based teaching requires teachers to continuously engage in a study mode (e.g., Pinar, 2004a, 2004b), which is more likely the

**Figure 7.1. Relationship and Interconnectedness Among Teacher's Study-Based Pedagogical Practice, Inner and Outer Dialogue, Negotiation, and Teacher Reflectivity**

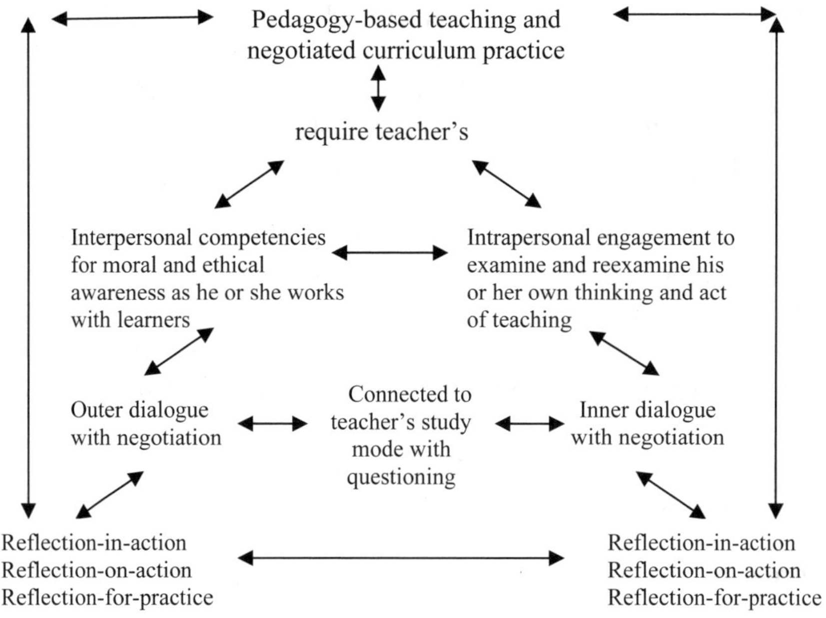


disciplined study of study as learning (Henderson, 2005) using a reflective pondering and questioning within oneself (inner dialogue) to reassess teachers' previous and preplanned thoughts of teaching in order to reach out to the learners' meaningful learning during or before/after the teaching. Examples of the reflective and contemplative questions might be "what is [forms of] the knowledge the learner knows that I do not know? What different kind of connection does the learner make that is meaningful to him/her in line with the current content that I did not know? How should I adapt my thoughts and teaching at this moment to be meaningfully responsive to the learner's counternormative knowledge? How can I negotiate with the learners to equally cover the basic content prepared and the learner's new emerging set of counternormative knowledge? How should I share the power with the learners so that an equal level of knowledge sharing and co-construction of new adapted knowledge can occur?" These kinds of contemplative questionings are examples of *inner dialogues* that occur during reflection-in-action (during the teaching) and reflection-on-action (after the teaching) by the teacher (see reflection-in-action, reflection-on-action, and reflection-for-practice in Chapter 9).

During the teaching, the teacher also attempts to promote multiple forms of open communications (i.e., the artistry of teaching) with learners to enact socially just, ethically sound, and academically empowering action of teaching and learning. For example, the teacher might be asking the learner "What others ways can you use and/or interpret the content (knowledge) that we have not discussed/explored yet? What other kind of knowledge/idea do you have that you think is related to the content we should also explore?" These kinds of questionings are examples of *outer dialogues* happening together with reflection-in-action. This kind of outer dialogue helps the teacher reconceptualize content standards in a holistic mode.

*Inner dialogue* means examining and reexamining one's own thoughts and actions within oneself during the action of teaching (reflection-in-action) as the new reality emerges or after the action of teaching (reflection-on-action and reflection-for-practice) when the new reality was shared. During the inner dialogue the individual revisits and questions the limitation of preexisting normative knowledge structures and simultaneously negotiate with a new emerging reality with counternormative knowledge structures within oneself coupled with reflection-in-action, reflection-on-action, and reflection-for-practice. Inner dialogue is a part of negotiation. *Outer dialogue* means examining and reexamining one's own thoughts and actions with others during the action of teaching (reflection-in-action) as the new reality emerges. Outer dialogue is a form of negotiation to construct collective understanding and new agreement between and among the teacher and learners.

Pedagogy-based teaching always requires inner and outer dialogues among the teacher, learner(s) and others in the context. This could be an example of Pinar's (2004a, 2004b) notion of "curriculum and study" in action that illuminates a study-based pedagogical practice (as discussed in Chapter 2). For pedagogy-based teaching be study-based, socially just, ethically sound, and academically empowering action, *negotiation between the teacher and learners with sharing the power* must be inherent in the process of inner and outer dialogues. Thus, in pedagogy-based teaching, there is always interdependent relationships among study-based teaching, inner and outer dialogues, and negotiation.

**A Closer Look**

In Syler's case, for example, the teacher engaged in an inner dialogue for the initial negotiation within oneself (it is articulated as reflection-*in*-action driven by first-person perspective-taking within oneself) (see perspective-taking in Chapter 9):

> What makes Syler believe that there are more than the four directions—north, south, east, and west? Why do we (Syler and I) have different views of such an obvious fact? What does Syler know that I don't?

Furthermore, the teacher analyzed the nature of children's expressions from the individual child's perspective. In the example of Syler, the teacher engaged in an inner dialogue for inner negotiation (it is articulated as reflection-*in*-action driven by second-person perspective-taking from the individual child's perspective):

> If I were Syler, what would I expect from my teacher at this moment? How might I try to have her respect my knowledge?

Third, the teacher realized the need to make changes in the children's learning contexts, the curriculum, and their teaching practices—a habit of reflection Kincheloe, Slattery, and Steinberg call "spiritual dynamics that intensifies consciousness and delineates the purposes of teaching as living" (2000, p. 70). At this point Syler's teacher engaged in an inner and outer dialogue in negotiation, simultaneously re-conceptualizing or deepening the understanding of content standards (it is articulated as reflection-*on*-action for further practice driven by third-person/multiple perspective-taking from the children's perspectives in a diverse learning community):

> As I read the book Syler brought, I realize that I am unconsciously limiting my students' learning experiences. Syler's voice allows other children and me to learn more than our "already-known knowledge" [the content stan-

> dards]. Sharing his story with us will give him a congruent and powerful personal learning experience and offer a broader understanding of our world experiences for everyone in the class.

The teacher who encourages and permits children to change instruction-oriented teaching always nurtures students' learning and meaning-making that leads to pedagogy-based teaching (Greene, 1975, 1978, 1995). Thus, curriculum becomes a negotiation-oriented lived experience. This pedagogy-based teaching is a form of lived organic curriculum practice that requires the teacher's continuation of critical inner dialogue (within oneself) and outer dialogue (with the student, parents, and other children), conscious awareness, and willingness to change in an effort to promote learners' active and relevant personal and social meaning-making experiences. Within pedagogy-based teaching teachers continuously realize that their knowledge is always incomplete and that they, too, are participating in a constant journey of studying and learning with the diverse learners. This realization is extremely important to the teachers in a diverse and pluralistic society. In that process, the teacher is no longer the ultimate power holder instead the teacher and the learners negotiate to share the power: Balancing the power between the teacher and learners is an inherent aspect in the inner and outer dialogue. As a result pedagogy-based teaching becomes a negotiation-oriented lived curriculum. Pre-planned, teacher-driven, instruction-oriented curriculum representing a set of intended learning outcomes produced by others can never be a fully lived curriculum for learners who represent the multidirectional, multidimensional, and multiethnic sociocultural world. The children's knowledge of four directions (north, south, east, and west for map reading) and the other three directions (earth, sky, and the judging of right and wrong) have become meaningful facts and meaningful truths as well as living operational and further spiritual knowledge. In negotiation-oriented curriculum practice, teaching does not need to operate in the service of established social order. Instead, teaching is questioning, pondering, studying, emancipating, liberating, and empowering. That becomes pedagogy-based teaching.

## Balancing Power Toward Shared Ownership in Curriculum Negotiation

According to Cook (1992), children are capable of being successful negotiators as adults are. Like adults, children have needs, interests, desires, and perspectives of their own, and they can make inquiries to influence the learning experience, the curriculum. They tend to work hard to get what they want if their inquiry and motivations are self-generated, and they can understand and engage in trade-off, exchange, and bargaining, involving the recognition of inevitable constraints and the impossible within the school curriculum if the shared ownership and decision-making space with the teacher is available. Cook argued that when the opportunity to exhibit abilities is unavailable, those abilities will remain hidden and underdeveloped. Refusal to recognize children as capable of sharing ownership inhibits effective curriculum delivery in any form. The key to negotiation lies in the ownership principle: people are inclined to strive hardest for things they wish to own or to keep and enhance things they already have owned (Cook, 1992).

Boomer et al. (1992) discussed negotiating curriculum, finding ways of equalizing power imbalances between teachers and students, making space for the learning intentions of students. In doing so students begin to co-develop teaching and learning guides (templates) and procedures (protocols) with teachers, helping teachers to break away from the conventional one-way (teacher to students) instruction-oriented curriculum practice to mutually shared and meaningfully power-balanced, pedagogy-based curriculum experiences. In pedagogy-based teaching negotiating the curriculum and negotiation-oriented discourse are inevitable phenomena that ought to be inherent in nature. The recognition that negotiation occurs in the classroom implies that all participants, that is, students, teachers, and parents (family members), have the power to create, modify, engage, study, and evaluate the learning process. In the process of sharing the power, contents are psychologized (meaning internalized) by the learner (Dewey's notion, see Chapter 2), and the teacher's intention of reaching out to the learner occurs (Eisner's notion, see Chapter 2). Rather than the traditional conception of the teacher as the sole source of classroom power in instruction-oriented teaching, a relationship of reciprocal power between students and teachers exists in pedagogy-based teaching that shapes negotiation-oriented curriculum practice.

In any human society various relations of power always permeate, characterize, and constitute the social body, and these relations of power cannot themselves be established, consolidated or implemented without the production, accumulation, circulation, and function of a discourse (Foucault, 1997). According to Foucault, we as human beings are subjected to the production of "truth" through power, and we cannot exercise power except through the production of "truth"; but the relationship among power, "right," and "truth" is organized in a highly specific fashion (e.g., instruction-oriented school curriculum). Foucault's triangular relationship among power, "right," and "truth" always exists in a typical classroom context, in which teaching and learning (production) are expected to occur. In classrooms teachers who practice instruction-oriented curricula are forced to produce the "truth" of power that the society demands (i.e., content standards), of which it has the need in order to function. However, students are also required to produce the true (as personally meaningful subjective truth) discourse which, at least partially, decides, transmits, and itself extends upon the effects of power (as it happened in Syler's story). If this reality of power-sharing is alive in a pervasive and inherent fashion, classroom discourse shapes curriculum that holds negotiation as a key element to transform instruction-oriented teaching into pedagogy-based teaching.

Pedagogy-based teaching is highly reflective inquiry-driven, study-oriented, negotiation-oriented, discourse-based, and supposed to be conversational for all members in the classroom. In reality, all members of the classroom have different knowledge, beliefs, skills, and dispositions (attitudes), which both reflect the culture from which each person comes and which enter into the conversation. Teachers need to demonstrate their beliefs through their actions. Furthermore, teachers must modify their vision of current and future possibilities in light of learners' cultural identities, emerging questions, current beliefs and dispositions. "It is so hard when you believe so deeply in the importance of particular ideas or activities to let those go when students tell you that what they hold is incompatible. Nonetheless, it is important for teachers to strive to be sensitive to students' needs and to keep focused on finding compatibilities that can be built on rather than focusing only on resistances" (Onore & Lubetsky, 1992, p. 260).

The teacher is not perceived as the ultimate power holder like a dictator but as a curriculum negotiator, whose main task is studying one's own thinking of teaching in light of the diverse students' multiple forms of voices and negotiating with students to produce a meaningful curriculum experience for learning with them. In that sense the teacher is still in charge. The teacher's goals, objectives, and responsibilities may not be different from the original teacher agenda driven by the characteristic of school curriculum, whatever it may be; but the mode (study, methodology, style, approach, interaction, dialogue) for achieving goals and objectives has changed depending upon the teacher's pedagogical study of the students' voices—desires, needs, interests, and perspectives driven by individual learners' developmental characteristics and cultural identities. The teacher's inner and outer dialogue for negotiation with the students should be driven by the notion of power-sharing. Thus, the students also hold some level of power (possibly an equal level of power with the teacher) in decision-making that leads to students' realizing ownership of the experience as the result of negotiation in which developmentally meaningful and culturally congruent learning occurs in diverse learners' schooling experiences. Then, teaching becomes inherently pedagogy-based in that ethical, socially just, and morally sound teaching and curriculum practice.

## Characteristics and Key Concepts in Negotiation-Oriented Curriculum

Negotiation-oriented curriculum is teaching and learning processes that inherently and pervasively allow teacher and students to open up and lead to share and achieve goals of one's own. Negotiation-oriented curriculum has several characteristics such as power-sharing, shared authority, and co-governance between teacher and learner(s). It values *power with* instead *power over* in teaching and learning context. Negotiation-oriented curriculum practices collaborative decision-making, democratic deliberation over policy, and co-development of learning content and procedures (e.g., syllabus, lesson plan) (Shor, 1996). Rather than simply studying (receiving) a body of content knowledge (e.g., math, science, social studies, language arts content standards), negotiation-oriented curriculum practice provides a public space for learners to ponder the social order, authority of the knowledge and make critical connections with the knowledge by questioning who the learners are in relation to the subject matter and how the learners act in the world with the set of knowledge individually as well as collectively. Act of change that is autonomous and meaningful by the learners is a core part of the curriculum practice. In that process, the learners problematize the previously organized body of knowledge through a particular cultural lens and possibly alter (transform) the knowledge that makes sense to them as developmentally meaningful and culturally congruent knowledge construction and use. In negotiation-oriented curriculum, teachers look for this particular kind of moment as a teachable moment that is equally a learnable moment.

According to Shor, a negotiated curriculum can certainly produce surprising and discomforting outcomes (sometimes even losing the class) from teacher perspective. On the other hand, negotiation-oriented curriculum can offer students and teachers "alternative social development, alternative ways of being, knowing, speaking, relating, and feeling, beyond and against traditional classroom arrangements" (p. 62). These alternatives can be both appealing and threatening, promising hope, novelty, validation, and relief, as well as conflict, loss, risk, responsibility, and so many possibilities of the unknown.

Negotiation-oriented curriculum is also interpreted as a critical-democratic pedagogy. It challenges the traditional and stifled construction of self, society, power, and institutional identities between teacher and learner that are shaped by the culture of traditional method of curriculum delivery. Any form of negotiation is always concerned with culture (Avruch, 2000). Negotiation-oriented curriculum questions unknown possibilities of human potential and dynamics by imagining a situation that would undo the existing power structure in classroom culture. As a result, it leads to transform the traditional institutional identities into teacher as learner and learner as teacher.

Under the massive movement of standardized content standards requirements and assessments (testing) starting even from preschool age, teachers are forced to teach according to a prepackaged curriculum, without engaging the interests of the learners, and as a result the quality of learning suffers. Teachers who strive to promote learner-centered teaching and curriculum practice support as well. Here, negotiation-oriented curriculum practice could come into play with two folds: First of all, as Dewey indicated (1902), the teacher must be an expert in seeing the ends in the beginnings. The teacher initially negotiates with the preprogrammed curriculum via deliberately planning to invite students to question/ponder, to contribute to, and to modify the educational program, so that the learners will have a real investment both in the learning journey and in the outcomes; second, engaging in negotiation with learners by making explicit, and then confronting, the constraints of the learning context and the non-negotiable requirements that apply. Once the teacher acts upon the belief that learners should share them with a commitment to the entire learning and teaching processes, negotiation between the teacher and learners will follow naturally.

In the process of negotiation-oriented curriculum, students seek to uncover who the learners are and how they and the subject of study might grow to relate. Subject matter is thus a beginning, an end, and the means to the end, all at once. Learners are likewise beginnings, ends, and means (Onore & Lubetsky, 1992). Because of this particular nature, negotiation-oriented curriculum practice may work well with any school curriculum culture that is either traditional or progressive, and whether the classroom is open or closed by the architectural design. Negotiation-oriented curriculum practice promotes the teacher's re-conceptualization of complying content standards and going beyond the political scrutiny of prepackaged, standardized curriculum and testing ("one size fits all"). It is politically savvy, academically challenging, and pedagogically sound practices that promote developmentally meaningful and culturally congruent learning experiences from the ever-changing diverse learners' points of view.

## Critical Aspects in Negotiation-Oriented Curriculum Practice

Although the degree of interaction may vary, the teaching process itself is interactive in nature and is built on a social relationship between teacher and students. A social relation exists in a continuum that extends from consent to domination. Consent is the ideal relation because it is based on a mutually recognized purpose on which all members agree and that result in few conflicts of interest as the group collectively interacts. By contrast, domination at the other end of the continuum has a very high degree of conflict with little concern for group members' mutual relations (Burbules, 1986; Cothran & Ennis, 1997).

According to Cothran and Ennis, consent and domination rarely occur at the classroom level. Instead, a range of student compliant behaviors is manifested in classroom contexts. Compliance relies on the willingness of participants to act cooperatively (different from collaboratively; see Lester, 1992) despite their conflict of interest. Because the learners must give cooperation, it can also be suspended. Rather than obey, participants can resist. Consequently, the teacher-student relationship can be and frequently becomes a battle to manage the conflicts of interest. In that context a process of bargaining (a negotiation) needs to occur that allows for the release of tensions created by conflicting interests (Ennis, 1995; Sedlak, Wheeler, Pullin, & Cusick, 1986).

Perhaps because of the obligatory nature of schooling or because adults have a mandate to teach or because society has designs on what is to be learned, by and large, a reality of power or adult privilege is in place when children enter school. In general, all knowledge is perceived as transmittable and the student's mind as a passive receptacle. Teachers are assumed to have the knowledge, and students are assumed to have none; the have-nots depend upon the haves—the teacher/adults identified with adult privilege (Boomer, Lester, Onore, & Cook, 1992; Cannella, 1997). As a result, instruction-oriented teaching and curriculum practice become prevalent.

Even if the teacher may call his or her practice child-centered, the teacher claims to take a largely facilitative role, still retaining significant, ultimate power over students by limiting decision-making opportunities to the students under the guise of giving choices, which is the hallmark of a child-centered approach. Without realizing or acknowledging the hidden injury that may result from child-centered curriculum practices, teachers expect students to cooperate with the teaching agenda to gain knowledge; thus, cooperative learning has become identified as an effective instructional teaching strategy, not as effective learning strategy created by pedagogy that seeks out students' autonomous engagement, emergent learning, and interests (i.e., hidden curriculum of cooperative learning; see Lester, 1992).

Within this power-related reality, as children move through the school culture, they tend to act more upon their teachers' expectation than upon their own autonomous learning derived from their own inquiry. As children become familiar with the culture of school curriculum, they reject or become nonparticipants for active learning within the teacher's agenda—instruction-oriented teaching. Teachers who strive to consciously engage in developmentally meaningful and culturally congruent curriculum work bargaining or negotiating with learners becomes necessary in order to be responsive of the diverse learners' multiple forms of voices and encourage their autonomous learning, emerging interests and thoughts, and simultaneously to achieve the standardized and mandated learning goals. Thus, curriculum negotiation is inevitable.

Another critical issue is related to "values" operated by the dominant culture within the context. We often acknowledge that values can vary with cultural context, thus we (teachers, dominant power holders, and so on) allow admitting cultural preferences into the curriculum practice but preserving its essential character of rational choice by the dominant power as it happened in the early stage of Syler's case. Avruch (2000) argues that this is the usual tack taken by those who see culture operating only at one level of values in a conflict or surface level negotiation. Only if the negotiation evolves with intra and inter-cultural manners via multiple/multiethnic perspective-taking (Hyun & Marshall, 1997), the conflict moves to a higher level of human understanding and new knowledge construction:

> When interests are shared intra-cultural manner, people certainly operate like motives, offering a readily available account of why people behave as they do. It is only when we consider cross-cultural encounters that, the difference between interests and motives is more significant. Sometimes in such intercultural encounters, in fact, we may have difficulty even interpreting their (apparent) motives as rational interest at all. Serious misunderstandings may result when the culturally constituted motives of one party do not match the assumed universal interest posited by the other (Avruch, 2000, pp. 342–343).

Negotiation is discourse-driven. Language must be allowed to work for the students, who must talk into clarifications, understanding and decisions. Talk is the language mode closest to thinking, and the small group of peers is the structure that most facilitates talk (Boomer et al., 1992). "Working class" children as well as "minority" children from diverse ethnic, cultural, and language backgrounds, however, do not have the same access to the dominant cultural artifacts that have shaped the standardized curriculum content and discourse. These children may not well attribute the layers of meaning to things they read and see because they just do not have the same kind of background knowledge, the target language for active academic discourse as other children do in the classroom. In regard to this particular phenomenon, Rose (1989) argues that the academic discourses are full of influential talks that are both a foreign tongue and also a foreign set of concepts for so many underprivileged minority children. Negotiation in the classroom is never just about getting the children to do and talk about what interests them. Negotiation-oriented curriculum practice should always be fluent in support of diverse learners' various forms of nonverbal discourses. Negotiation in learning and teaching takes account of the unexpected interaction introduced by diverse learners' multiple forms of voices, accommodates emerging thoughts of the learners, and co-constructs immediate goals with equally shared power to enhance meaningful and congruent achievements that support the learners' growth.

## Conclusion

The principle of negotiation-oriented curriculum practice starts with believing that learners bring a set of knowledge that is reflection of their own identity and personal experiences (e.g., five-year- old Angelo in Chapter 5), and the learners always seek to make connection with what they already know and what they are about to learn (e.g., seven-year-old Syler), and hence their knowledge is relevant to the content they will be learning. Students are already viewed as knowledge holders. Each form of knowledge holds a culturally inflicted structure. Knowing the background of the knowledge and cultural investigation about the knowledge are critical components of any study because of what culture conceals is what it reveals. Thus, students need to examine not only their own questions but also cross-examine the cultural origins of their own questions. In doing so, the cultural origins of the teacher's questions and the ways of knowing embodied in any organized subject matter are also objects of investigation.

Moreover, these particular inquiries are at the heart of a negotiation-oriented curriculum that supports critical pedagogy and education processes that are meaningfully (truly) multicultural.

Learners are viewed as knowledge (wisdom) holders, knowledge (wisdom) seekers, knowledge (wisdom) creators, knowledge (wisdom) challengers, and knowledge (wisdom) changers. Therefore, negotiation-oriented curriculum may be viewed as education for resistance, teaching for standing in opposition, or understanding things to change knowledge. Thus, negotiating the curriculum is the real learning (e.g., Lester & Boomer, 1992). As a result, schools produce resisters, critics, and questioners, in other words, inquiring minds, and prospective leaders.

Further articulation on the key characteristics of negotiation-oriented curriculum practice in comparison with teachable moment-oriented curriculum and emergent-oriented curriculum is discussed in Chapter 10.

## Chapter Ending Questions

- What are critical aspects in negotiation-oriented curriculum practice that classroom teachers need to be fully aware of as they implement the curriculum practice into teaching?
- What does negotiation mean to you as a teacher in an early childhood classroom setting (Pre-K-3$^{rd}$ )?
- How can you capitalize a teachable moment to bring a curriculum negotiation with learners in the classroom?
- How can you reconceptualize content standards driven by teacher accountability as you familiarize with negotiation-oriented curriculum practice?

# Section III: Curricula Re-conceptualization and Interconnectedness

# Chapter Eight

## Recursive Movement Among Positions

### Initial Inquiries

- How do teachers' manifestations of constructivism relate to their sense-making of teachable moments? How does it shape their curriculum practice?
- What drives teachers to engage in the recursive mode of de-construction, re-construction, and new construction of their teaching? How does it lead to changes in their curriculum practice?

Like many prospective teachers, the teachers introduced in the previous chapters (i.e., Kevin's teacher in Chapter 4, Mrs. Englishwill in Chapter 5, LD in Chapter 5, Lynn in Chapter 6, and Syler's teacher in Chapter 7) value constructivism as their teaching philosophy and classroom practice, particularly in conjunction with the notion of developmentally appropriate practice (DAP). Whenever the teachers shared their stories of constructivist developmentally appropriate effective teaching, they all mentioned finding or capturing teachable moments and the way they capitalized on them to maintain the constructivist child-centered element in their teaching and curriculum.

Depending on "who is the teacher" (i.e., background, identity, philosophy, beliefs, and personal experiences, and so on) and how the teacher articulates an understanding of what curriculum *is* and *does*, her or his manifestation of developmentally appropriate practice would differ from that of other teachers. When thoughtful teachers with constructivist orientations ordinarily deal with developmentally appropriate practice, they are highly encouraged to contemplate critically "whose appropriateness" and "whose guidelines of appropriateness they refer to" and to ponder that appropriateness in responding to children's contemporary multidimensional, multidirectional, and multiethnic realities, which influence their growth and learning. As a result of this kind of contemplation, the teacher's own meaning-making of developmentally appropriate practice for children will bring forth developmentally meaningful and culturally congruent learning experiences from the children's point of view.

## Various Types of Constructivism Manifested in Teaching and Teachable Moments

Moshman (1982) identified three different types of constructivism: endogenous, exogenous, and dialectical. This section contains a discussion of the various types and interpretations of constructivism manifested in teachers' teaching and the teachable moments that shape their curricula.

*Endogenous constructivism* emphasizes learner exploration of and interaction with materials/manipulatives/environment that leads to the learner's knowledge construction and development. The teacher may expect the learner's level of constructive exploration with materials based on the typical developmental theory and learning (e.g., Piaget's theory). The teacher who values this type of constructivism may reveal teacher-centered manifestations of effective teaching and curriculum practice: The teacher's perspective and adult privilege control the selection of materials and learning experiences as well as the interpretation of the child's capability to experience the materials. Mrs. Englishwill's practice (in Chapter 5) provides an example of endogenous constructivism:

> We know from Piagetian theory how important playing with manipulatives is for young children's development. That was apparently missing in Angelo's home setting, I think. Based on this observation, I concluded that Angelo had very limited eye-hand coordination and a lack of small muscle development. As soon as I knew that his developmental delay was not an intellectual but a physical matter, I needed to consider providing some play-oriented activity for him to exercise his coordination and small muscle development. The next day, during morning free playtime, I saw that Angelo playing with Play-doh and building a very detailed truck. He said to me, "It's my truck!" At that moment I saw that his fine motor skills seemed very well adjusted, so I decided to take advantage of that moment and showed him ways to make other kinds of cars.

Within endogenous constructivism the way teachers capture and capitalize on teachable moments derives from their own knowledge of child development influenced by first-person perspective-taking. Teachers are contemplative observers relying on their own knowledge of child development and learning, subject matter content, and effective teaching. The teacher's expression of teachable moments may not coincide with the learner's learnable moments. The assessment the teacher makes regarding teachable moments may not be fair to the child's true learner capability as in the case of Angelo. The teacher's curriculum practice could be segmental (poorly connected, less integrated, less authentic) and based on the teacher's perspective and interests instead of the individual learner's. This particular concern can be exacerbated by a cultural divide between the child and the teacher unless the teacher is fully aware of and knowledgeable about cultural differences and able to respond thoughtfully to that reality by using multiple/multiethnic perspective-taking (e.g., by asking, "If I were Angelo, what would I have done differently? How would I have used an idea of my own [e.g., my own 1st language] that I can relate to what we are doing now? What is the thing that Angelo knows or can do that I as a teacher do not know or cannot do?). If that happens, the teacher's constructivist teaching would assume another form that would allow the curriculum to evolve.

*Exogenous constructivism* involves direct instruction as a teacher responsibility but with an emphasis on learners actively constructing their own knowledge representations (e.g., Dewey's perspective). As in endogenous constructivism, a certain level of teacher-centered teaching may be found in exogenous constructivist teaching: The teacher's manifestation of teacher responsibility reflects culturally endorsed constructivist practice that gives power to the teacher in making curriculum decisions; thus, infusing learners' diverse voices into the curriculum decision-making may be limited. The teacher's approach in Kevin's story (in Chapter 4) illustrates an example of exogenous constructivism manifested in teaching:

> *Teacher*: Listening quietly and being able to comprehend and understand stories are important skills for kindergartners to develop. When I finish reading a book with the children, we talk about the story before each child engages in further activities, such as creating his or her own book using "sound spelling" or drawing a picture of his or her favorite part of the story. To conclude the activity, each child explains what he or she did. Kevin always physically acts out the story as I read and bothers the other children who are listening to the story. I am not sure whether he really understands the story because he is always so busy pretending to be one of the characters. . . . [Speaking to Kevin's father] Did you ever consider testing him to find out whether he is some type of special needs child with Autism, ADD, or ADHD?

The teacher's approach exemplifies a well thought out and culturally endorsed constructivist practice for early childhood literacy experience. Within exogenous constructivism, the way a teacher captures and capitalizes on teachable moments can derive from formal curriculum content expectations, social-culturally oriented teacher responsibilities, and required content and teaching standards (i.e., culturally endorsed constructivist practices). The teacher is a contemplative observer and facilitator with knowledge of child development and learning, interpretation of what children can or cannot do, content knowledge, and culturally endorsed constructivist meaning-making of thoughtful and effective teaching. Even though the teacher values and emphasizes learner-constructed knowledge and experiences, his or her teachable moments may reflect a teacher's agenda influenced by external expectations (system/political/cultural) and requirements like curriculum mandates. If "what children can do and experience" does not seem to be related to the culturally endorsed constructivist learning style, neither the teacher nor the learners can fully engage in a meaningful constructivist teaching and curriculum as evidenced in Kevin's case. The teacher can construct and present an integrated curriculum in which all subjects/contents are well connected, including culturally endorsed curriculum mandates and constructivist teaching practices based on the teacher's perspective instead of diverse learners' pluralistic perspectives on their learning processes. The effects of this particular issue increase if cultural differences (e.g., ethnic or gender difference) and different forms of intellectual processes (e.g., creativity) exist among the children, the teacher, and the system unless the teacher is fully aware of and knowledgeable about those differences and able to respond thoughtfully to that reality, using critical, multiple/multiethnic perspective-taking. If that happens, the teacher's constructivist teaching and curriculum practice would take a different form, one requiring *negotiation* to *balance* the mandated content standards, culturally endorsed constructivist teaching, and the different perspectives needed to enrich the learners with pluralistic curriculum experiences.

*Dialectical constructivism* (also known as social constructivism) emphasizes the role of interaction among learners, their peers, and teachers: Learners require scaffolding provided by teachers or experts as well as collaboration with peers (cf. Vygotsky's perspective). Teachers who value this type of constructivism may capitalize on teachable moments and strive for pedagogy-based teaching because scaffolding requires individualized pedagogical adaptation for each learner in a learner-meaningful context (see Chapter 2). An individual does indeed construct her or his own knowledge, but the process of knowledge construction inevitably takes place in a social cultural context with negotiation; therefore, knowledge is in fact socially constructed. As shown below, parts of Lynn's story (in Chapter 6) and parts of Syler's story (Chapter 7) contain examples of dialectical constructivism manifested in teaching:

> [from Lynn's story] When the children saw a display of the Valentine's cards they had made, several of them pointed to the green diamond-shaped card and asked the teacher why Jeffery's card looked different and why he had made it in that way. A teachable moment emerged. Because of the children's interest in Jeffery's card and knowing Jeffery's mom's story, the next day Lynn and the cooperating teacher decided to give the children the opportunity to talk about the cards that they had made. After Jeffery talked about his special card, another child asked, "Can I make another card? A different one?" Other children agreed, "Yeh!" After the children heard the reason that Jeffery had made a green diamond-shaped card for his mom, they all decided to create their own unique cards with various shapes and colors, but the original idea of expressing their special feelings to special person was much clearer to all the children in the classroom. Even one of the Korean children, who had absolutely no idea about what Valentine's Day meant, was able to create his own special cards for his mother and grandfather. The project was transformed.

> [From Syler's story] The following day Syler and his father Jeffray read the book together to the class. Syler's classmates and teacher listened to the story and learned about seven directions. When Syler and his father finished reading the book, the teacher captured a teachable moment and asked the children to tell what they knew about the new directions, how they differed from the first four directions, and what they thought about the other three directions. The children requested that the teacher add the three new directions to the original four on the bulletin board. Later the children talked about not only which directions Christopher Columbus took to get to North America but also which direction they should take to make good decisions for building (not "keeping") peace on earth and in their classroom.

In the cases of both Lynn and Syler, the teacher was not the only one who was "mature," "knowledgeable," or "expert" in a teaching and learning context. In fact, the learner presented, shared, negotiated, and thus taught counternormative knowledge, reaching beyond "normative" knowledge structures. As a result, each member of the learning community engaged in continuous reinterpretation of knowledge (e.g., de-construction, re-construction, and new construction of the knowledge), that is, a personally meaningful experience: *currere*, the experience of oneself in regard to knowledge (see Chapter 1).

In the process of negotiating counternormative knowledge with the teacher, learners engage in *exploratory talk*; its initiation may be challenged and counterchallenged with suggestions developing from that initiation. Progress then rests on the joint acceptance of one of the suggestions or of a modification of what has been put forward (Fisher, 1993, p. 255).[1]

Thus, one of the key elements in dialectical constructivism is the classroom discourse culture that values learners' exploratory talk (Hyun, 2005b; Hyun & Davis, 2005). In exploratory talk, de-construction, re-construction, and new construction of the knowledge occur in the learners' learning as well as the teacher's (as shown in the teachers' stories presented in Chapters 5, 6, & 7). In order not only to be comfortable with but also take full advantage of learners' exploratory talk from the learners' points of view, the teacher must be fluent in reflective multiple perspective-taking. Fisher argued that exploratory talk offers a potential for learning and that in exploratory talk we may find evidence of learners' extending their learning within Vygotsky's (1978) Zone of Proximal Development (ZPD).[2]

Teachers are identified as agents for change and draw children into language as it is used in their culture. Numerous studies of classroom discourse have indicated that many teachers control the content and direction of the discourse by asking questions, by rephrasing, and by reformulating learners' responses (Fisher, 1993; Mercer & Fisher, 1993). In successful constructivist teaching, teachers' discourse strategies, such as scaffolding, should be carefully and reflectively employed so as to offer students developmentally meaningful and culturally congruent assistance at crucial teachable moments without discouraging them from autonomously seeking their own meaning-making of the learning.

Within dialectical constructivism, the way the teacher captures and capitalizes on teachable moments may derive from reflectivity influenced by her or his multiple, multidimensional, and multiethnic perspective-taking as happened in Lynn's (Chapter 6) and Syler's cases (Chapter 7). The teacher is a contemplative observer, negotiator, and facilitator, continuously de-constructing and re-constructing his or her own knowledge of child development and learning; content knowledge, both required subject matter as well as the teacher's and the children's personal knowledge of the content; and reflective critical thinking (e.g., What knowledge does the child have that I do not? How can I simultaneously support both the child's counternormative knowledge and the knowledge that I need to provide?). As a result the teacher's teaching is pedagogy-based, and the curriculum is negotiation-oriented. Within negotiation-oriented curriculum, teachable moments and learnable moments interlock.

Glasersfeld (1984) discussed radical constructivism, which is an epistemological construct also known as postepistemological constructivism. Knowledge is not something that can merely be conveyed from teacher to students (e.g., Syler's story: *"When the teacher and the textbook referred only to four directions [north, south, east, and west, based on the Florida Sunshine State Social Studies Content Standards], Syler disagreed, explaining to his teacher and classmates that he knew about three other directions: earth, sky, and the judging of right and wrong."*), and any pedagogical approach that presumes otherwise must be rejected. Radical constructivism is grounded in the belief that an individual's knowledge can never be a "true" representation of reality, but is instead an ongoing and recursive construction of the world that the individual experiences (Windschitl, 2002). Thus, radical constructivism supports postmodern curriculum scholars' definition of curriculum as *currere* (e.g., Pinar & Grumet, 1976; see Chapter 2). Because curriculum is viewed as a continuous reinterpretation by the learner via de-construction, re-construction, and new construction, curriculum is understood as the active verb *currere*. In Chapter 6, Lynn's story illustrates this particular concept of *currere* through Jeffery's experience of making a green diamond-shaped Valentine's Day card for his mother and young children's continuous reinterpretation of the meaning of card-making as they engaged in different emerging experiences.[3]

Table 8.1 illustrates the possibility of evolving constructivist teaching accompanied by various curricular practices. Teachable moments can occur in any kind of constructivist teaching. Depending on how the teacher inherently and pervasively captures and capitalizes on teachable moments derived from her or his own perspective on constructivist teaching, the characteristics of classroom curricular phenomena differ and could evolve.

Neither Lynn (Chapter 6) nor the teacher in Syler's story (Chapter 7) started with dialectical or postmodern constructivist teaching.

**Table 8.1. Teacher's Constructivist Teaching Accompanied by Various Curricular Practices**

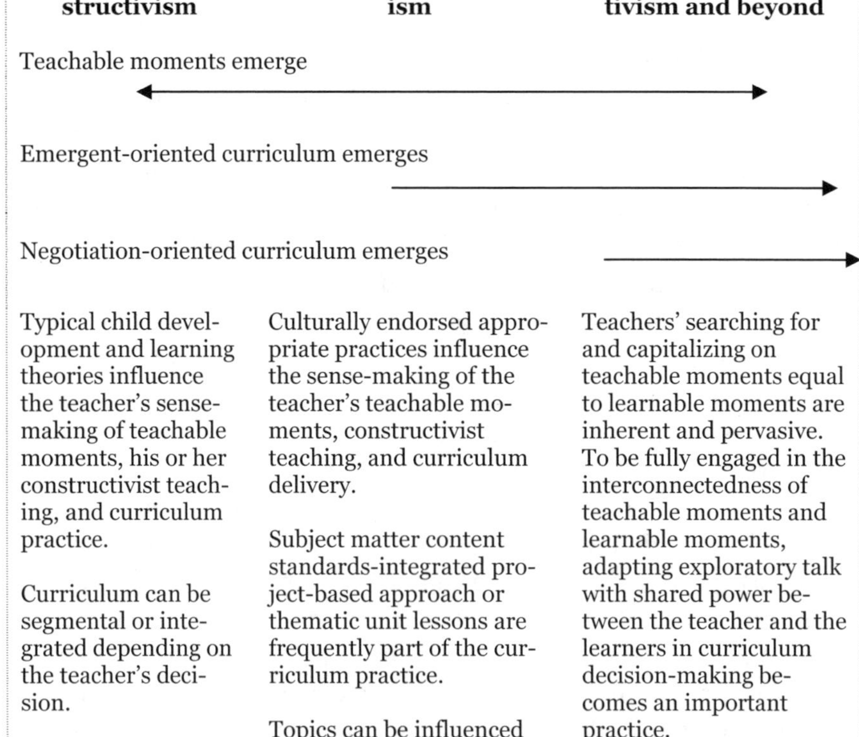

| Endogenous constructivism | Exogenous constructivism | Dialectical constructivism and beyond |
|---|---|---|
| Teachable moments emerge ← | → | → |
| | Emergent-oriented curriculum emerges → | → |
| | | Negotiation-oriented curriculum emerges → |
| Typical child development and learning theories influence the teacher's sense-making of teachable moments, his or her constructivist teaching, and curriculum practice.<br><br>Curriculum can be segmental or integrated depending on the teacher's decision. | Culturally endorsed appropriate practices influence the sense-making of the teacher's teachable moments, constructivist teaching, and curriculum delivery.<br><br>Subject matter content standards-integrated project-based approach or thematic unit lessons are frequently part of the curriculum practice.<br><br>Topics can be influenced by the learners' emerging | Teachers' searching for and capitalizing on teachable moments equal to learnable moments are inherent and pervasive. To be fully engaged in the interconnectedness of teachable moments and learnable moments, adapting exploratory talk with shared power between the teacher and the learners in curriculum decision-making becomes an important practice. |

| | | |
|---|---|---|
| | interests, experiences, and interpretations; simultaneously contents can be controlled, guided, or managed by the teacher's culturally endorsed constructivist teaching approaches.<br><br>The teacher's sense-making of teachable moments can support learners' learnable moments if the teacher and learners share similar backgrounds and have shared understandings. | Initially, teaching content and learning content can be segmental or subject-integrated based on "required/mandated" curriculum. Through exploratory talk, learners' counternormative knowledge is equally negotiated with normative knowledge. The teacher and learners can still cover the mandates, the teacher's content interests, and diverse learners' counternormative knowledge. |

Lynn's initial approach was more likely an endogenous constructivist practice. Syler's teacher started her lesson with exogenous constructivist practice. Their constructivist teaching evolved as they faced unexpected moments and were willing to explore the new, emerging reality by engaging in self-reflective critical thinking and questioning, inner and outer dialogue, and multiple/multiethnic perspective-takings. In that process both teachers and learners experienced the recursive mode of de-constructing, re-constructing, and new constructing of the reality that was meaningful to them; thus, real learning occurred individually as well as collectively.

## Teacher's Recursive Mode of De-construction, Re-construction, and New Construction in Curricular Practices

Even within the parameters of a teacher's constructivist beliefs, if a learner-initiated learnable moment is not captured or capitalized on as a meaningful teachable moment from the teacher's point of view in a pervasive and natural manner, the teacher's teaching and the curriculum can easily become teacher-centered and instruction-oriented. In contrast, if the teacher is fully aware of and knowledgeable about the critical differences and able to respond thoughtfully to that reality using reflective multiple/multiethnic perspective-taking, the teacher's constructivist teaching would be de-constructed, re-constructed, and new-constructed in a recursive mode. Thus, the teacher would continue to grow as a change agent, that is, as an ethical, moral, effective, and thoughtful professional.

What drives the teacher's constructivist teaching as it evolves from endogenous or exogenous to dialectical and beyond to postmodern constructivist teaching? As discussed in Chapter 7, teachers' self-reflective critical thinking and questioning, inner and outer dialogue, and multiple/multiethnic perspective-takings could be the elements that lead them to engage in the cycle of de-construction, re-construction, and new construction in a recursive mode, which in turn leads them to evolving experiences of their own constructivist teaching and curriculum practice (see Figure 8.1).

In Lynn's case (Chapter 6), for example, the prospective teacher started with an existing knowledge and perceived reality, in this case, the reality regarding Valentine's Day cards.

> It's Valentine's Day card making! Heart, red, and pink, don't you know? What do you mean "Why only heart shaped and red and pink? I don't understand your questions." The children had already seen red or pink heart-shaped Valentine symbols in the decorations in their classroom. For 3- to 5-year-olds, drawing or cutting a heart shape is developmentally a very difficult task. They are still working on drawing a closed-circle shape as I learned from child development class, so I am going to make the shape for them prior to the activity.

The teacher's endogenous constructivist teaching approach based on typical knowledge about child development theory and taken-for-granted perceived reality (commercial culture) was de-constructed when one of her students rejected the teacher's original lesson and when she learned more about the child's family background and culture.

> Lynn learned that Jeffery's single mother just became engaged. Her boyfriend, who happened to be Jeffery's best friend, gave his mom a diamond ring. This made Jeffery's mother very happy. So was Jeffery. Green was the favorite color of both Jeffrey and his mom. Jeffery had recently learned how to draw a diamond shape. He had practiced drawing diamond shapes and other shapes at home with his mom for a couple of weeks. He was very excited about the fact that he could draw a diamond shape all by himself!

**Figure 8.1. Recursive Cycle**

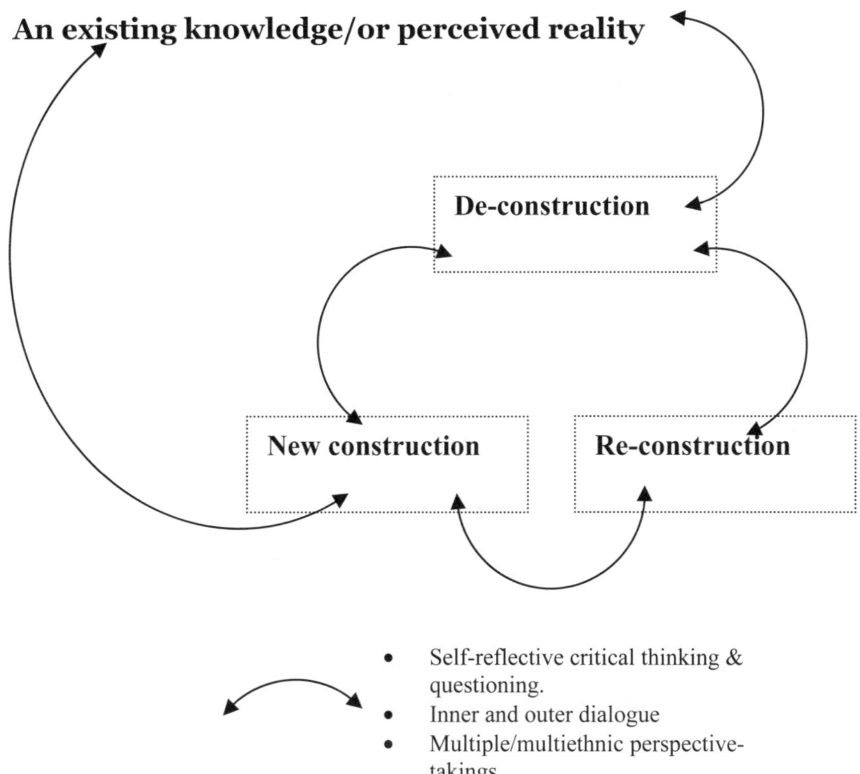


During the experience the teacher engaged in

- honest, humble, and self-reflective critical thinking and questioning (e.g., *Was my pre-assumption of "what 3-year-old children can and cannot do" developmentally fair to and culturally congruent for them? What is the limitation of my teacher knowledge? In order to be an effective and thoughtful teacher, how can I remain continuously conscious and honest about the limitations of my professional knowledge and overcome them?*);

- inner dialogue with oneself (e.g., *What makes the child see the learning materials differently from the way I do? What does the child know that I do not know?*) and outer dialogue with the learner and the parent (e.g., direct, open, and honest communication with others in the context); and
- multiple/multiethnic perspective-taking (e.g., *If I were the child, why would I have done the task differently from the way my teacher imagined or expected but in a way that made more sense and had more meaning for me. If I were the child, how could I have expressed my perspectives to my teacher and classmates?*).

Teacher contemplation like this led to the teacher's discovery of *what the child can do* and subsequently to the re-construction of her knowledge of child development as it affected the child's learning and growth. The teacher's de-construction and re-construction also influenced the way she captured teachable moments driven by learnable moments, capitalizing on them for further learning that motivated other learners in the classroom to engage in de-construction and re-construction of their own previous learning:

> At first, they all made the Valentine cards, using the intern's materials. They were all the same. When the children saw a display of the Valentine's cards they had made, several of them pointed to the green diamond-shaped card and asked the teacher why Jeffery's card looked different and why he had made it in that way. A teachable moment emerged. Because of the children's interest in Jeffery's card and knowing Jeffery's mom's story, the next day Lynn and the cooperating teacher decided to give the children the opportunity to talk about the cards that they had made. After Jeffery talked about his special card, another child asked, "Can I make another card? A different one?" Other children agreed, "Yeh!" After the children heard the reason that Jeffery had made a green diamond-shaped card for his mom, they all decided to create their own unique cards with various shapes and colors, but the original idea of expressing their special feelings to special person was much clearer to all the children in the classroom. Even one of the Korean children, who had absolutely no idea about what Valentine's Day meant, was able to create his own special cards for his mother and grandfather.

During the experience the teacher also witnessed the children's capability of engaging in dialectical constructivist learning with negotiation:

- children's emerging self-reflective critical thinking by reassessing their previously made cards and questioning whether they could make others that would make more sense to them through inner dialogue within themselves and outer dialogue with the teacher, the other matured peer, and others; and
- using multiple/multiethnic perspective-takings of the person who may receive the card (e.g., thinking of grandfather, aunt, goldfish, what he/she may like).

Once the experiential processes of de-construction and re-construction became autonomous and meaningful to both the teacher and the learners, a new form of construction emerged. New construction occurred in the form of the card-making table that was continuously used by the children as their classroom experiences became socially meaningful living:

> The classroom had a new card-making table next to the art area. The children wanted to continue the card-making activity any time they wanted to or thought it was needed. For example, they made a "We love you, Goldfish" card for the new goldfish in their classroom. One of neighbors who lived near the school had donated three goldfish in a small fishbowl before he moved away. The children also made a card for the mother of a classmate who brought them snacks: "We like your cupcakes and the decorations." These demonstrate that what is being taught and learned had taken on a serious significance: New curriculum was formed by the children and existed in the classroom.
>
> One day Jin Min brought two books to school. They came from Seoul, South Korea, and were written in two different languages: English and Korean. Jin Min's mother and grandfather came to school and read the books to the children. Jin Min's mom read the book in English as his grandfather read it in Korean. Jin Min tried hard to explain in English how excited he was when he discovered the package containing the book in his home mailbox. Classmate Susan said, "Why don't we make a thank-you card for the person who sent the book to Jin Min? She will be also excited to find the mail in her mailbox. It will make her happy like Jin Min." A small group of children—Jin Min, Jeffery, Susan, and Asa—made a card during the activity time.

Within this particular group of learners and their teacher, the fluency of new construction becomes a pattern of their classroom practice as a classroom learning culture. Once the teacher and learners are comfortable with and empowered by the process of de-construction, reconstruction, and new construction, the cycle recursively continues as either unexpected or expected moments arise.

**Conclusion: Depending on the Teacher**

Depending on how the teacher perceives what curriculum *is (or should be)* and *does* and his or her reflectivity and multiple perspective-taking, the teacher's sense-making of teachable moments and how to use teachable moments to support his or her curriculum practice will differ.

If the teacher believes that curriculum is to pass or practice a set of culturally endorsed knowledge within a prescribed timeline with a standardized outcome (e.g., school readiness), then the curriculum will shape every learner's knowledge and developmental capacity reflecting the set of knowledge (e.g., appropriate vs. inappropriate). A clear distinction always exists between the teacher (knowledge transmitter, provider, "facilitator") and the learners (knowledge receivers). Learning can be segmental, delivered by the teacher's instruction-oriented teaching, even if it is a culturally endorsed constructive learner-centered approach (i.e., adult privilege). The teacher's way of capturing and capitalizing on teachable moments would lie within the parameter of the prescribed curriculum. Learner-originated learnable moments can be systematically muted. The teacher's multiple/multiethnic perspective-taking to learn and explore other points of view and to engage in self-reflective critical thinking and questioning can also lie within this boundary and would then preclude open and honest inner dialogue reflecting self-doubt, limiting an effective and thoughtful teacher. Outer dialogue with learners and others to expand knowledge and experience would be hindered.

All curriculum and curriculum work are biased. In curriculum work in a complex society with pluralistic and democratic ideas, if the teacher believes that curriculum *is* and thus should comprise holistic and authentic learning experiences run by individual learners, then the curriculum will serve as social and individual public space, which supports and treats all the members of the learning community as wisdom holders, wisdom seekers, and wisdom creators, even if they are three-year-olds. No clear distinction exists between teacher and learners; transformation of the identities of "student" and "teacher" will occur inherently and pervasively as active and engaged learning takes place. In order to capture and capitalize on learners' emerging and evolving interests and inquiries, teachers search for teachable moments to motivate further learnable moments at higher levels from the learners' points of view within the learning context. Thus, teachable moments and learnable moments interlock. A teacher's teaching naturally becomes pedagogy-based, illuminating study-based, socially just, and ethically sound democratic practices. This kind of curriculum understanding and practice necessitates teachers who are fluent in diverse forms of reflective thinking (reflectivity) and multiple/multiethnic perspective-taking. Chapter 9 contains a discussion of this issue.

## Chapter Ending Questions

- How can teachers freely and fluidly employ the three curricular notions in light of their relative identities and responsibilities?
- In curriculum practice, how can teachers promote exploratory talk with the characteristics of dialectical and postmodern constructivist teaching?

## Notes

[1] Fisher (1993) categorized three types of talk occurring among children:

*Disputational talk*, characterized as an initiation in various forms, such as suggestion or instruction, followed by a challenge, either a direct rejection or a countersuggestion. This results either in a lack of any clear resolution or a resolution that does not build directly on previous utterances.

*Cumulative talk*, in which initiations are accepted either without discussion or with additions or superficial amendments.

*Exploratory talk*, in which the initiation may be challenged and counterchallenged with suggestions that are developments of that initiation. Progress then rests on the joint acceptance of one of the suggestions or of a modification of what has been put forward (p. 255).

[2] Learning in the Zone of Proximal Development (ZPD) commonly refers, first, to what takes place between individuals, where one is more "expert" than the other; and

second, to joint consciousness of the participants, where two or more minds collaborate to solve a problem. Vygotsky (1978) argued that learning would most likely be achieved voluntarily in the ZPD with the help of more experienced, "matured," or metacognitively sophisticated persons. He emphasized the important function of language in learning, theorizing that learning occurs initially in a social linguistic (interpsychological) context prior to its becoming internalized or individualized within an intrapsychological context (Fisher, 1993; Vygotsky, 1978; Wegerif & Mercer, 1996). The intrapsychological thought processes influence individuals' internalization of learning. In order to engage in more advanced thought, individuals require the presence of "matured" others in a social linguistic context. If linguistic discourse is well guided by the strategic scaffolding of matured individuals (e.g., teacher or matured learner with acquired subject matter knowledge), high levels of learning are likely to occur (Bodrova & Leong, 1996).

[3] Epistemological social constructivism reflects social phenomenology (Schutz, 1970), in which individuals who constantly construct, de-construct, and re-construct unique understanding of their own reality from experiences. This intersubjectivity becomes objectified as the experiential world that people take for granted. Thus, multiple ways of interpreting objectified intersubjectivities are inevitable to constitute the reality of individuals' work, experience, and life itself. Finally, classic scientific constructivism is known as scientific knowledge construction, or scientific constructivism, that is both symbolic in nature and also socially negotiated. The basic objectives of science are not phenomenal in nature but constructs that are advanced by the scientific community's act of interpreting the uncovered nature (Driver, Asoko, Leach, Mortimer, & Scott, 1994)

# Chapter Nine

# Reflectivity and Multiple Perspective-Taking

## Initial Inquiries

- How does multiple perspective-taking coincide with teachers' reflectivity?
- What is reflectivity? What is reflection-in-action? What is reflection-on-action? What is reflection-for-practice?

The teacher's multiple/multiethnic perspective-taking coinciding with reflectivity (reflective functions) is the foundation to the varied teaching and curricula practices in light of teachable moments. Chapter 9 contains a discussion of interconnected, recursive relationships between multiple/multiethnic perspective-taking and the teacher's reflectivity.

## Multiple/Multiethnic Perspective-Taking

In order to construct a curriculum practice that supports all diverse learners' developmentally meaningful and culturally congruent learning experiences from the learners' points of view, each teacher must be fluent in multiple and multiethnic perspective-taking in an inherent and pervasive mode in light of teaching (Hyun & Marshall, 1997). Developing multiple and multiethnic perspective-taking involves coordinating and integrating various psychological perspectives—specifically, first-, second-, and third-person perspectives. The ability to assume a second-person perspective allows people psychologically to step out of their egocentrism (first-person perspective-taking) or cultural myopia to comprehend that another person might have a different, although equally reasonable, perspective. Teachers who have the ability to integrate their first- and second-person perspectives can see themselves through the eyes of others and evaluate learners' behavior through those eyes. Hyun and Marshall (1997, p. 191) illustrated perspective-taking phases:

> Soonja doesn't know how to greet people properly. One is expected to say "How are you?" or "How do you do?" when you meet people. She must be a shy person or doesn't know this type of social interaction well (first-person/single-ethnic perspective-taking).

> Instead she bows and/or simply says "Hi" or "Hello" and drops her eyes for a short moment. I notice that Soonja greets others in a style different from mine, yet it seems to be socially appropriate and personally meaningful [thus cultural] behavior from her point of view (second-person/bi-ethnic perspective-taking).
>
> In some cases, Soonja uses "How are you?" with a person who is personally closer to her than others whom she simply knows or meets. But even when she has a close relationship, if the person is older than she, it seems to me she does not use "How are you?" but rather "Hello" or "Hi." Somehow, these distinctions seem to reflect appropriate [culturally congruent] social distinctions. Now that I think about it, many people use different greeting styles in their social contacts while maintaining an appropriate [culturally congruent] degree of social interaction. I guess my style is just one of many different greeting practices (third-person/multiple/multiethnic perspective-taking).

As illustrated above, the third-person perspective permits teachers to add another dimension to their social-cognitive abilities by stepping out of their own cultural paradigms, which tend to be collections of individually distinct elements. Cognition of their own culture becomes less context-specific as they generalize across distinct, culturally pluralistic situations. In addition, this third-person perspective allows individuals to generalize multiple perspectives across the groups or members they encounter in social contexts. Ethnic perspective-taking as socially constructed cognition can, therefore, lead to multicultural perspectives that require one to understand others within a context of interethnic and intraethnic dynamics (Hyun & Marshall, 1997; Quintana, 1994).

Realizing the existence of multiple realities inevitably leads to divergence in all human endeavors. This divergence can be found in human development, cultural and educational values, and even in ways of learning and teaching. According to Quintana (1994) a person with little bicultural experience may have limited development of his or her own ethnic perspective-taking ability; that is, many children and adults may experience a lag in the development of their social perspective-taking, depending on the extent of their experiences with, understanding of, and appreciation for their own and other ethnic groups. People limited to monocultural experiences may be significantly delayed in the development of ethnic perspective-taking ability, relative to their social-cognitive abilities. Cannella and Reiff (1994) reported that prospective teachers with largely monocultural experiences exhibit significant limitations in their multiethnic perspective-taking ability. This is unfortunate because it is a fundamental ability for the reflective teacher's pedagogy-based teaching and curricular practices.

As teachers exercise multiple and multiethnic perspective-taking, interpersonal and intrapersonal negotiation skills become important elements. The assumption underlying Selman and Schultz's (1990) model of interpersonal and intrapersonal negotiation strategies suggests that coordination of social perspectives is intrinsic to the process of balancing intrapersonal and interpersonal needs in ongoing relationships and that matured negotiation is based on the increasing ability to coordinate (i.e., differentiate and integrate) the perspectives of self and other.

When development and learning are inseparable from the social-cultural context, new assumptions related to responsible teacher preparation clearly emerge. In a diverse society teachers must deal with multiple perspectives, value systems, and various forms of human learning that are divergent, multidirectional, multidimensional, and multicultural. Developing multiple/multiethnic perspective-taking ability for use in everyday pedagogical practices ought to be standard practice in teacher preparation. Teachers in contemporary society require a high level of cognitive capacity that allows them to understand how to connect with all learners' unique capacities to make sense of the learners' meaningful learning. Viewing this sense-making as a social capacity can lead teachers to construct developmentally meaningful and culturally congruent pedagogy from the learners' point of view, and that creates equal and fair learning experiences for all individuals in light of democratically accountable curriculum practice.

To develop this multiple/multiethnic perspective-taking ability, teachers must first examine and come to understand their own monocultural experiences, then expand to include bicultural/cross-cultural and multicultural experiences. This is particularly important for those with limited ethnic or cultural experiences. To be successful perspective takers in a diverse society, teachers should develop their multiple/multiethnic perspective-taking ability during their initial teacher preparation experience. To accomplish this, it may be helpful to consider a conceptual construction that points out a parallel dynamic between perspective-taking and ethnic perspective-taking ability within the phenomena of interpersonal and intrapersonal negotiation strategies. Table 9.1 introduces this parallel dynamic. The stages (more like mental positions) are *recursive* given the nature of a person's inner dialogue; that is, a person may move back and forth among the positions instead of following the stages in an invariant sequence from first to last. Individuals will constantly reconstruct diverse perspective-taking in light of their various social and cultural contacts. Consequently, self-awareness of one's own cultural paradigm becomes the cornerstone upon which to build one's own multiple/multiethnic perspective-taking (as happened with the prospective teacher Lynn in Chapter 6).

Because each new social contact may bring cultural conflict, most adolescents and adults initially think from a first-person/single-ethnic perspective; however, knowing that their interpretation of others may limit a genuine understanding of those individuals, self-conscious, reflective persons deliberately remain willing to expand their own perspective-taking to second- and third-person/multiple perspective-taking. Individuals' self-examination of their own cultural paradigm, coupled with an ongoing inner dialogue are, therefore, key to bringing about this recursive dynamic and producing teachers with multiple/multiethnic perspective-taking abilities.

## Table 9.1. Parallel Dynamics of Perspective-Taking

*First-person perspective-taking = Single-ethnic perspective-taking*
Egocentrism, ethnocentrism, and cultural myopia direct an individual's thinking and behavior. Knowing about self and examining her or his own cultural paradigm, which has formed thinking and behavior, are limited. Expectations of others' sense-making of living, learning, problem-solving approaches, and so on, are based on the individual's point of view, which is derived from her or his own family cultural background. Inappropriate or unfair value judgments regarding others may occur in the individual's social interaction.

*Second-person perspective-taking = Bi-ethnic/cross-ethnic perspective-taking*
The individual has the ability to comprehend and assume that another person might have a different but equally reasonable perspective. Knowing about self and examining one's own cultural paradigm are simultaneously active and ongoing in a one-to-one interaction. Expectations of others' sense-making of liv-

ing, learning, problem-solving approaches, and so on, which are based on the individual's point of view, are reconstructed and changed. Personal inner negotiation with the other person who is in contact occurs frequently, leading the individual to develop cross-cultural competencies and willingness to solve conflicts with others.

*Third-person perspective-taking = Multiple/multiethnic perspective-taking*
The individual has the ability to step out of his or her own cultural paradigm and to assume that the existence of multiple realities inevitably leads to divergence in all human endeavor. Expecting diverse and multiple ways of making sense of living or learning provides problem-solving approaches in any social context. Realizing that the continuous presence of diverse human perspectives derives from each person's unique family ethnicity, the individual values and treats everyone's family ethnicity equally. This realization leads to a willingness to explore, learn about, and respect diverse perspectives from various ethnic family practices.

In order for teachers to provide a fair, developmentally meaningful and culturally congruent education that serves all individuals, teachers need to pay attention to the dynamics of the perspective-taking abilities in their thinking and action in conjunction with their various interpersonal/intrapersonal negotiation strategies. Table 9.2 presents examples of teachers' perspective-taking ability implemented in their pedagogical reflective thinking and action.

## Table 9.2. Teacher's Perspective-Taking Implemented in Pedagogical Reflective Thinking and Action

**First-person perspective-taking = Single-ethnic perspective-taking**
(Coincides with instruction-oriented teaching and curriculum practice)

| **Thinking** | **Action** |
|---|---|
| Intrapersonal reasoning: *Students should use only English because that is the only language I as their teacher can understand.* | Interpersonal interaction: *Akia! You should be using English in the classroom. Then I will understand what you say.* |
| Use power-oriented negotiations including one-way commands and orders or conversely, simple and unchallenging accommodations (giving in) to the perceived needs and de- | This type of interpersonal strategy may lead teachers to the habit of high levels of survival/task focus in their instructional (not pedagogical) practices. In this case we can easily observe teachers |

mands of the other person.

who are overly concerned with classroom management, content standards management, and control. A high frequency of teacher directive, one-way instruction, and limits in learner-oriented reflective practices become main elements of classroom culture. Teachers expect students to adjust to teaching styles rather than modify instruction to fit students' learning needs. Instruction-oriented and teacher-centered teaching and curriculum practice are apparent.

**Second-person perspective-taking =**
**Bi-ethnic/cross-ethnic perspective-taking**
(Coincides with pedagogy-based teaching and curriculum practice)

**Thinking**

Intrapersonal reasoning*: Maybe Akia feels somewhat uncomfortable using only English in the classroom. If I were Akia, I would feel more comfortable using my own familiar language at first.*

Use psychologically based reciprocal exchanges that coordinate the perspectives of both the self and the other in the ability to reflect upon negotiation from a second-person perspective. It is understood that both the self and the other are planful and self-reflective, and that the thoughts, feelings, and actions of each influence those of the other. The self may defer to the other without yielding completely.

**Action**

Interpersonal interaction: *As teacher I should not adhere strictly to the use of one language—English—in the classroom. Instead I support Akia's code-switching between two different languages and cultures as she engages in learning. "You may use your first language/community language as needed in order for you to connect (or make meaning) between the subject concept and yourself."*

Teachers examine means and goals by asking themselves questions in order to make independent, individual decisions about pedagogical issues. Strategies include psychological trades and exchanges, verbal persuasion or deference, convincing others, making deals, and other forms of self-interested co-operation. The teacher attempts to connect the learner and subject, simultaneously considering the individualized teaching approach; thus, the teacher's practice becomes pedagogy-based.

**Third-person perspective-taking =**
**Multiple/multiethnic perspective-taking**
(Coincides with pedagogy-based teaching and curriculum practice)

| **Thinking** | **Action** |
|---|---|
| Intrapersonal reasoning: *Maybe other children want to know or learn about Akia's home language and her own unique ideas, too. Maybe there are other languages the children know/use from their family /community culture that I have not noticed yet. The children may also want to share those. With an invitation to share their own family culture/practices, they will be able to create a congruent learning experience between home and school. It would also benefit other children to expose them to diverse language expressions, divergent learning experiences, and various ways to solve problems.* | Interpersonal interaction: *Ask the children in the classroom about what other languages we are using/can use/want to use. Let's count the numbers in Akia's home language. Can we think about any other languages we can use to count the numbers? Encourage the children to learn about each other's languages, unique ideas to solve a problem, etc. Then let them share their observations within the formal peer interaction or formal instructional learning events.* |
| Represents a consideration of the need for an integration of the interests of self and other so that the negotiation is viewed from a third-person perspective. These strategies involve compromise, dialogue, process analysis, and the development of a shared goal of mutual understanding. There is an understanding that concern for the continuity of the relationship over time is a necessary consideration for the adequate and optimal solution of any immediate problem. | Teachers are both process- and outcome-oriented. They examine classroom phenomena from multiple perspectives and recognize how the decisions they make influence the learning that occurs. Teachers look critically at the ethnical bases of what happens in the classroom and determine how exact practices affect all learners. The teacher's action is not bound by required content knowledge but by the moral and ethical reality of one's own action for the diverse learners' meaningful learning; thus, the teacher's teaching and curriculum would be filled with inter- and intranegotiation leading to pedagogy-based practice. |

Teachers who are mainly in the habit of first-person/single-ethnic perspective-taking often feel that some children are "especially" different from others, based on group ethnicity, physical traits, or socioeconomic status, and naively hope that these different learners will follow the teachers' instruction and "fit in" some day as others do. Because culturally diverse learners are surrounded by mainstream or dominant culture, teachers usually believe that it is correct to move children toward the mainstream (i.e., the teacher's) learning expectations. This type of "power pedagogy" creates hidden teachable moments and a hidden curriculum in which individuality goes unrecognized, and an unfair learning environment is inherently accepted within the classroom culture. Within this classroom culture, the true meaning of an equal education thus becomes subconsciously muted. Democratically accountable curriculum practice becomes questionable.

Once teachers elect to expand their pedagogical perspective-taking from first-person/single-ethnic perspective-taking to second-person/bi-ethnic perspective-taking, developmentally meaningful and culturally congruent learning and teaching can begin to take place for each individual child. If the teacher's mental mode is second-person perspective-taking at the emergence of a teachable moment, the teachable moment has the potential to be an equally learnable moment initiated and led by the learner. As a result the moment of teaching has the capacity to become pedagogy-based. Simultaneously, more equal power-sharing tends to be present between the teacher and individual learners within the classroom culture that welcomes negotiation and exploratory talk. If teachers can learn to move in and out of first- and second-person perspective-taking, the traditional institutionalized power struggles between teacher ("adult privilege") and learners and between "minority" learners and teachers from the dominant culture may eventually fade away.

Ultimately, teachers' ability to develop third-person/multiple/multiethnic perspective-taking will result in developmentally meaningful and culturally congruent practice within the classroom. Teachers who initiate and encourage multiple power-sharing by inviting all learners' voices, ideas, and decision-making opportunities into the learning experiences become members of multiple peer interactions instead of the sole power holder of students' learning. Learners are encouraged to create their own developmentally meaningful and culturally congruent learning experiences by incorporating their own languages, experiences, identities, and knowledge through a pedagogy that welcomes exploratory talk and negotiation between the teacher and learners. Teachers who are fluent in third-person/multiple/ multiethnic perspective-taking seek out informed teachable moments that would facilitate learners' learning of the standardized content knowledge, simultaneously and intentionally inviting learners to negotiate counternormative knowledge-sharing and construction resulting in learning that goes beyond the parameters of standardized knowledge receiving. Thus, the teacher's use of third-person/multiple/ multiethnic perspective-taking coincides with pedagogy-based teaching and curriculum practice.

Developmentally meaningful and culturally congruent learning and teaching reflect reciprocal, diverse, and fair power-sharing through the expression of each individual learner's unique presence, which is presented through a learner-oriented, continuously negotiable, democratically accountable, and socially constructed curriculum. The teacher may also facilitate *critical teachable moments*, responding to what is going on outside the classroom apart from the scheduled content knowledge learning (e.g., in the school building, in the community, in the world, and so on), giving learners the opportunity to learn and engage in socially responsible and morally sound knowledge and action (e.g., What is the difference between "peace-keeping" and "peace-building?" During the Hurricane Katrina disaster in 2005, what kind of social act would you like to have been part of? Why? How?).

## Reflectivity and Types of Reflection

Reflectivity is defined here as the intellectual capacity to engage in relatively complex thought about one's own action that may or may not be voiced through inner or outer dialogue. Reflection is a fundamental aspect of educational theory and practice, and in that sense it becomes synonymous with thinking about teachers' pedagogical practices (Bowman, 1989; Grant & Zeichner, 1984; Hyun & Marshall, 1996; Lasley, 1992; van Manen, 1991). There are three different types of reflectivity: reflection-in-action, reflection-on-action, and reflection-for-practice (Hyun & Marshall, 1996; Schön, 1983; Sparks-Langer & Colton, 1991). Depending on individual teachers' desire to engage in different levels of multiple perspective-taking (mental positions), the nature of their reflectivity differs (see Figure 9.1).

*Reflection-in-action*, a cognitive element that refers to reflection in the midst of practice, is concerned with knowledge that teachers need in order to make "good" decisions in and about classroom situations. The way the teacher captures and capitalizes on teachable moments coincides with reflection-in-action. If the teacher's reflection-in-action at the emergence of teachable moments is driven by first-person perspective-taking, the teacher may tend toward the teacher-centered instruction-oriented approach. The possibility of having curriculum practice that is emergent-oriented or negotiation-oriented will be limited. If the teacher's mental position on his or her multiple perspective-taking runs freely and recursively through first-person, second-person, and third-person perspective-taking during reflection-in-action, the teacher's teachable moments represent pedagogy-based teaching with the capacity to construct negotiation-oriented curriculum. Exploratory talk (see Chapter 8) would be apparent in the classroom discourse.

**Figure 9.1. Recursive and Interconnected Relationship Between Reflectivity and Perspective-Taking**

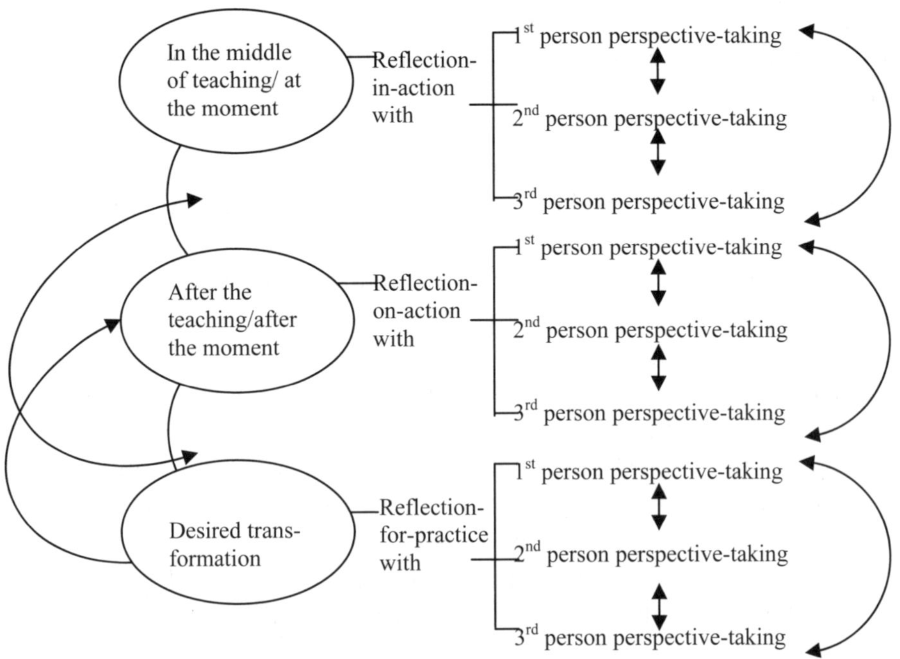

*Reflection-on-action* is a narrative element that is essentially reactive with reflection-in-action. It provides a much richer understanding of what takes place in classrooms and in teachers' re-construction of reality. It could and should happen after the teacher utilizes teachable moments. Again, if the teacher's mental position on his or her multiple perspective-taking runs freely and recursively among the three perspective-takings during reflection-on-action, the teacher may reconceptualize the content standards in an integrated mode, and the teacher's lesson planning would be more inquiry-oriented. If the teacher engages in the reflection-on-action with a collaborative (e.g., colleague) or some students, this would provide a richer context for the teacher's analysis on the teaching and the effectiveness of the curriculum. If the teacher's reflection-on-action was not well analyzed contextually in light of second- and third-person perspective-takings, his or her teaching and curriculum practice would be instruction-oriented instead of pedagogy-based; thus an emergent curriculum or curriculum negotiation would not be apparent in the classroom.

*Reflection-for-practice* holds a critical element, particularly coinciding with third-person/multiple/multiethnic perspective-taking. It is a deeper understanding of one's own reflection-in-action and reflection-on-action for further articulated curriculum enactment. It is the desired transformative outcome of reflection-on-action and reflection-in-action. It is concerned with students' learning in light of the moral and ethical aspects of social compassion and justice, thus essential to pedagogy-based teaching and curriculum practice (Hyun & Marshall, 1996; Schön, 1983). In reflection-for-practice, teachers contemplate their own sense-making of teachable moments with learner-initiated learnable moments and negotiated moments with the learners. Depending on how teachers engage in their own reflection-for-practice using different perspective-takings, their next reflection-in-action at the emergence of teachable moment would differ. Thus, these three different types of reflectivity are and should be recursive, curriculum experience organically growing from the perspectives of both teachers and learners.

Reflective phenomena include three elements that foster teachers' reflective thinking: cognitive, narrative, and critical. The cognitive element fosters concern regarding broad teaching principles and strategies of classroom management and organization that appear to transcend subject matter (Shulman, 1987). This element coincides with the most personal form of reflective practice—the "inner dialogue" that teachers have with themselves. First-person perspective-taking is the dominant mental mode in teachers' elementary cognitive level reflection. Table 9.3 presents examples of the teacher's inner dialogue at the elementary cognitive level:

**Table 9.3. Examples of the Teacher's Inner Dialogue at the Elementary Cognitive Level with First-Person Perspective-Taking**

- Are all the children following my directions?
- Are their eyes all on me?
- Do they seem to understand my directions?
- Am I missing anything from what I have planned in the [written] lesson plan?
- Do I have to make some changes? Why? Do I want to change?
- Does the change still cover the required content standards?

The immediacy of teaching precludes others from participating in reflection-in-action, but the reflective teacher can learn to bring multiple perspectives into this process as shown in the examples of reflection-in-action from Table 9.4:

**Table 9.4. Examples of the Inner Dialogue Occurring in Reflection-in-Action with Second-Person Perspective-Taking**

- If I were the child who seems to have some difficulties following the directions or who seems to have some conflicts with me or peers, what/how would I feel about this activity/lesson/materials/situation?
- What individually meaningful change do I need to make for the child? Is there any other child who seems to have a problem or difficulty with my lesson ideas/procedures/directions?
- What are the needed changes that I have to make in this lesson to be equally and fairly meaningful to the individual learners?

The major aspect of the narrative element of reflection is that it serves to contextualize the classroom experience for teachers and others, thus providing them with a much richer understanding of what takes place in the classroom and in the teacher's construction of reality (Reagan, 1993). Key to the resulting narrative are questions designed to uncover the teacher's decisions *during* the teaching act. This narrative element of reflection provides one of the most effective ways in which developmentally meaningful and culturally congruent practice can be encouraged: by suggesting that the teacher reexamine classroom phenomena from multiple perspectives. Table 9.5 provides examples of narrative elements in the inner dialogue occurring in reflection-on-action.

**Table 9.5. Examples of Narrative Elements in the Inner Dialogue Occurring in Reflection-on-Action with First-Person Perspective-Taking**

- What had happened during the lesson delivery?
- What occurred during the lesson that was unexpected? For what was I unprepared?
- What changes did I make for the unexpected reactions from the children in order for me to provide not only developmentally meaningful but also culturally congruent individual learning experiences to the learners?
- What made me change in that particular way in that situation?
- Was it developmentally meaningful and culturally congruent for the individual child? How did I come to that conclusion or realization?
- After I made some alterations, what changes improved my previously planned approach?
- How did I know that the children were learning and engaging in equal, fair, and congruent learning experiences?

These inquiries allow prospective teachers to be both process- and transformative outcome-oriented. It helps them to recognize how the decisions they make influence the learning that occurs.

Reflection-for-practice represents a habit of mind that enables practitioners to call upon what they have learned through their personal (cognitive) and shared (narrative) reflections in a more deliberative sense as they plan future teaching episodes. Ideally, this planning includes a critical element of reflection, often identified with critical pedagogy and pedagogical theory that prompts teachers to analyze critically various instructional perspectives and to use them to understand and act responsively on revealed inconsistencies (McLaren, 1989; Nieto, 1992; Reagan, 1993). Suggested inquiries for this reflection-for-practice appear in Table 9.6:

**Table 9.6. Examples of Critical Elements in the Inner Dialogue Occurring in Reflection-for-Practice**

- What did I learn from my previous teaching?
- What do I have to prepare or know more about regarding the individual child's unique learning style, communication style, interests, needs, and so on?
- How should I extend or change my teaching style, interaction style, or materials that would affect all learners' development and learning experiences fairly?
- What are the critical elements that I should consider and prepare for my next lesson that would allow me to support fully and be responsive to the individual learners' developmentally meaningful and culturally congruent experience and that would allow all of us to have an equal and fair learning experience?

This critical element of reflection influences teachers to be democratically accountable educators.

## Conclusion

The recursive and interconnected relationship between reflectivity and perspective-taking entails complex thinking by teachers. It influences the teacher's teaching and overall quality of curriculum practice. We need to introduce to both in-service and prospective teachers multiple/multiethnic perspective-taking (different mental positions) coinciding with reflectivity (reflective functions) as the foundation to varied teaching and curricula practices. Teachers' contemplation of this particular complex relationship between perspective-taking and reflectivity could help them see their curriculum practice—what it *is* and *does* for the learners at a much deeper level—and it might help them to engage in teaching and curriculum practices beyond the political scrutiny of standardized curriculum practice and teaching.

**Chapter Ending Questions**

- How do you see inner and outer dialogue related to the teacher's reflectivity and multiple/multiethnic perspective-taking?
- What kind of relationship do you see between the teacher's reflectivity and pedagogy-based teaching as she or he strives for developmentally meaningful and culturally congruent curriculum practice from the learners' points of view?

# Chapter Ten

# Summary and Conclusion

## Initial Inquiry

- How do we compare and contrast the three different curricular understandings in conjunction with teachable moments, power-sharing, and negotiation?

In conclusion, based on the discussions in previous chapters on different types of curricular approaches in light of teacher reflectivity and multiple perspective-taking, Chapter 10 summarizes, compares, and contrasts the three different curricular understandings in conjunction with teachable moments, power-sharing, and negotiation. Starting in the late 1980s, we have faced conflicting realities and paradoxical behaviors in curriculum practices influenced by the law and politics (e.g., The U.S. No Child Left Behind Act, 2001; The U.K. National Curriculum, 1988) that heavily emphasize standardized and instruction-oriented curriculum practices and assessments (Bassey, 2003; Hyun, 2003). As well-informed educators we need to learn how to negotiate and go beyond the political scrutiny of narrowly defined curriculum implementation in order to cultivate and enhance democratically well-grounded and pedagogically sound curriculum leadership for all learners.

## Comparison Among the Three Different Curricular Understandings

Table 10.1 illustrates key characteristics of negotiation-oriented curriculum practice in comparison with teachable moment-oriented curriculum and emergent-oriented curriculum. As illustrated in the table, negotiation-oriented curriculum practice

- could be a short event based on content or a prolonged engagement driven by the topic of learners' interests;
- can change teacher-driven instruction-oriented teaching into pedagogy-based teaching;
- can go beyond expected outcomes of standards- or content-based subject-matter learning, objectives, and achievement;

- takes into account the unexpected interaction, accommodates emerging thoughts of the people, and constructs immediate goals to enhance achievement; and
- may work well with any school curriculum culture that is either traditional or progressive, and whether the classroom is architecturally open or closed.

Similar to emergent-oriented curriculum practice, negotiation-oriented curriculum practice emphasizes the following:

- developing a classroom culture based on trust between and among students and teacher;
- inquiry based, negotiation-oriented curriculum practice requires both teacher and students as knowledge seekers to push the envelope to resist and question the authority and origins of the knowledge and to become knowledge constructors. Thus, negotiation-oriented curriculum practice emphasizes questions like "Why should we do it in that way?" "What are the reasons you can come up with?" "Why is it the way it is? "Why does it have to be in that way?"
- discourse-based negotiation;
- active parents and family involvements especially for young children; and
- teachers' multiple/multiethnic perspective-taking, risk-taking and ongoing action research as well as trust and respect for the unknown and unexpected possibilities of diverse learners' capabilities and potential.

Both teachable moment-oriented curriculum and negotiation-oriented curriculum practice could entail short events based on content, highly depend on teacher decision, and appear in both teacher-directed and child-centered approaches.

## Table 10.1. Negotiation-Oriented Practice in Comparison with Teachable Moment-Oriented and Emergent-Oriented Practice

**Teachable Moment-Oriented Practice (TMOP): Key ideas**
A short event focused on a child's interests or readiness of child as interpreted by teacher.
It may not be equal to a learner-motivated learnable moment.
It can have a purely individual base: a teacher and a child experience one-to-one interaction. Thus, it has the possibility of limiting the social learning context.

**Similarity between TMOP and NOP**
Based on a short event.
Depends on teacher decision.
Listening and observing the learners.
Can appear in both teacher-directed and child-centered approaches.

**Negotiation-Oriented Practice (NOP): Key ideas**
It could be a short event or a prolonged engagement.
Can change teacher-driven instruction-oriented teaching into pedagogy-based teaching.
Standards- or content-based subject-matter learning, objectives, and achievement modified in the process of negotiation that goes beyond expected outcome.
It takes account of the unexpected interaction, accommodates emerging thoughts of those involved, and constructs immediate goals to enhance achievement.
It may work well with any school curriculum culture that is either traditional or progressive and whether the classroom is architecturally open or closed.

**Similarity between NOP and EOP**
Negotiation emerges.
Discourse-based.
Power-sharing occurs.
Active parent and family involvements.
Teacher has to be a multiple/multiethnic perspective-taker, risk-taker and ongoing action researcher as well as trust and respect unknown and unexpected possibilities of diverse learners' capabilities and potential.
Listening to and observing the learners.

**Emergent-Oriented Practice (EOP): Key ideas**
A longer period of activity initiated by child interests.
Acculturating and cultivating learners' process-oriented learning.
Thought-provoking learning environment characterized by collaboration. It creates serendipitous moments.
Teacher as a multiple/multiethnic perspective-taker, risk-taker and ongoing action researcher.
Trust, respect unknown and unexpected possibilities of diverse learners' potential.

A teachable moment-oriented curriculum (Chapter 5) is sensitive to the issues of "true" ownership of the moment: Is this moment equally learnable for the learner? An emergent-oriented curriculum (Chapter 6) is highly sensitive to learners' prolonged engagement with their emerging and evolving interests and inquiries. In order to capture and capitalize on learners' emerging and evolving interests and inquiries, thoughtful teachers' searching for teachable moments for further and higher levels of learnable moments within the learning context is one of the key elements in emergent-oriented curriculum practice. The negotiation-oriented curriculum (Chapter 7) is highly sensitive to power sharing between teacher and learners. More precisely, it entails ownership of learning—a democratic curriculum process operating from a continuous, shared power relationship among teachers, learners, parents, and political forces that shape formal curriculum. Here, learners and teachers initiate learning expectations within constraints and negotiate lessons and learning experiences. Teachers who strive to enhance their negotiation-oriented curriculum practice look for a teachable moment in which learners create, express, share, and teach their counternormative knowledge, and they capitalize on the moment for counternormative knowledge co-construction together with the learners. Thus, within negotiation-oriented curriculum practice teachable moments and learnable moments interlock. The three curricular practices are distinctively different from one another in classroom practice; however, they are interconnected through different intention of the teacher's capitalizing on their teachable moments (see Table 10.2).

One particular aspect that theoretically differentiates the three curricular practices is related to power issues. In teachable moment-oriented practice the teacher tends to be the ultimate power-holder because he or she has to make the decision about whether an incident constitutes a teachable moment or not. In emergent-oriented practice the teacher deliberately promotes the initiating power of the learner. Learners seem or tend to hold more power than the teachers in the learning process. In negotiation-oriented practice equal power-sharing between teacher and learners emerges in the process of negotiation and learning; furthermore, teachable moments always exist in the three forms of curriculum practice with a different teacher intention depending on the teacher's understanding of what curriculum *is* and *does* (see Table 10.3, and Figure 10.1).

## Table 10.2. Teachable Moments in the Three Different Curricular Practices

| Teachable Moment-Oriented Curriculum Practice | Negotiation-Oriented Curriculum Practice | Emergent-Oriented Curriculum Practice |
|---|---|---|
| The learner indicates a readiness or interest through his or her own play, action, or expression. The teacher, in turn, captures the moment, observes, recognizes, and interprets it by filtering the moment through his or her own personality, knowledge, and beliefs, then considers, creates, and presents some spontaneous purposeful learning experience accordingly. On a continuum, the teacher observes the child's response and interacts with or intervenes in the child's learning moment. | Teachers who strive to enhance their curriculum practice that is negotiation-oriented look for a teachable moment in which learners create, express, share, or teach their counternormative knowledge, and the teachers capitalize on the moment for counternormative knowledge coconstruction together with the learners. Thus, within negotiation-oriented curriculum practice teachable moments and learnable moments interlock. | In order to capture and capitalize on learners' emerging and evolving interests and inquiries, teachers search for teachable moments for further and higher levels of learnable moments within the learning context. Teacher's manifestations of teachable moments tend to be much more complex and multidimensional than any other linearly defined curriculum practice. (see more detail in Chapter 6) |

If a teacher believes that the purpose of curriculum is to present and reinforce the knowledge, skills, and dispositions that best represent the needs of the society; and to present and clarify the "dominant" core knowledge tentatively established by society (dominant culture's cultural knowledge and mandated standardized curriculum) as well as its values while simultaneously ignoring or minimizing the coexistence of other forms or sets of knowledge, then the teacher, either consciously or unconsciously muting other voices (views, knowledge), would prepare learners for what the dominant culture and society needs through his or her curriculum practice as manifested in teachable moments. Thus, instruction-oriented teaching and curriculum delivery would coincide with the teacher's teachable moment-oriented curriculum practice.

## Table 10.3. Power Issues in the Three Different Curricula Practices

| Teachable Moment-Oriented Curriculum Practice | Negotiation-Oriented Curriculum Practice | Emergent-Oriented Curriculum Practice |
|---|---|---|
| Teacher is the ultimate power-holder capturing and capitalizing on teachable moments. Teacher's sense-making of teachable moments may not be an equally learnable moment. The kind of moment the teacher captures and capitalizes on for intervention purposes or new emerging learning experiences depends upon the teacher's privilege. | Teacher is fully aware of his or her teaching and expectation toward learner performances within a political or system constraint. At the same time, the teacher acknowledges the learners' counternormative knowledge construction and constant meaning-making of their own meaningful learning derived from the knowledge teacher provided and their own personal experiences and interests. Thus, teacher deliberately strives for an equal power-sharing between the teacher and the learners in curriculum decision-making. Thus, curriculum becomes negotiated. Power-sharing emerges in the process of negotiation. | Teacher always deliberately intends to promote learner-initiated and learner-maintained power in curriculum decision-making of at least "what" to learn. Through negotiation, "why" to learn, "how" to learn, and "what" to learn emerges mainly led by the learner(s). As a result learners seem to hold more power than the teacher. |

If a teacher believes that curriculum provides an educational opportunity to address and extend the knowledge, skills, and dispositions inherent in each human being (each child) and to realize and illustrate how individuals can came together to promote the social well-being, the teacher's curriculum practice manifested in his or her teachable moments would enable learners to become all that they possibly can become (the traditional notion of child-centered) by capitalizing on individual learners' emergent interests leading to learning and growth. The teacher's curriculum belief and practice would be best supported if there were no or very limited expectations of standardized and mandated curriculum requirements from the society's formal educational system. Only then, the teacher's curriculum practice would be ultimately emergent-oriented based on the individual learner's emerging interests and voices.

**Figure 10.1. An Illustration of Power Issues and Teachable Moments in the Three Different Understandings of Curriculum**

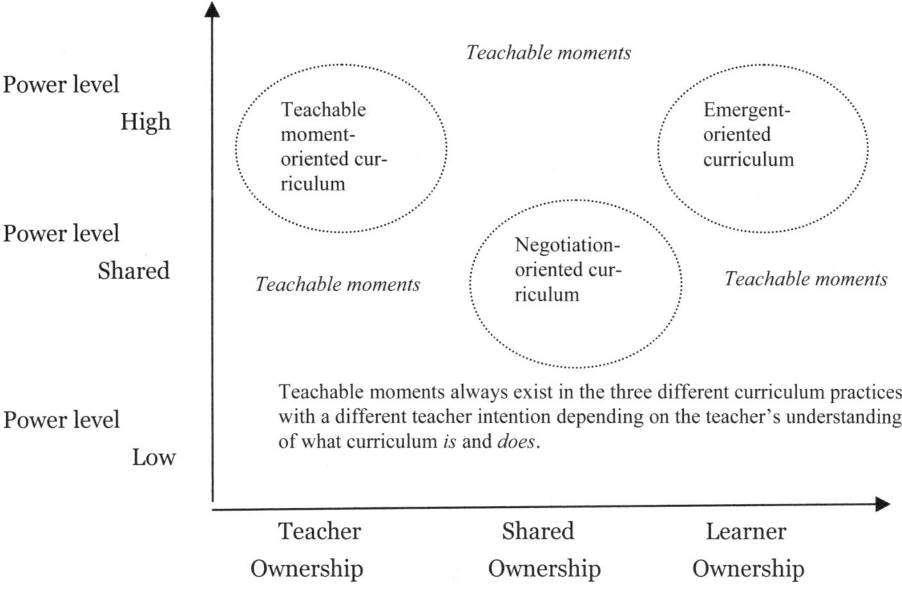


If a teacher believes that curriculum provides a systematic educational opportunity to learn, negotiate, and appreciate those with different ideas (both "dominant" core knowledge and co-existence of other forms/sets of knowledge) in order to succeed in society; to realize and illustrate the manner in which humankind collectively promotes social progress; and to expose and overlap the awareness and ability of each learner to question critically *what is* in light of *what might be* (to share counternormative knowledge), the teacher's curriculum practice manifested in his or her teachable moments would enable learners to thrive and contribute to a pluralistic society; to become leaders in tomorrow's world; to become the best (socially and individually responsible) citizens that they can become; and to prepare learners to shape and control their world. In this kind of curriculum belief (what curriculum *is*) and practice (what curriculum *does*), both the teacher and learners need to be familiar with inherent and pervasive negotiation-oriented classroom discourse that would bring a balanced support between learner-centered curriculum decision-making and standardized or mandated curriculum delivery. If the society has a strong curriculum movement that is standardized and mandated by political and economic forces, the notion of curriculum negotiation and negotiation-oriented curriculum practice should be an inevitable phenomenon. In that endeavor the teacher's reconceptualizing standard would occur, leading beyond the narrowly defined curriculum implementation (delivery and management) and moving toward curriculum leadership (empowerment, enactment, and shared ownership).

## Final Remarks

We cannot and should not depend on more than half-century-old developmental theories as we strive to provide developmentally meaningful and culturally congruent curriculum experiences for contemporary young children's meaningful learning, growth, and change. In order for teachers to go beyond developmentally and culturally mismatched curriculum practice and to engage in responsive and awakened educational practice, we as teachers need to critically and continuously engage in examining and understanding our own perspective of what curriculum *is* and *does* to and for diverse learners by becoming fluently accustomed to multiple perspective-takings and critical reflectivity.

A teachable moment-oriented curriculum (Chapter 5) is sensitive to the issues of "true" ownership of the moment: Is this moment equally learnable to the learner? An emergent-oriented curriculum (Chapter 6) is highly sensitive to learners' prolonged engagement with their emerging and evolving interests and inquiries. A negotiation-oriented curriculum (Chapter 7) is highly sensitive to power sharing between teacher and learners. Negotiation-oriented curriculum has to do with ownership of learning—a democratic curriculum process operating from a continuous, shared power relationship among teachers, learners, parents, and political forces that shape a formal curriculum. Here, learners and teachers initiate learning expectations within constraints (e.g., NCLBA, standardized content standards and assessment/testing) and negotiate lessons and learning experiences.

Within the formal educational environment, curriculum for developmentally meaningful and culturally congruent practice becomes a shared, organic, mutually created, and lived experience blending elements of teachable moments, emergent curriculum, and curriculum negotiation. As teachers are exposed to and become familiar with the notions of a teachable moment-oriented curriculum, emergent-oriented curriculum, and the negotiation-oriented curriculum, it is hoped that they will freely borrow from these three curricular traditions while attempting to become critical thinkers, ethical care givers, careful listeners, and active learners themselves; moreover, teachers, parents, and learners all share the power and responsibilities inherent in the process of making decisions for the lived curricula experiences it promises.

## Chapter Ending Question

- How would an informed educator practice toward democratically accountable and pedagogically sound curriculum leadership for young children?

# References

Apple, M. (1979). *Ideology and curriculum.* London: Routledge and Kagan Paul.

________ (1985). Teaching and women's work: A comparative historical and ideological analysis. *Teachers College Record, 86*(3), 455–473.

________ (1999). *Power, meaning, and identity: Essays in critical educational studies.* New York: Peter Lang.

Astington, J. W. (1998). Theory of mind goes to school. *Educational Leadership, 56* (3), 46–49.

Avruch, K. (2000, October). Culture and negotiation pedagogy. *Negotiation Journal,* 339–346.

Ayers, W. (1989). *The good preschool teacher: Six teachers reflect on their lives.* New York: Teachers College Press.

Baker, G. C. (1994). *Planning and organizing for multicultural instruction.* New York: Addison-Wesley.

Banks, J. (1994). *Multiethnic education: Theory and practice.* Boston: Allyn & Bacon.

Bassey, M. (2003). More advocacy: Give back autonomy to teachers. *Research Intelligence, 84,* 26–30.

Beans, J. A. (1997). *Curriculum integration: Designing the core of democratic education.* New York: Teachers College Press.

Beck, C., & Kosnik, C. (2001). Reflection-in-action: In defense of thoughtful teaching. *Curriculum Inquiry, 31*(2), 217–227.

Becker, W. C., Engelmann, S., Carnine, D. W., & Rhine, W. R. (1981). Direct instruction model. In W. R. Rhine (Ed.), *Making schools more effective: New directions from follow through* (pp. 95–154). New York: Academic Press.

Bennett, W. (1995). *Book of virtues: A collection of moral stories.* New York: Simon and Schuster.

________ (1997). *The James Madison elementary school: A curriculum for American students.* Washington, DC: U.S. Government Printing Office.

________ (1984). *To reclaim a legacy: A report on the humanities in higher education.* Washington, D.C.: National Endowment for the Humanities.

Bereiter, C., & Engelmann, S. (1966). *Teaching disadvantage children in the preschool.* Engelwood Cliffs, NJ: Prentice-Hall.

Berk, L. (2000). *Child Development.* Needham Heights, MA: Allyn and Bacon.

Best, F. (1988). The metamorphoses of the term pedagogy. *Prospects, 18*(2), 157–166.

Bhabha, H., & Parekh, B. (1989, June). Identities on parade: A conversation. *Marxism Today,* 3.

Biber, B. (1984). *Early education and psychological development.* New Haven, CT: Yale University Press.

Biber, B., Shapiro, E., & Wickens, D. (1977). *Promoting cognitive growth: A developmental interaction point of view* (2nd ed.). Washington, DC: National Association for the Education of Young Children.

Block, A. (2004). *Talmud, curriculum, and the practical: Joseph Schwab and the Rabbis.* New York: Peter Lang.

Bodrova, E., & Leong, D. (1996). *Tools of the mind: The Vygotskian approach to early childhood education.* Upper Saddle River, NJ: Prentice Hall.

Boomer, G., Lester, N., Onore, C., & Cook, J. (Eds.). (1992). *Negotiating the curriculum.* Bristol, PA: Falmer Press.

Booth, C. (1997). The fiber project: One teacher's adventure toward emergent curriculum. *Young Children, 52 (5),* 79–85.

Bowman, B. (1989). Self-reflection as an element of professionalism. *Teachers College Record, 90*, 444–451.

_______ (1992). Reaching potentials of minority children through developmentally and culturally appropriate program. In S. Bredekamp & T. Rosegrant (Eds.), *Reaching potentials: Appropriate curriculum and assessment for young children* (pp. 128–138). Washington, DC: National Association for the Education of Young Children (NAEYC).

_______ (1994). Thoughts on educating teachers. In S. G. Goffin & D. E. Day (Eds.), *New perspectives in early childhood teacher education: Bringing practitioners into the debate* (pp. 210–214). New York: Teachers College Press.

Bredekamp, S. (Ed.). (1987). *Developmentally appropriate practice in early childhood programs serving children from birth through age 8.* (rev. ed.). Washington, DC: NAEYC.

Bredekamp, S., & Copple, C. (Eds.). (1997). *Developmentally appropriate practice in early childhood* programs (rev. ed.). Washington, DC: NAEYC.

Bredekamp, S., & Rosegrant, T. (1992). *Reaching potentials: Appropriate curriculum and assessment for young children*, Vol. 1. Washington, DC: NAEYC.

_______ (1995). *Reaching potentials: Transforming early childhood curriculum and assessment*, Vol. 2. Washington, DC: NAEYC.

Britzman, D., & Pitt, A. (1996). Pedagogy and transference: Casting the past of learning into the presence of teaching. *Theory Into Practice, 35*(2), 117–123.

Brown, J., & Moffett, C. (1999). *The hero's journey: How educators can transform schools and improve learning*. Alexandria, VA: Association for Supervision and Curriculum Development.

Brown, R. C. (1998). The teacher as contemplative observer. *Educational Leadership, 56* (4), 70–73.

Bruce, J., & Weil, M. (1972). *Models of teaching*. Englewood Cliffs, NJ: Prentice Hall.

Bruchac, J, & Locker, T. (1996). *Between earth and sky*. San Diego, CA: Harcourt Brace and Company.

Burbules, N. (1986). A theory of power in education. *Educational Theory, 36*, 95–114.

Cannella, G. (1997). *Deconstructing early childhood education: Social justice and revolution*. New York: Peter Lang.

_______ (1998). Early childhood education: A call for the construction of revolutionary images. In W. Piner (Ed.), *Curriculum toward new identities* (pp. 157–184). New York: Garland.

Cannella, G., & Reiff, J. (1994). Preparing teachers for cultural diversity: Constructivist orientations. *Action in Teacher Education, 16*(3), 37–45.

Cannella, G., & Viruru, R. (1999). Generating possibilities for the construction of childhood studies. *Journal of Curriculum Theorizing, 15* (1), 13–22.

Cassidy, D., & Lancaster, C. (1993). The grassroots curriculum: A dialogue between children and teachers. *Young Children, 48* (6), 47–51.

Chard, S. C. (1992). *The project approach: A practical guide for teachers*. Edmonton, Alberta: University of Alberta Printing Services.

Cheney, L. (1989). *50 hours: A core curriculum for college students*. Washington, D.C.: National Endowment for the Humanities.

Cobb, S. (2000, October). Negotiation pedagogy: Learning to learn. *Negotiation Journal*, 315–319.

Coles, R. (1992). *Anna Freud: The dream of psychoanalysis.* Reading, MA: Addison-Wesley.

Coles, R., & Nixon, N. (1998). *School.* New York: Little, Brown and Company.

Constas, M. (1998). The changing nature of educational research and a critique of postmodernism. *Educational Researcher, 27*(2), 26–33.

Cook, J. (1992). Negotiating the curriculum: Programming for learning. In G. Boomer, N. Lester, C. Onore, & J. Cook (Eds.), *Negotiating the curriculum: Educating for the 21st century* (pp. 15–31). Bristol, PA: Falmer Press.

Cornett, C. E. (1999). *The arts as meaning makers: Integrating literature and the arts throughout the curriculum.* Upper Saddle River, NJ: Merrill.

Cothran, D. J., & Ennis, C. D. (1997). Students' and teachers' perceptions of conflict and power. *Teaching and Teacher Education. 13*(5), 541–553.

Davis, B. (2004). *Inventions of teaching: A genealogy.* Mahwah, NJ: Lawrence Erlbaum Associates.

Davis, B., & Sumara, D. (2004). Becoming more curious about learning. *Journal of Curriculum and Pedagogy, 1*(1), 26-30.

Delpit, L. D. (1988). The silenced dialogue: Power and pedagogy in educating other people's children. *Harvard Educational Review, 58*(3), 280–287.

________ (1995). *Other people's children: Cultural conflict in the classroom.* New York: The New.

Derman-Sparks, L. (1992). Reaching potentials through antibias multicultural curriculum. In S. Bredekamp, & T. Rosegrant (Eds.), *Reaching potentials: Appropriate curriculum and assessment for young children* (pp. 114–127). Washington, DC: NAEYC.

Derman-Sparks, L., & the A.B.C. Task Force. (1989). *Anti-bias curriculum: Tools for empowering young children.* Washington, DC: NAEYC.

Dewey, J. (1879). My pedagogic creed. *The School Journal, 54*(3), 77–80.

________ (1902). *The child and the curriculum.* Chicago: University of Chicago Press.

________(1938a). *Experience and education.* New York: Collier/ Macmillan.

________ (1938b). *Logic, the theory of inquiry.* New York: Henry Holt.

Diamond, M., & Hopson, J. (1998). *Magic trees of the mind: How to nurture your child's intelligence, creativity, and healthy emotions from birth through adolescence.* New York: Penguin Putnam.

Dodge, D. T. (1988). *A guide for supervisors and trainers on implementing the creative curriculum for early childhood.* (2nd ed.). Washington, DC: Teaching Strategies, Inc.

Dodge, D. T., & Colker, L. J. (1990). *The creative curriculum for family child care.* Washington, DC: Teaching Strategies, Inc.

________ (1992). *The creative curriculum for early childhood* (3rd ed.). Washington, DC: Teaching Strategies, Inc.

Dodge, D. T., & Phinney, J. (1990). *A parent's guide to early childhood education.* Washington, DC: Teaching Strategies, Inc.

Driver, R., Asoko, H., Leach, J., Mortimer, E., & Scott, P. (1994). Constructing scientific knowledge in the classroom. *Educational Researcher, 23* (5), 5–12.

Edwards, C., Gandini, L., & Forman, G. (1993). *The hundred languages of children: The Reggio Emilia approach to early childhood education.* Norwood, NJ: Ablex.

Eeds, M., and Wells, D. (1989) Grand conversations: An exploration of meaning construction in literature study groups. *Research in the Teaching of English, 23*, 4–29.

Eisner, E. (1994). *The educational imagination: On the design and evaluation of school programs* (3rd ed). Upper Saddle River, NJ: Merrill Prentice Hall.

Ennis, C. D. (1995). Teachers' responses to noncompliant students: The realities and consequences of negotiated curriculum. *Teaching and Teacher Education, 11*(5), 445–460.

Epstein, A., Schweinhart, L., & McAdoo, L. (1996). *Models of early childhood education*. Ypsilanti, MI: High/Scope Press.

Fisher, E. (1993). Distinctive features of pupil-pupil classroom talk and their relationship to learning: How discursive exploration might be encouraged. *Language and Education, 7* (4), 239–257.

Foucault, M. (1997). Power, right, truth. In R. Goodin & P. Pettit (Eds.), *Contemporary political philosophy: An anthology* (pp. 543–550). Cambridge, MA: Blackwell.

Freeman, E. (1994). Families: Teachable moments in school-community practice. *Social Work in Education, 16*(3), 139–142.

Freire, P. (1971). *Pedagogy of the oppressed. (M.B. Ramos Trans.).* New York: Seaview.

Gardner, H. (1983). *Frames of mind: The theory of multiple intelligences*. New York: Basic Books.

________ (1989). Preface. In M. Reynolds (Ed.), *Knowledge base for the beginning teacher* (pp. ix–xii). New York: Pergamon.

________ (1999). Are there additional intelligences? In J. Kane (Ed.), *Education, information, and transformation* (pp. 111–131). Engelwood Cliffs, NJ: Prentice Hall.

________ (2000). *The disciplined mind: Beyond facts and standardized tests, the K-12 education that every child deserves*. New York: Penguin Books.

Gesell, A. (1940). *The first five years of life: A guide to the study of the preschool years*. New York: Harper & Row.

Gesell, A., & Ilg, F. L. (1940). *The child from five to ten*. New York: Harper & Row.

Giroux, H. A. (1988). *Schooling and the struggle for public life: Critical pedagogy in the modern age*. Minneapolis: University of Minnesota Press.

________ (1992). *Border crossings: Cultural workers and the politics of education.* New York: Routledge.

________ (1997). *Pedagogy and the politics of hope: Theory, culture, and schooling.* Boulder, CO: Westview.

Giroux, H. A., & Simon, R. (1989). Schooling, popular culture, and a pedagogy of possibility. *Journal of Education, 170*(1), 9–26.

Glasersfeld, E. (1984). An introduction to radical constructivism. In Paul Watzlawick (Ed.), *The invented reality: How do we know what we believe we know?* (pp. 17–40). New York: Norton.

Goldstein, L. (1997). *Teaching with love: A feminist approach to early childhood education*. New York: Peter Lang.

Gollnick, D. & Chinn, P. (1998). *Multicultural education in a pluralistic society* (5th ed.). Upper Saddle River, NJ: Merrill/Prantice Hall.

Goodlad, J. (1966). *The development of a conceptual system for dealing with problems of curriculum and instruction.* Washington, DC: Cooperative Research Program, US. Office of Education. ERIC ED 010064.

Gordon. W. (1972). On being explicit about the creative process. *Journal of Creative Behavior, 6,* 295–300.

Grant, C. A. (1981). Education that is multicultural and teacher preparation: An examination from the perspectives of preservice students. *Journal of Education Research, 75* (2), 95–101.

________ (1992). (Ed.). *Research and multicultural education: From the margins to the mainstream.* Bristol, PA: Falmer.

Grant, C. A., & Zeichner, K. M. (1984). On becoming a reflective teacher. In C. A. Grant (Ed.), *Preparing for reflective teaching* (pp. 1–18). Boston: Allyn and Bacon.

Greene, M. (1975). Curriculum and consciousness. In W. Pinar (Ed.), *Curriculum theorizing: The reconceptualist.* Berkeley, CA: McCutchan Publishing.

________ (1978). *Landscapes of learning.* New York: Teachers College Press.

________ (1995). *Releasing the imagination: Essays on education, the arts, and social change.* New York: Teachers College Press.

Greenfield, P. M., & Cocking, R. (Eds.). (1994). *Cross-cultural roots of minority child development.* Hillsdale, NJ: Lawrence Erlbaum.

Held, D. (1980). *Introduction to critical theory: Horkheimer to Habermas.* Berkeley, CA: University of California Press.

Helm, J. H., & Katz, L. (2001). *Young investigators: The project approach in the early years.* New York: Teachers College.

Henderson, J. (2005). Conversation with JCP editors. Paper presented at the 4th Annual meeting of the American Association for the Advancement of Curriculum Studies (AAACS), Montreal, Canada.

Henderson, J. & Hawthorne, R. (2000). Transformative curriculum leadership. Upper Saddle River, NJ: Merrill/Prentice Hall.

Hendrick, J. (1997). (Ed.). *First steps toward teaching the Reggio way.* Upper Saddle River, NJ: Merrill/Prentice Hall.

Hirsch, E. D., Jr. (1987). *Cultural literacy.* Boston, MA: Houghton Mifflin.

Hohmann, M., Banet, B., & Weikart, D.P. (1979). *Young children in action: A manual for preschool educators.* Ypsilanti, MI: High/Scope Press.

Hohmann, M., & Weikart, D. P. (1995). *Educating young children: Active learning practices for preschool and child care programs.* Ypsilanti, MI: High/Scope Press.

Hyson, M. (2003). (Ed.). *Preparing early childhood professionals: NAEYC's standards for programs.* Washington, DC: NAEYC.

Hyun, E. (1996). New directions in early childhood teacher preparation: Developmentally and culturally appropriate practice (DCAP). *Journal of Early Childhood Teacher Education, 17* (3), 7–19.

________ (1998). *Making sense of developmentally and culturally appropriate practice (DCAP) in early childhood education.* New York: Peter Lang.

________ (2003). The No Child Left Behind Act of 2001: Issues and implications for early childhood teacher education. *Journal of Early Childhood Teacher Education, 24*(2), 119–126.

_______ (2004). *Transforming instruction into pedagogy through negotiation-oriented curriculum practice.* Paper presented at the Curriculum and Pedagogy Conference, Oxford, Ohio.

_______ (2005a). How is young children's intellectual culture of perceiving nature different from adults? *Environmental Education Research, 11* (2), 199–214.

_______ (2005b). A study of 5- to 6-year old children's peer dynamics and dialectical learning in a computer-based technology-rich environment. *Computers & Education, 44*(1), 69-91.

_______ (2006). *Critical perspectives on instruction vs. pedagogy in curriculum studies.* Paper presented at the 2006 AERA Annual Conference. San Francisco, CA.

_______ (in press). Transforming instruction into pedagogy in curriculum negotiation. *Journal of Curriculum and Pedagogy, 3* (1).

Hyun, E., & Davis, G. (2005). Kindergartners' Conversations in a Computer-Based Technology Classroom. *Communication Education, 54*(2), 118–135.

Hyun, E., DiPento, S., Duarte, G., Matthews, C., Morales, R. & Smrekar. J. (2000). DCAP-Based Early Childhood Teacher Preparation Movement Through DCAP Research Net Activity. *Journal of Early Childhood Teacher Education, 21*(2), 215–226.

Hyun, E., & Marshall, J. D. (1996). Inquiry-oriented reflective supervision for developmentally and culturally appropriate practice. *Journal of Curriculum and Supervision, 11* (2), 127–144.

_______ (1997). Theory of multiple/multiethnic perspective-taking ability for teachers' developmentally and culturally appropriate practice (DCAP). *Journal of Research in Childhood Education, 11*(2), 188–198.

_______ (2003a). Teachable moment-oriented curriculum practice in early childhood education (ECE). *Journal of Curriculum Studies, 35*(1), 111–127.

_______ (2003b). Critical inquiry into emergentoriented curriculum practice. *Journal of Early Childhood Teacher Education, 24*(1), 37–59.

Hyun, E., & Marshall, J. D., & Dana, N. F. (1995, June). New direction in early childhood teacher preparation for DCAP. Paper presented at the annual meeting of the National Association of Early Childhood Teacher Educator. Washington, DC.

Jipson, J. (1991). Developmentally appropriate practice: Culture, curriculum, connections. *Early Education and Development, 2*(2), 120–136.

Johnson, M. (1967). Definitions and models in curriculum theory. *Educational Theory, 17,* 127–140.

_______ (1977). *Intentionality in education.* Albany, NY: Center for Curriculum Research and Services.

Jones, E., Evans, K., Rencken, S., Stringer, C., & Williams, M. (2001). *The lively kindergarten: Emergent curriculum in action.* Washington, DC: NAEYC.

Jones, E., & Nimmo, J. (1994). *Emergent curriculum.* Washington, DC: NAEYC.

Kamii, C., & DeVries, R. (1977). Piaget for early education. In M. C. Day & R. K. Parker (Eds.), T*he preschool in action: Exploring early childhood programs* (2nd ed., pp. 365–420). Boston: Allyn & Bacon.

_______ (1978/1993). *Physical knowledge in preschool education: Implications of Piaget's theory.* New York: Teachers College Press. (Original work published by Prentice-Hall 1978).

_______ (1980). *Group games in early education: Implications of Piaget's theory.* Washington, DC: National Association for the Education of Young Children.

Kandel, E., & Hawkins, R. (1992). The biological basis of learning and individuality. *Scientific American. 267*(3), 78–86. EJ 458266.

Karp, S. (2002). Let them eat tests. *Rethinking Schools, 16*(4), 3–4.

Katz, L. (1990). Impressions of Reggio Emilia preschools. *Young Children, 47*(1), 11–12.

_______ (1994a). *The project approach.* ERIC Digest. EDO-PS-94–6. Urbana, IL: ERIC Clearinghouse on Elementary and Early Childhood Education.

_______ (1994b). Knowledge of child development and the competence of developing teachers. In S. Goffin, & D. Day (Eds.), *New perspectives in early childhood teacher education: Bringing practitioners into the debate* (pp. 124–128). New York: Teachers College Press.

Katz, L., & Chard, S. (1989). *Engaging children's minds: The project approach.* New York: Ablex.

_______ (1993). The project approach. In J.L. Roopnarine & J. E. Johnson (Eds.), *Approaches to early childhood education* (2nd ed., pp. 209–222). New York: Macmillan.

_______ (2000). *Engaging children's minds: The project approach* (2nd ed.). Stamford, CT: Ablex.

Kellogg, R. (1969). *Analyzing children's art.* Palo Alto, CA: Mayfield Publishing.

Kessler, S., & Swaddener, B. (Eds.). (1992). *Reconceptualizing the early childhood curriculum: Beginning the dialogue.* New York: Teachers College Press.

Kincheloe, J. (1993). *Toward a critical politics of teacher thinking: Mapping the postmodern.* Westport, CT: Bergin & Garvey.

Kincheloe, J., Slattery, P., & Steinberg, S. (2000). *Contextualizing teaching.* New York: Longman.

Kliebard, H. M. (1995). *The struggle for the American curriculum* (2nd ed.). New York: Routledge.

Kneller, G. (1984). *Movements of thought in modern education* (2nd ed.). New York: John Wiley and Sons.

Kolb, D. (2000). More than just a footnote: Constructing a theoretical framework for teaching about gender in negotiation. *Negotiation Journal, 16(3),* 347–356.

Kumabe, K. T., Nishida, C., & Hepworth, D.H. (1985). *Bridging ethnocultural diversity in social work and health.* Honolulu: University of Hawaii, School of Social Work.

Ladson-Billings, G. (1992). Culturally relevant teaching: The key to making multicultural education work. In C. Grant (Ed.), *Research and multicultural education: From the margins to the mainstream* (pp. 106–121). Bristol, PA: Falmer.

_______ (1994). Who will teach our children? Preparing teachers to successfully teach African American students. In E. Hollins, J. King, & W. Hayman (Eds.), *Teaching diverse populations: Formulating a knowledge base* (pp. 231–245). New York: SUNY Press.

Lasley, T. (1992). Promoting teacher reflection. *Journal of staff Development, (13),* 1, 24–29.

Lather, P. (1986). Research as praxis. *Harvard Educational Review, 56,* 257–277.

_______ (1991). *Getting smart: Feminist research and pedagogy with/in the postmodern.* New York: Routledge

Lester, N. (1992). All reforms are not created equal: Cooperative learning is not negotiating the curriculum. In G. Boomer, N. Lester, C. Onore, & J. Cook (Eds.), *Negotiating the curriculum: Educating for the 21st century* (pp. 198-215). Bristol, PA: The Falmer Press.

Lester, N., & Boomer, G. (1992). Negotiating the curriculum: Archeologists in search of meaning. In G. Boomer, N. Lester, C. Onore, & J. Cook (Eds.), *Negotiating the curriculum: Educating for the 21st century* (pp. 266–275). Bristol, PA: Falmer Press.

Lincoln, Y. (1998). The ethics of teaching in qualitative research. *Qualitative Inquiry, 4* (3), 315–328.

Lindauer, S. L. K. (1987). Montessori education for young children In J. L. Roopnarine, & J. E. Johnson (Eds.), *Approaches to early childhood education* (pp. 109–126). Columbus, OH: Merrill.

_______ (1993). Montessori education for young children. In J.L. Roopnarine & J.E. Johnson (Eds.), *Approaches to early childhood education* (2nd ed., pp. 243–259). New York: Macmillan.

Loewenstein, J., & Thompson, L. (2000, October). The challenge of learning. *Negotiation Journal*, 399–408.

Lowenfeld, V., & Brittain, W. L. (1987). *Creative and mental growth*. New York: Macmillan.

Lubeck, S. (1996). Deconstructing "child development knowledge" and teacher preparation. *Early Childhood Research Quarterly, 11* (2), 147–167.

Malaguzzi, L. (1993). History, Ideas, and Basic Philosophy. In C. Edwards, L. Gandini, and G. Forman (Eds.), *The hundred languages of children: The Reggio Emilia Approach to early childhood education*. Norwood, NJ: Ablex. ED355034.

Mallory, B., & New, R. (Eds.). (1994). *Diversity and developmentally appropriate practices: Challenges for early childhood education*. New York: Teachers College Press.

Marshall, J. D., & Sears, J. (1990). *Teaching and thinking about curriculum*. New York: Teachers College Press.

Marshall, J. D., Sears, J., & Schubert, W. (2000). *Turning points in curriculum: A contemporary American memoir*. Upper Saddle River, NJ: Merrill.

Martin, A. (1994). Deepening teacher competence through skills of observation. In S. Goffin & D. Day (Eds.), *New perspectives in early childhood teacher education: Bringing practitioners into the debate* (pp. 95–197). New York: Teachers College Press.

McAdoo, H. P. (Ed.). (1993). *Family ethnicity: Strength in diversity*. Newbury Park, CA: SAGE.

McClintock, R. (1971). Toward a place for study in a world of instruction. *Teachers College Record, 73* (2), 161–205.

McLaren, P. (1989). *Life in schools*. New York: Longman.

Mercer, N., & Fisher, E. (1993). How do teachers help children to talk? An analysis of teachers' interventions in computer-based activities. *Learning and Instruction, 2*, 339–355.

Mitchell, L.S. (1950). *Our children and our schools*. New York: Simon and Schuster.

Montessori, M. (1964). *The Montessori method*. New York: Schocken.

_______ (1973). *From childhood to adolescence*. New York: Schocken.

Morrison, J. (2000). *Fundamentals of early childhood education.* Upper Saddle River, NJ: Merrill.

Moshman, D. (1982). Exogenous, endogenous, and dialectical constructivism. *Developmental Review, 2*, 371–384.

National Association for the Education of Young Children. (1997). *Guidelines for preparation of early childhood professionals.* Washington, DC: Author.

National Council for Accreditation of Teacher Education. (1979). *Approved curriculum guidelines.* Washington, DC: Author.

________ (2002). *Professional standards for the accreditation of schools, colleges, and departments of educations.* Washington, DC: Author.

New, R. (1993). *Reggio Emilia: Some lessons for U.S. educators.* ERIC, EDO-PS-93–3.

Nieto, S. (1992). *Affirming diversity: The sociopolitical context of multicultural education.* White Plains, NY: Longman.

No Child Left Behind Act. (2001). U.S. Department of Education. Washington DC: The Author.

Noddings, N. (1992). *The challenge to care: An alternative approach to education.* New York: Teachers College Press.

________ (1995a). *Philosophy of education.* Boulder: Westview.

________ (1995b, May). Teaching themes of care. *Phi Delta Kappan, 76*(9), 675–679.

________ (1995c, January). A morally defensible mission for schools in the 21st century. *Phi Delta Kappan, 76*(5), 365–368.

O'Loughlin, M. (1992). Engaging teachers in emancipatory knowledge construction. *Journal of Teacher Education, 43*(5), 336-347.

Onore, C., & Lubetsky, B. (1992). Why we learn is what and how we learn: Curriculum as possibility. In G. Boomer, N. Lester, C. Onore, & J. Cook (Eds.), *Negotiating the curriculum: Educating for the 21st century* (pp. 253–265). Bristol, PA: Falmer Press.

Pagliaro, M. (1991) Using crises for cognitive development: A case study. *Education, 111* (3), 339--346.

Pearce, J. C. (1977). *Magical child: Rediscovering nature's plan for our children.* New York: E. P. Dutton.

Peters, T., & Schubeck, K. (1995). The thematic approach. *Phi Delta Kappan, 76* (8), 633–667.

Peterson, B. (2002). Write the truth. *Rethinking Schools, 16* (4), 10–12.

Piaget, J. (1952). *The origins of intelligence.* New York: International Universities Press.

Pinar, W. (Ed.). (1988). *Contemporary curriculum discourses.* Scottsdale, AZ: Gorsuch Scarisbrick.

________ (2004a). Curriculum and study. *Journal of Curriculum and Pedagogy, 1*(1), 21–23.

________ (2004b, October). *Curriculum and Study: Not curriculum and pedagogy.* Paper presented at the Curriculum and Pedagogy Conference. Oxford, OH.

Pinar, W., & Grumet, M. (1976). *Toward a poor curriculum.* Dubuque, IA: Kendall/Hunt.

Pinar, W., Reynolds, W., Slattery, P., & Taubman, P. (1995). *Understanding curriculum: An introduction to the study of historical and contemporary curriculum discourses.* New York: Peter Lang.

Posner, G. (1995). *Analyzing the curriculum* (2nd ed.). New York: McGraw-Hill.

Pourdavood, R., and Fleener, J. (1997) Impact of a dialogic community on the development of classroom sociocultural norms. *Journal for Just & Caring Education, 3*(4), 399—418.

Quintana, S. (1994). A model of ethnic perspective-taking ability applied to Mexican-American children and youth. *Journal of Intercultural Relations, 1*(18), 419–448.

Ramsey, P. (1987). *Teaching and learning in a diverse world: Multicultural education for young children.* New York: Teachers College Press.

Reagan, T. (1993). Educating the reflective practitioner: The contribution of philosophy of education, *Journal of Research and Development in Education, 26* (4), 189–196.

Rose, M. (1989). *Lives on the boundary.* New York: Penguin.

Rousseau, J. (1933, 1979). *Emile* (A. Bloom, Trans.). New York: Basic.

Schiller, M. (1995, May). Reggio Emilia: A focus on emergent curriculum and art. *Art Education*, 48, 45–50.

Schnur-Laughlin, J. (1999), Pantry math. *Teaching Children Mathematics, 6*(4), 216—219.

Schön, D. (1983). *The reflective practitioner: How professionals think in action.* New York: Basic Books.

Schubert, W. (2004). Curriculum and pedagogy for reconstruction and reconceptualization. *Journal of Curriculum and Pedagogy, 1*(1), 19–21.

Schutz, A. (1970). *On phenomenology of the social relations.* Chicago, IL: University of Chicago Press.

Sedlak, M. W., Wheeler, C. W., Pullin, D. C., & Cusick, P. A. (1986). *Selling students short.* New York: Teachers College Press.

Seefeldt, C. (Ed.). (1999). *The early childhood curriculum: Current findings in theory and practice.* New York: Teachers College Press.

Selman, R., & Schultz, L. H. (1990). *Making a friend in youth: Developmental theory and their pair therapy.* Chicago, IL: Chicago Press.

Sheerer, M., Dettore, E., & Cyphers, J. (1996). Off with a theme: Emergent curriculum in action. *Early Childhood Education Journal, 24*(2), 99–102.

Shepard, L., & Smith, M. (1989). *Escalating kindergarten curriculum.* Urbana, IL: ERIC Clearnighouse on Elementary and Early Childhood Education.

Shor, I. (1996). *When students have power: Negotiating authority in a critical pedagogy.* Chicago, IL: University of Chicago Press.

Shore, B. (1996). *Culture in mind: Cognition, culture, and the problem of meaning.* New York: Oxford University Press.

Shore, R. (1997). *Rethinking the brain: New insights into early development.* New York: Families and Work Institute.

Shulman, L. (1987).Knowledge and teaching: Foundation of the new reform, *Harvard Educational Review, 57* (1), 1–22.

Silin, J. G. (1995). *Sex, death, and the education of children: Our passion for ignorance in the age of AIDS.* New York: Teachers College Press.

Sipe, L. (2000). The construction of literacy understanding by first and second graders in oral responses to picture storybook read-alouds. *Reading Research Quarterly, 35* (2), 252—276.

Slattery, P. (1995). *Curriculum development in the postmodern era*. New York: Garland.

Sleeter, C. (1991). *Empowerment through multicultural education*. New York: SUNY Press.

Sleeter, C., & Grant, C. (1994). *Making choice for multicultural education: Five approaches to race, class, gender* (2nd ed.). New York: Macmillan.

________ (1999). *Making choices for multicultural education: Five approaches to race, class, and gender* (3rd ed.). Upper Saddle River, NJ: Merrill/Prantice Hall.

Smith, J. (1983). Quantitative versus qualitative research: An attempt to clarify the issue. *Educational Researcher, 12*, 6–13.

Sowell, E. (2005). *Curriculum: An integrative instruction*. Upper Saddle River, NJ: Merrill Prentice Hall.

Sparks-Langer, G., & Colton, A. (1991). Synthesis of research on teachers' reflective thinking. *Educational Leadership, 48* (6), 37–44.

Spodek, B., & Brown, P. (1993). Curriculum alternatives in early childhood education: A historical perspective. In B. Spodek (Ed.), *Handbook of research on the education of young children* (pp. 91–104). New York: Macmillan.

Stark, J. S., & Lattuca, L. R. (1997). *Shaping the college curriculum: Academic plans in action*. Needham Heights, MA: Allyn & Bacon.

Stewart, E., & Bennett, M. (1991). *American cultural patterns: A cross-cultural perspective*. Yarmouth, ME: Intercultural.

Swadener, B. B., & Miller-Marsh, M. (1993). *Antibias early childhood education: Toward a stronger teacher voice in research*. Eric Document Reproduction Series No. 362290.

Takanishi, R. (1987). Childhood as a social issue: Historical roots of contemporary child advocacy movements. *Journal of Social Issues, 34*(2), 8–28.

Taylor, C. (1971). Interpretation and the sciences of man. *Review of Metaphysics, 25*, 3–51.

Tinworth, S. (1997). Whose good idea was it?: Child initiated curriculum. *Australian Journal of Early Childhood, 22*(3), 24–29.

Tyler, R. (1949). *Basic principles of curriculum and instruction*. Chicago, IL: University of Chicago Press.

U.K. National Curriculum. (1988). *Education Reform Act 1988*. http://www.opsi.gov.uk /acts/acts1988/Ukpga_19880040_en_1.htm, last visit made on January 16, 2006.

van Manen, M. (1977). Linking ways of knowing with ways of being practical. *Curriculum Inquiry*. *12*(6), 1–12.

________ (1991). *The tact of teaching*. London, ON: Althous Press.

________ (1996). Phenomenological pedagogy and the question of meaning. In D. Vandenberg (Ed.), *Phenomenology and educational discourse* (pp. 39–64). Durban: Heinemann Higher and Further Education.

Vygotsky, L. S. (1978). *Mind and society: The development of higher mental processes*. Cambridge, MA: Harvard University Press. (Original work published in 1930).

Wegerif, R., & Mercer, N. (1996). Computer and reasoning through talk in the classroom. *Language and Education, 10* (1), 47–64.

Weikart, D. P., & Schweinhart, L. J. (1987). The high/scope cognitively oriented curriculum in early education. In J. L. Roopnarine & J. E. Johnson (Eds.), *Approaches to early childhood Education* (pp. 253–268). Columbus, OH: Merrill.

________ (1993). The High/scope curriculum for early childhood care and education. In J. L. Roopnarine & J. E. Johnson (Eds.), *Approaches to early childhood education* (2nd ed., pp 195–208). New York: Macmillan.

Windschitl, M (2002). Framing constructivism in practice as the negotiation of dilemmas: An analysis of the conceptual, pedagogical, cultural, and political challenges facing teachers. *Review of Educational Research, 72*(2), 131–175.

Wolfe, P., & Brandt, R. (1998). What do we know from brain research? *Educational Leadership, 56*(3), 8–13.

Woodhead, M. (1990). Psychology and the cultural construction of children's needs. In A. James and A. Prout (Eds.), *Constructing and reconstructing childhood* (pp. 60–78). New York: Falmer Press.

Wortham, S. C. (1998). *Early Childhood Curriculum: Developmental bases for learning and teaching* (2nd ed.). Upper Saddle River, NJ: Merrill/Prentice Hall.

York, S. (1991). *Roots and wings: Affirming culture in early childhood programs*. St. Paul, MN: Readleaf.

Zeichner, K. (1981–1982). Reflective teaching and field-based experience in teacher education. *Interchange, 12*, 1–22.

________ (1993). Connecting genuine teacher development to the struggle for social justice. *Journal of Education for Teaching, 19*(10), 5–16.

Zeichner, K., & Grant, C. (1998). A research informed vision of good practice in multicultural teacher education: Design principles. *Theory into Practice, 37*(2), 163–172.

Zeichner, K., & Liston, D. (1987). Teaching student teachers to reflect. *Harvard Educational Review, 57*(10), 23–48.

Zimiles, H. (1987). The Bank Street Approach. In J. L. Roopnarine & J. E. Johnson (Eds.), *Approaches to early childhood education* (pp. 164–178). Columbus, OH: Merrill.

________ (1993). The Bank Street Approach. In J. L. Roopnarine & J.E. Johnson (Eds.), *Approaches* to early childhood education (2nd ed., pp. 261–273). New York: Macmillan.

# Author Index

**A**
Apple, M. 25, 82
Asoko, H. 150
Avruch, K. 116, 127, 130
Ayers, W. 71

**B**
Baker, G. C. xvi, 12
Banet, B. 47
Banks, J. xvi, 3, 12
Bassey, M. xxiii, 167
Beans, J. 89
Beck, C. 116
Becker, W. 37, 44
Bennett, M. 12
Bennett, W. 24
Bereiter, C. 37, 44
Berk. L. 38
Best, F. 17
Bhabha, H. 5
Biber, B. 45
Block, A. 30
Bodrova, E. 41, 150
Boomer, G. 115, 116, 117, 124, 131, 132
Booth, C. 90, 98
Bowman, B. xv, xvii, xviii, 5, 14, 159
Brandt, R. 11
Bredekamp, S. xv, 5, 33, 34, 48, 90
Brittain, W. 95
Britzman, D. xvi, 86
Brown, J. 58
Brown, P. xv
Brown, R. xvi
Bruce, J. 17
Bruchac, J. 7, 118
Burbules. N. 129

**C**
Cannella, G. xv, xvi, xvii, xviii, 5, 33, 34, 52, 64, 81, 129, 152
Carnine, D. 37, 44
Cassidy, D. 89
Chard, S. 48, 89, 99, 108
Cheney, L. 24
Chinn, P. 3, 4,
Cobb, S. 116
Cocking, R. xix
Coles, R. xxi, 86, 104
Colker, L. 47
Colton, A. 157
Constas, M. xviii, 61
Cook, J. 115, 117, 124, 129
Copple, C. xv, 5, 33, 48, 89
Cornett, C. 95
Cothran, D. 129
Cyphers, J. 89

**D**
Dana, N. xvi
Davis, B. 21, 22, 119
Davis, G. 140
Delpit, L. xv, xix, 5, 12, 57, 64
Derman-Sparks, L. xv, 5
Dettore, E. 89
DeVries, R. 47
Dewey, J. 18, 19, 24, 28, 42, 62, 70, 86, 87, 128, 137
Diamond, M. 11
DiPento, S. 71
Dodge, D. 47
Driver, R. 150
Duarte, G. 71

**E**
Edwards, C. 49, 89, 102
Eeds, M. 70
Eisner, E. 18, 20, 28, 30, 82, 124
Engelmann, S. 37, 44
Ennis, C. 117, 129
Epstein, A. 33, 34, 49,
Evans, K. 89

**F**
Fisher, E. 140, 149
Fleener, J. 70
Forman, G. 49, 89, 102
Foucault, M. 125
Freeman, E. 70
Freire, P. 18, 21, 29

**G**
Gandini, L. 49, 89, 102
Gardner, H. 5, 11, 50
Gesell, A. 38, 42, 47, 70, 80, 95
Giroux, H. 3, 4, 5, 12, 13, 18, 21, 22, 25, 28, 29, 30, 61, 62

Glasersfeld, E. 141
Gollnick, D. 3, 4
Goodlad, J. 24, 62
Gordon. W. 21, 22
Grant, C. xvi, 3, 4, 12, 22, 159
Greene, M. 24, 60, 123
Greenfield, P. xix
Grumet, M. 19, 20, 24, 59, 62, 141

**H**
Hawkins, R. 48
Hawthorne, R. 25
Held, D. 28
Helm, J. 89
Henderson, J. 25, 30, 120
Hendrick, J. 49
Hepworth, D. 12
Hirsch, E. D., Jr. 24, 62
Hohmann, M. 33, 47
Hopson, J. 11
Hyson, M. xv
Hyun, E. xv, xvi, xvii, xviii, xix, xxi, xxii, xiii, 5, 12, 17, 22, 24, 28, 29, 50, 64, 70, 71, 85, 92, 104, 159, 109, 112, 116, 117, 130, 140, 151, 152, 161, 167

**I**
Ilg, F. 38

**J**
Jipson, J. xv, 5
Johnson, M. 24, 62
Jones, E. 89

**K**
Kamii, C. 47
Kandel, E. 48
Karp, S. 112
Katz, L. 48, 89, 99, 108
Kellogg, R. 95
Kessler, S. 36
Kincheloe, J. xvi, 12, 24, 25, 28, 61, 122
Kliebard, H. 4
Kneller, G. 28
Kolb. D. 116
Kosnik, C. 116
Kumabe, K. 12

**L**
Ladson-Billings, G. 3, 5
Lancaster, C. 89
Lasley, T. 159
Lather, P. xviii, 12, 13, 61
Lattuca, L. 24
Leach, J. 150
Leong, D. 40, 147
Lester, N. 115, 116, 117, 129, 132
Lincoln, Y. 70
Lindauer, S. 45
Liston, D. 3
Locker, T. 7, 118
Loewenstein, J. 116
Lowenfeld, V. 95
Lubeck, S. xviii, 39
Lubetsky, B. 126, 128

**M**
Malaguzzi, L. 89
Mallory, B. xv, xviii, 5
Marshall, J. xvi, xix, xxi, xxii, 12, 29, 34, 62, 70, 92, 104, 109, 116, 130, 151, 152, 159, 161
Martin, A. 33
Matthews, C. 71
McAdoo, H. 12, 51
McAdoo, L. 33, 34
McClintock, R. 29
McLaren, P. 164
Mercer, N. 140, 150
Miller-Marsh, M. xv, 5
Mitchell, L. 45
Montessori, M. 42, 45
Morales, R. 71
Morrison, J. 36
Mortimer, E. 147
Moshman, D. 136

**N**
NAEYC. xv
NCATE. xv, 3
New, R. xv, xviii, 5, 49, 89
Nieto, S. xvi, 12, 13, 22, 164
Nimmo, J. 89
Nishida, C. 12
Nixon, N. xxi, 104
Noddings, N. 24

**O**
O'Loughlin, M. 13
Onore, C. 115, 117, 126, 128, 129

**P**
Pagliaro, M. 70
Parekh, B. 5
Pearce, J. 11
Pestalozzi, J. 42, 69
Peters, T. 89
Peterson, B. xxi, 104
Phinney, J. 47
Piaget, J. 39, 40, 42
Pinar, W. 20, 24, 29, 30, 31, 34, 59, 60, 62, 119, 121, 141
Pitt, A. xvi, 86
Posner, G. 24, 25
Pourdavood, R. 70
Pullin, D. 129

**Q**
Quintana, S. 152

**R**
Ramsey, P. 3
Reagan, T. 163, 164
Reiff, J. 152
Rencken, S. 89
Reynolds, W. 24, 29, 34
Rhine, W. 37, 44
Rose, M. 131
Rosegrant, T. xv, 33, 34
Rousseau, J. 42, 44, 69

**S**
Schiller, M. 99
Schnur-Laughlin, J. 70
Schön, D. 116, 159, 161
Schubeck, K. 89
Schubert, W. 20, 34, 59, 62
Schultz, L. 153
Schutz, A. 150
Schweinhart, L. 33, 34, 47, 49
Scott, P. 150
Sears, J. 34, 62

**T**
Takanishi, R. 81
Taubman, P. 24, 29, 34
Taylor, C. 116
Thompson, L 116
Tinworth, S. 108
Tyler, R. 24, 34, 62

**V**
van Manen, M. 21, 159
Viruru, R. 33, 52, 64
Vygotsky, L. 40, 42, 70, 140, 150

**W**
Wegerif, R. 150
Weikart, D. 33, 47
Weil, M. 17
Wells, D. 70
Wheeler, C. 127
Wickens, D. 45
Williams, M. 89
Windschitl, M. 141
Wolfe, P. 11
Woodhead, M. 80
Wortham, S. 39

**Y**
York, S. xv

**Z**
Zeichner, K. 3, 159
Zimiles, H. 45

# Subject Index


**A**
academic discourses, 131
adult privilege, xv, 129, 136, 148, 158
age-appropriateness, 38, 43, 44
anti-bias curriculum, 58
appropriateness, xvii, 43, 48, 135
artistry of teaching, 20, 23, 121
autobiographical, 12, 24, 35, 63, 83

**B**
Bank Street Approach, 42, 45
bargaining, 117, 124, 127, 130
Behaviorism, 26, 27, 36, 42
bicultural, 152, 153
bi-ethnic/cross-ethnic perspective-taking, 154, 156
bilingual (bilingual capability), 37, 79
bilingualism, 82
boundaries, 21, 60, 95
bureaucratic school culture, 110

**C**
child-centered curriculum, 129
child development, 11, 74, 75, 77, 79, 80, 81, 82, 84, 85, 136, 138, 131, 144, 146
child studies, 33 , 66
child's perspective, xvi, 122
child's point of view, xvii, 80
classroom discourse culture, 140
classroom (learning) culture, 56, 127, 158
clinical supervision, 92
code-switching, 37
conscious framework, 59, 60, 62, 66
consent, 128, 129
Constructivism, 136–141
Constructivists, 30, 43
  constructivist interactionism, 36
  constructivist teaching, 137, 138, 140, 142, 143, 144
contemplation, 135, 146, 164
contemplative observer, 136, 138, 141
contemplative question (-ing), 120, 121
core knowledge, 26, 65, 171, 173
counternormative knowledge, 21, 23, 59, 62, 63, 120, 121, 140, 141, 143, 159, 170, 171, 172, 174
Creative Curriculum, 42, 47, 49
critical pedagogy, xix, 12, 13, 18, 21, 22, 23, 28, 29, 30, 57, 132, 164
critical-democratic pedagogy, 127
critical theorists, 21
cultural diversity, 94
cultural myopia, 12, 13, 151, 154
cultural studies, 33, 51, 66
cultural transmission tradition, 36
culturally bounded teacher knowledge, 101
culturally endorsed constructivist practice, 137, 138
culturally endorsed knowledge, 148
*Currere*, 20, 35, 59, 60, 61, 140, 141
Curriculum, 11, 12, 13, 33, 53, 69, 89,115
  Behaviorists' learning theory-based curriculum, 43
  conscious curriculum, 60, 64, 65
  Constructivists' child-centered curriculum, 43
  curriculum as a conscious frame work, 59, 60, 62, 66
  curriculum *does*, 37, 39, 41, 43, 60
  curriculum *is*, 20, 34, 39, 41, 43, 60
  curriculum negotiation, 14, 22, 23 , 115, 119, 124, 130, 161, 174
  curriculum negotiator, 113, 126
  Emergent curriculum, 14, 89
  Emergent-oriented curriculum, 89
  Instruction-oriented curriculum, 28
  learner-centered curriculum, 174
  learner-generated curriculum, 84
  lived curriculum, 36, 57, 59, 60, 61, 63, 64, 65
  Maturationists' child-centered cur riculum, 39, 43
  monocultural curriculum, 100
  Negotiation-oriented curriculum, 115
  neoconservative understanding of curriculum, 26, 27
  Postmodern curriculum, xxi, 21, 53, 141
  Teachable moment-oriented curriculum, 69
  What curriculum *does*, 27, 31, 174
  What curriculum *is*, 26, 31, 32, 60, 174
  What curriculum *is* and *does*, xv,

xix, xx, xxi, 14, 24, 25, 26, 31, 33, 35, 41, 51, 59, 135, 171, 174
curriculum and study, 30, 31, 121
curriculum framework, 14, 41, 51, 57, 58, 59, 60, 65, 66
curriculum leadership, xxii, 165, 174
curriculum ownership, 58

**D**
de-construction, 140, 143–148
deliberative inquiries, 63
democratic, 4, 12, 21, 24, 28, 31, 35, 50, 126, 127, 148, 149, 170
democratically accountable, 153, 158, 159, 164
democratization, 18
democratic curriculum, 170, 175
democratic educational practice, 31
democratic pedagogy, 127
developmental delay, 50, 78, 136
Developmentally and Culturally Appropriate Practice (DCAP), xvi, xvii, xx
Developmentally Appropriate Practice (DAP), xv, xvii, xviii, xix, 5, 89, 135
    DAP-based curriculum, 42, 47
Developmentally meaningful and culturally congruent-
    assistance, 30, 140
    curriculum, xv, xvi, xvii, xx, 3, 12, 51, 66, 70, 71, 130, 174
    learning experience, xv, 119, 128, 135, 151, 158
    pedagogy, 153
    practice, xviii, xix, xx, xxi, xxii, 14, 62, 63, 69, 75, 80, 82, 85, 158, 163, 175
developmental psychology, 59, 65, 79, 80, 81
dialectical, 21, 136, 142, 144
    dialectical constructivism, 138, 139, 140, 141, 142
    dialectical constructivist learning/teaching, 21, 146
DISTAR, 37, 42, 44
direct instructional model, 37
disciplined study of study, 30, 120
discourse strategies, 140
doubled inquiry logic, 30
dual learning, 97, 105, 111, 163

**E**
ecological brain, 11, 57
Education that is multicultural (ETM), xv, 4,6, 11, 22
emancipatory knowledge, 12
emergent, 59
    emergent (-oriented) curriculum (see Curriculum)
    emergent moments, 59, 60
endogenous, 136, 144
    endogenous constructivism, 136, 137, 142
    endogenous constructivist teaching, 143, 144
epistemological, 29, 41, 141, 150
ESOL(English Speaker of Other Languages), 4, 5, 108
Ethnocentrism, 62, 154
exogenous, 136, 144
    exogenous constructivism, 137, 138, 142
    exogenous constructivist practice, 143
    exogenous constructivist teaching, 137
exploratory talk, 140, 142, 143, 149, 158, 160

**F**
field experience, 90, 110
first-person/single-ethnic perspective-taking, 155, 157, 158

**G**
gender identity, 116
giving choices, 129
group-orientation/ -oriented, 5, 10
grouping, 3, 6

**H**
Head Start, 42, 45
Hereditarian tradition, 37, 38
hidden curriculum, 25, 37, 82, 129, 158
High/Scope curriculum, 46
home culture, 54, 56, 65, 94, 103

## I

implicit curriculum, 82
individualized pedagogical adaptation, 139
influential talks, 131
inner and outer dialogue, 23, 29, 118, 119, 120, 121, 122, 123, 126, 143, 144
inner and outer negotiation, 31, 115, 118
inner dialogue, 119–123, 146, 147, 148, 154, 162, 163, 164
inner negotiation,119, 122, 155
institutionalized patronization, 6
Instruction, 17–32, 35, 37, 70, 137, 143, 157, 160, 161, 164
    instruction-oriented curriculum (see Curriculum)
    instruction-oriented teaching, 17–33, 37, 43, 44, 50, 65, 118, 119, 123, 124, 125, 129, 130, 148, 167, 169, 172
integrated curriculum, 58, 138
interlock(-ing), 117, 141, 149, 170, 171
interpersonal and intrapersonal negotiation, 153, 154
interpersonal competencies, 18, 119, 120

## K

Kamii-DeVries curriculum, 42, 47
knowledge (wisdom) creators, 132, 148
knowledge (wisdom) holders, 132, 148
knowledge (wisdom) seekers, 132, 148

## L

learnable moments, xxi, xxii, 59, 64, 66, 69, 74, 75, 82, 84, 86, 104, 107, 115, 127, 137, 141, 142, 143, 146, 149, 158, 161, 169, 170, 171, 172
learner-constructed knowledge, 138
learner-generated curriculum (see Curriculum)
learners' points of view, xv, 31, 51, 81, 133, 117, 120, 128, 140, 149, 151, 153
lived curriculum (see Curriculum)

## M

Maturationism, 36
Maturationists, 36, 38, 39, 43
mental mode, 158, 162
mental positions, 154, 159, 164
monocultural curriculum (see Curriculum)
monolingual, 79, 82
monolingual school culture, 82
monologue, 79
Montessori curriculum, 42, 45
multiculturalism, xviii, 4, 10, 11, 58
multiple/multiethnic, 11, 12
multiple/multiethnic
    perspective taker(s), 60, 106, 107, 110, 153, 169
multiple/multiethnic perspective-taking, xix, xxii, 12, 65, 66, 109, 137, 138, 143, 144, 146–149, 151–155, 157–159, 161, 164, 168

## N

narrative element, 161, 163
NAEYC (National Association for the Education of Young Children), xv, xvi, xvii, 5, 34, 48
NCATE (National Council for Accreditation of Teacher Education), xv
negotiated moments, 60, 161
negotiation, xxii, 22, 23, 29, 31,66, 112, 115–132, 138, 139, 146, 153–158, 160–175
Negotiation-oriented curriculum (see Curriculum)
negotiator, 113, 124, 126, 141
neoconservative understanding, 26, 27, 28
null curriculum, 25, 37
NCLBA, 17, 27, 49, 50, 65, 175

## O

organic, xiv, 14, 20, 23, 98, 102, 104, 105, 123, 161, 175
outer dialogue, 23, 29, 118–123, 126, 143–148, 159
ownership, 58, 195, 108, 113, 124, 126, 173–176

## P

parallel dynamic, 154
Pedagogy, xv–xxii, 12, 13, 17–32, 35, 43, 50, 51, 57, 84, 103, 115, 117, 119–127, 129, 132, 139, 141, 149, 153, 156–161,

164, 167, 169
pedagogical adaptation, 20, 21, 28, 30, 139
pedagogical constraints, 84
pedagogical culture, 112
pedagogical framework, xv
pedagogical methods, 30
pedagogical practices, xvi, 5, 28, 73, 89, 99, 153, 155, 159
pedagogically sound curriculum leadership, xviii, 167
pedagogical theory, 164
pedagogy-based teaching/practice, xv, xx, xxi, xxii, 20–23, 25, 28, 29, 31, 33, 43, 50, 51, 115, 117, 119–125, 139, 153, 157, 159–161, 167, 169
perpetual skeptics, 64
perspective takers, 60, 106, 107, 110, 153, 169
Perspective-taking, xix, xxii, 12, 65, 66, 109, 137, 138, 143, 144, 146–149, 151–155, 157–159, 161, 164, 168
First-person perspective-taking, 79, 122, 136, 154, 155, 160, 162, 163
Second-person perspective-taking, 75, 80, 85, 86, 122, 154, 156, 158, 162
Third-person/multiple perspective-taking, 122, 155, 157, 160, 161
Piagetian constructivism, 36
Piagetian orientation, 79, 80
Piagetian perspective, 40
plasticity, 11
pluralistic multiculturalism, 4
pluralistic orientation, 5, 13
pluralistic perspective, 138
pondering, 120, 123
Positivism, 28
postepistemological constructivism, 141
postmodern, xv, xviii, xxi, 21, 35, 51, 53, 59, 61, 62, 141, 142, 144
postmodern critical discourse, xiii
postmodern constructivist teaching, 142, 144
Postmodern curriculum (see Curriculum)
Postmodernism, xviii, 61, 62
poststructuralist perspective, 21
Power, 30, 41, 42, 71, 81, 82, 86, 87, 112, 125, 172, 173, 174
power-balanced, 124
power holder(s), 4, 65, 84, 126, 130, 158, 170, 172
power neutral, 86
power over, 126, 129
power pedagogy, 158
power struggle, 4, 10, 13, 25, 28, 37, 158
power with, 121, 126
power-related reality, 130
power-sharing, xxii, 18, 29, 30, 123, 125, 126, 158, 159, 167, 169, 170, 172, 175
reciprocal power, 124
shared power, 65, 66, 131, 142, 170, 173, 175
ultimate power, 65, 81, 84, 123, 126, 129, 170, 172
proctor/proctoristic, 17, 27, 28, 59
project approach, 42, 89, 93, 98, 108–111
purposeful action, 63, 75, 80, 83, 97
purposeful learning, 80, 81, 171

**Q**

questioners, 132

**R**

radical constructivism, 139
re-construction, 31, 39, 135, 140, 145, 146, 161
recursive, 62, 135, 141, 143, 144, 145, 148, 151, 154, 160, 161, 164
recursive cycle, 145
Reflection, 13, 35, 76, 80, 82, 122, 131, 151–165
Reflection-*for*-practice, 65, 120, 121, 151–165
Reflection-*in*-action, 65, 116, 120–122, 151–165
Reflection-*on*-action, 65, 120, 121, 122, 151–165
reflective clinical supervision, 92
reflective critical thinking, 141, 143, 144, 145, 147, 148
reflective inquiry, 116, 126
reflective phenomena, 161
reflective pondering, 120
reflective questioning, 29, 30

reflectivity (reflective functions), 65, 119, 120, 141, 151–165
Reggio Emilia approach, 42, 90, 100, 111
retention, 39
risk-taker(s), 102, 103, , 105, 106, 107, 169
risk-taking, 20, 95, 110, 111, 168
Romantic Approach, 42, 44

**S**

scaffolding, 138, 139, 140, 150
second-person/bi-ethnic perspective-taking, 152, 158
self-monitoring, 65, 66
self-reflective critical thinking, 143, 145, 147, 148
serendipitous moment, 100, 106, 169
shared power (see Power)
single-ethnic perspective-taking (see first-person perspective-taking)
situational questions, 64
Social constructivism, 26, 138, 150
social constructivist orientation, 41
social reconstructionist perspective, 4
socially constructed curriculum, 159
study-based pedagogical practice/pedagogy, 29, 31, 120, 121
sustained teacher, 29
superficial pluralism, 4

**T**

teachable moments, 69–88
  critical teachable moments, 159
  hidden teachable moments, 158
Teachable moment-oriented curriculum (see Curriculum)
teacher-centered manifestations, 136
teacher-centered teaching, 137
teacher education, xv, xvi, xvii, xix, 3, 5, 76, 110, 112
teacher preparation, xv, xvi, 3, 153
teacher reflectivity (see Reflectivity)
teacher's privilege, 172
teaching *is*, 21
thematic approach, 89, 93
third-person/multiethnic perspective-taking, 155, 157
transformation, 19, 29, 86, 97, 98, 105, 117, 119, 149, 160
Transformative /transforming identities, 31, 87
transformative outcome, 161, 163
transforming identity, 29
Tyler Rationale, 34, 35

**U**

underprivileged minority children, 128

**V**

voice maker, 107
voice-raising, 105, 108, 110
Vygotskian constructivist orientation, 40
Vygotsky's perspective, 139

**W**

What curriculum *does* (see Curriculum)
What curriculum *is* (see Curriculum)
What curriculum *is* and *does* (see Curriculum)
wide-awakeness, 24, 60, 65

**Z**

Zone of Proximal Development (ZPD), 70, 140, 149

## Studies in the Postmodern Theory of Education

*General Editors*
*Joe L. Kincheloe & Shirley R. Steinberg*

Counterpoints publishes the most compelling and imaginative books being written in education today. Grounded on the theoretical advances in criticalism, feminism, and postmodernism in the last two decades of the twentieth century, Counterpoints engages the meaning of these innovations in various forms of educational expression. Committed to the proposition that theoretical literature should be accessible to a variety of audiences, the series insists that its authors avoid esoteric and jargonistic languages that transform educational scholarship into an elite discourse for the initiated. Scholarly work matters only to the degree it affects consciousness and practice at multiple sites. Counterpoints' editorial policy is based on these principles and the ability of scholars to break new ground, to open new conversations, to go where educators have never gone before.

For additional information about this series or for the submission of manuscripts, please contact:

Joe L. Kincheloe & Shirley R. Steinberg
c/o Peter Lang Publishing, Inc.
29 Broadway, 18th floor
New York, New York 10006

To order other books in this series, please contact our Customer Service Department:

(800) 770-LANG (within the U.S.)
(212) 647-7706 (outside the U.S.)
(212) 647-7707 FAX

Or browse online by series:

www.peterlang.com